REVISED EDITION

FIELD GUIDE TO THE LARGER

MAMMALS

OF AFRICA

FIELD GUIDE TO THE LARGER

MAMMALS

OF AFRICA

CHRIS & TILDE STUART

Struik Publishers

(a division of New Holland Publishing (South Africa) (Pty) Ltd)

Cornelis Struik House

80 McKenzie Street

Cape Town, 8001

South Africa

New Holland Publishing is a member of Johnnic Communications Ltd.

Visit us as at **www.struik.co.za** and view over 40 000 unique African images available to
purchase at Images of Africa photo library

First published in 1997

Second edition (new cover only) 2000

Third edition 2006

10 9 8 7 6 5 4 3

Copyright © text and maps: C.T. Stuart and M.D. Stuart, 1997, 2000, 2006

Copyright © photographs: C.T. Stuart and M.D. Stuart and individual photographers
as listed on page 305, 1997, 2000, 2006

Copyright © illustrations: M.D. Stuart and C.T. Stuart, 1997, 2000, 2006

Copyright © line and spoor drawings: M.D. Stuart, 1997, 2000, 2006

Copyright © published edition: Struik Publishers, 1997, 2000, 2006

Editors: Jonathan Spencer-Jones and Maggie Mouton

Publishing Manager: Pippa Parker

Concept design: Janice Evans

Designer: Patricia Lynch-Blom

Cartographer: Gillian Black

Reproduction by Hirt and Carter Cape (Pty) Ltd.

Printed and bound by Kyodo Printing Co (Singapore) Pte Ltd.

ISBN 1 77007 393 0

Front cover (clockwise): Plains zebra (C & T Stuart); 'King cheetah' (C & T Stuart); Chimpanzee mother and child
(N. Dennis); Nyala ewes and young (C & T Stuart);

Spine: Caracal (C & T Stuart)

CONTENTS

In the contents section under Family Bovidae we have divided the various groups into subfamilies. Through the body of the Bovidae text we have placed them in their relevant tribes, as some taxonomists favour the subfamily designation, whereas others prefer the tribe names. We are still undecided.

ACKNOWLEDGEMENTS

A book of this nature is, of necessity, a compilation not only of the work of the authors but also that of the countless field workers and observers who have published their findings, or deposited specimens in museums. We hope that this guide will be a credit to the hundreds of individuals who have contributed, unwittingly, to its compilation. However, the responsibility for any omissions or errors must lie in the hands of the authors.

The directors and curators of the mammal collections of the following museums are thanked for allowing us free access: British Museum of Natural History; Musée Royal de l'Afrique Centrale, Tervuren; South African Museum; National Museum, Pretoria; Amathola Museum.

A special word of thanks is due to H.H. Sheikh Saud of Qatar for permitting one of the authors to observe and photograph his private gazelle collection. The directors and curators of a number of zoological gardens, including Antwerp, Zoo Berlin and Tiergarten Berlin, were extremely helpful when we wished to observe rare African mammal species in their collections.

A number of people have helped to fill our photographic gaps and we thank them all; their names are listed under the photographic credits. Dr A. Gauthier of Station Biologique de Poiunpont, kindly provided some photographic material on primates.

Kyle Stuart is thanked for drawing the size comparison silhouettes, and Leigh Stuart for assisting with the typing of photo captions.

Our publishing manager, Pippa Parker, has had to put up with differences on both sides of the publishing fence, and we thank her for the professional way in which she has handled points of conflict. Lastly we wish to thank our editor Maggie Mouton, designer Darren MacGurk, and James Mills-Hicks who took the book through its final stages.

CHRIS AND TILDE STUART, LOXTON 2006

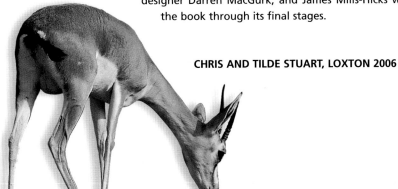

INTRODUCTION

1. Cape and Mediterranean evergreen scrub

2. Tropical rainforest

3. Desert

4. Southern semi-desert

Of the 4 000 to 4 500 living species of mammals worldwide, approximately 25%, or some 1 100, occur on the African continent. There is no absolute certainty as to how many species there are, particularly in the case of the bats, shrews and smaller rodents. Taxonomists are constantly revising and assessing the scientific status of many mammals, and with the development of more sophisticated methods of establishing genetic diversity, this can be expected to accelerate.

Apart from the ongoing taxonomic knot-tying and unravelling of known species, from time to time new, previously unknown species are found. During the early part of this century even some large species, such as the okapi and the giant forest hog, were first collected and described by scientists. Today, most new discoveries are of mice, shrews and bats, but in recent decades several species of small carnivores and monkeys have seen the 'scientific light', particularly from the tropical lowland forests. As there are still several areas of Africa that are unexplored in zoological terms, new discoveries can still be expected.

The conservation status and distribution of many species are as yet only poorly known, but more critical is the general lack of understanding of their requirements and behaviour. Even for the larger, widespread and abundant species, these aspects are surprisingly lacking. Nevertheless, we do have a vast storehouse of knowledge. Thus a field guide such as this is a product not only of the work of the authors but also of the many hunters, explorers, naturalists and scientists who have gathered information over long periods of time, and recorded and published their findings.

Mammals have a number of common characteristics that set them apart from other vertebrates: they have a four-chambered heart; there are three delicate bones in the middle ear; females have mammary glands that produce milk for suckling the young; and nearly all species have a covering of body hair.

The African continent covers some 30 million km², incorporating the world's largest desert (the Sahara), one of the largest tracts of lowland rainforest (the Congolean block), one of the longest rivers (the Nile), the second largest lake (Victoria) and the second deepest (Tanganyika). The diversity of habitats, climatic forms and species is impressive.

The following summary of the principal vegetation zones of the continent is of necessity a greatly simplified version of the real situation, and each of the broad divisions presented here is in fact composed of many different recognizable units. Many mammal species are restricted to one particular vegetation type or habitat, whereas others range over many. The reader should thus be aware that the following account is broad, in the broadest sense.

1. CAPE AND MEDITERRANEAN EVERGREEN SCRUB
These zones are found only in the extreme north-western and south-western corners of the continent, and are dominated by evergreen shrubs and bushes (sometimes referred to as heathland, fynbos or Macchia in the south). Very few mammal species are endemic to these zones.

2. TROPICAL RAINFOREST
In tropical rainforests, the rainfall is high and the trees are predominantly evergreen, or semi-deciduous, and frequently form a distinct canopy with a number of more, or less, discrete vegetation strata. In West Africa, particularly, but also elsewhere, large tracts of tropical rainforest have been destroyed by man. Many species are endemic to these forests.

3. DESERT
The two desert zones are the Sahara, which dominates the north of the continent, and the Namib stretching in a narrow belt along the south-western coastline. Deserts are characterized by very sparse vegetation, extremely low rainfall (less than 100 mm per annum) and a number of species that are highly adapted to survival in this harsh environment.

MAP OF PRINCIPAL VEGETATION ZONES

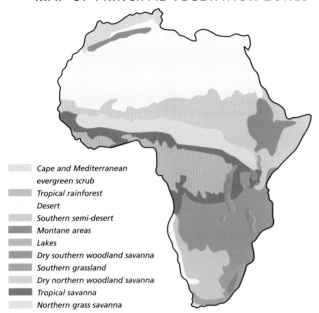

Cape and Mediterranean
evergreen scrub
Tropical rainforest
Desert
Southern semi-desert
Montane areas
Lakes
Dry southern woodland savanna
Southern grassland
Dry northern woodland savanna
Tropical savanna
Northern grass savanna

5. Montane areas

*6. Dry southern and northern
woodland savanna*

*7. Southern grassland and
northern grass savanna*

4. SOUTHERN SEMI-DESERT
This region includes the Kalahari, the Karoo, Bushmanland and Namaqualand. Rainfall is generally less than 500 mm and vegetation ranges from open thorn tree woodland to areas covered by short, woody shrubs and succulents.

5. MONTANE AREAS
These areas include the Atlas Mountains, the Ethiopian Highlands, Ruwenzoris, Mounts Kenya, Kilimanjaro and Meru, and the Drakensberg range. Vegetation varies considerably between ranges and at different altitudes, and includes forest types, bamboo thickets, woodland, grassland and subalpine zones.

6. DRY SOUTHERN AND NORTHERN WOODLAND SAVANNA
Woodland savanna contains elements of woodland, grassland and scrub, but in the south, trees are more abundant and the grass is often taller and denser. The northern areas tend to be drier than the southern. Some of the great savanna reserves and some of the world's greatest herds of game are located in these areas.

7. SOUTHERN GRASSLAND AND NORTHERN GRASS SAVANNA
Grass species dominate in these savannas, with scatterings of trees, including acacias. Previously these were occupied by great migratory game herds, which are now much diminished.

8. TROPICAL SAVANNA
Tropical savanna comprises mixed grass and tree savanna, and typically receives a fairly high rainfall. Some dense forest stands are scattered through these areas.

This guide covers the more visible and some of the more easily distinguished larger mammal species, as many of the smaller species are nocturnal, secretive and occupy inhospitable (to humans) habitats, and are seldom seen or known only from a few museum specimens and descriptions in scientific papers.

8. Tropical savanna

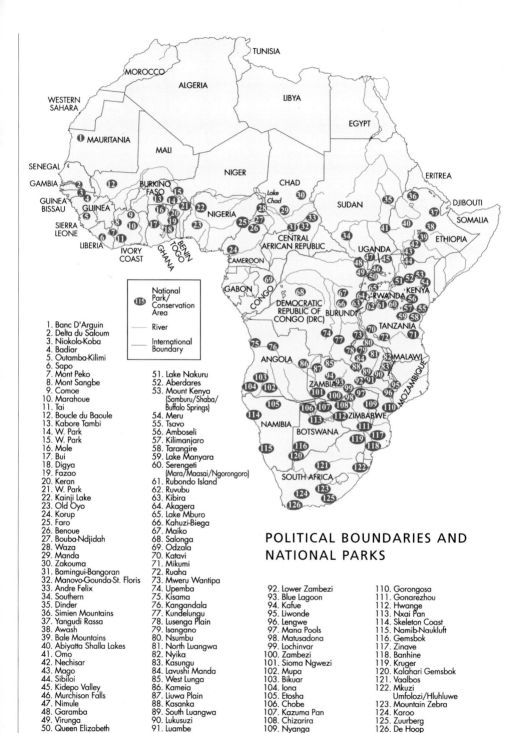

1. Banc D'Arguin
2. Delta du Saloum
3. Niokolo-Koba
4. Badiar
5. Outamba-Kilimi
6. Sapo
7. Mont Peko
8. Mont Sangbe
9. Comoe
10. Marahoue
11. Tai
12. Boucle du Baoule
13. Kabore Tambi
14. W. Park
15. W. Park
16. Mole
17. Bui
18. Digya
19. Fazao
20. Keran
21. W. Park
22. Kainji Lake
23. Old Oyo
24. Korup
25. Faro
26. Benoue
27. Bouba-Ndjidah
28. Waza
29. Manda
30. Zakouma
31. Bamingui-Bangoran
32. Manovo-Gounda-St. Floris
33. Andre Felix
34. Southern
35. Dinder
36. Simien Mountains
37. Yangudi Rassa
38. Awash
39. Bale Mountains
40. Abiyatta Shalla Lakes
41. Omo
42. Nechisar
43. Mago
44. Sibiloi
45. Kidepo Valley
46. Murchison Falls
47. Nimule
48. Garamba
49. Virunga
50. Queen Elizabeth

51. Lake Nakuru
52. Aberdares
53. Mount Kenya (Samburu/Shaba/Buffalo Springs)
54. Meru
55. Tsavo
56. Amboseli
57. Kilimanjaro
58. Tarangire
59. Lake Manyara
60. Serengeti (Mara/Maasai/Ngorongoro)
61. Rubondo Island
62. Ruvubu
63. Kibira
64. Akagera
65. Lake Mburo
66. Kahuzi-Biega
67. Maiko
68. Salonga
69. Odzala
70. Katavi
71. Mikumi
72. Ruaha
73. Mweru Wantipa
74. Upemba
75. Kisama
76. Kangandala
77. Kundelungu
78. Lusenga Plain
79. Isangano
80. Nsumbu
81. North Luangwa
82. Nyika
83. Kasungu
84. Lavushi Manda
85. West Lunga
86. Kameia
87. Liuwa Plain
88. Kasanka
89. South Luangwa
90. Lukusuzi
91. Luambe

POLITICAL BOUNDARIES AND NATIONAL PARKS

92. Lower Zambezi
93. Blue Lagoon
94. Kafue
95. Liwonde
96. Lengwe
97. Mana Pools
98. Matusadona
99. Lochinvar
100. Zambezi
101. Sioma Ngwezi
102. Mupa
103. Bikuar
104. Iona
105. Etosha
106. Chobe
107. Kazuma Pan
108. Chizarira
109. Nyanga

110. Gorongosa
111. Gonarezhou
112. Hwange
113. Nxai Pan
114. Skeleton Coast
115. Namib-Naukluft
116. Gemsbok
117. Zinave
118. Banhine
119. Kruger
120. Kalahari Gemsbok
121. Vaalbos
122. Mkuzi Umfolozi/Hluhluwe
123. Mountain Zebra
124. Karoo
125. Zuurberg
126. De Hoop

HOW TO USE THIS FIELD GUIDE

As with most field guides, the purpose of this book is to enable the observer to identify mammals observed in the wild. All of the larger mammals have been covered, and within this definition is included a number of species that weigh between 500 g and 1 kg, but excluded are the bats and virtually all of the insectivores and rodents. The species in the 'smaller' category include those that are frequently seen, such as the hyraxes, hares and rabbits, hedgehogs, ground squirrels and springhares. The definition of 'smaller' and 'larger' is totally subjective, as several of the antelope weigh less than 5 kg, and some of the carnivores weigh less than 2 kg, with a few, such as the dwarf mongoose, as little as 220 g.

The reasoning behind selecting 'larger' mammals is that these are usually, but not always, easier to see, and generally less problematic to identify.

Each species is discussed according to ten subheadings as follows:

MEASUREMENTS: In most cases, a range of measurements is given, from lowest to highest measurement, or alternatively, the average for that particular species. There will always be variation within a species, however. The most useful measurement in the field identification of the larger and medium-sized mammals is shoulder height. A useful method of learning to judge measurements is to cut pieces of wood into known lengths and place these at different distances. With practice, it should be possible to apply these estimates to mammals in the field. In the case of most antelope species, two horn measurements are provided: the average length, and the hunting record length.

IDENTIFICATION POINTERS: The main aids to identifying a species are highlighted.

SIMILAR SPECIES: Where one species is similar to, or could easily be confused with another, their distinguishing features are mentioned.

DESCRIPTION: The descriptions concentrate on external features that will assist the observer to identify a mammal to species level. The following six steps will serve as a guide when identifying a mammal:
1. Decide to which group the mammal belongs. (Is it an antelope, or does it belong to the dog or cat families?)
2. Estimate the shoulder height and the total and tail lengths if possible. (Is the tail shorter than the length of head and body? Is the mammal roughly as tall as a Shetland pony?)
3. Look for outstanding features. (Does it have black or white stripes, spots or a bushy tail, or is the back arched?)
4. Check the distribution map to determine whether the species occurs in the area.
5. Check the habitat preference of the mammal. (A klipspringer will not be seen on the open savanna, nor a cheetah in tropical forest.)
6. Make a note of any specific behaviour which may aid in identification. (Are there a large number of the same species together? Did the animal retreat into a burrow?)

Note that the young of some species may appear totally different to the adults, particularly in the case of antelope, where subadults of one species may be confused with the adults of another. Also, a number of species possess one or more subspecies or races that differ from each other in colour, pattern or size.

DISTRIBUTION: A glance at the distribution map will give a quick indication of the distributional range of a species. Remember that the scale of the maps is such that only general distribution patterns can be given. Always consult the notes on the habitat preference of a species in conjunction with the distribution map.

STATUS: This gives a broad indication of whether the species is common, rare or endangered.

HABITAT: This discusses the habitats favoured by each species. It is not definitive, however, and a species that is frequently encountered in one habitat may on occasion be encountered in another.

BEHAVIOUR: Behavioural characteristics which may aid in identification are given preference, but other aspects of interest are also given.

FOOD: Common foods are listed and in some cases this may assist identification.

REPRODUCTION: This may aid identification, but is mainly given for general interest.

KEY TO SYMBOLS

 E   ENDANGERED SPECIES

HABITAT SYMBOLS AND SILHOUETTES:

 SAVANNA, GRASSLAND/SCRUB   MOUNTAINS

 SAVANNA/OPEN WOODLAND   HILLS/ROCKY AREAS

 WOODLAND/BUSH   DESERT

 FOREST   ALL HABITATS

 FRESHWATER-RELATED HABITATS   SIZE OF ANIMAL RELATIVE TO MAN

ACTIVITY PERIODS:

 DIURNAL   NOCTURNAL

 CREPUSCULAR

Dominant activity periods are indicated but some variation must be taken into account. Activity periods can also be influenced by the season, food availability and in some cases habitat. In the case of the antelope, this becomes a little more complex, depending on such issues as levels of human disturbance and hunting pressure. For example, the greater kudu is predominantly diurnal in undisturbed areas but in areas where it is hunted this animal is mainly nocturnal.

FAMILY INTRODUCTIONS

The following entries provide brief key features of the mammal families and subfamilies of Africa which are covered in this book.

INSECTIVORES Order Eulipotyphla
HEDGEHOGS *Family Erinaceidae (p. 292)*
Five species; small size; short, banded spines cover back and sides; curl up if threatened; very short tail; nocturnal.

PRIMATES Order Primates
POTTOS AND GALAGOS (BUSHBABIES) *Families Lorisidae and Galagidae (pp. 16–21)*
Eleven to seventeen species. **Pottos:** small; 'bear-like'; very short tail. Well-developed hind limbs; large eyes and ears; nocturnal; arboreal. **Galagos/bushbabies:** 50 g–1,5 kg; long, well-haired tail; nocturnal; arboreal.
BABOONS AND MONKEYS *Family Cercopithecidae (pp. 22–62)*
More than 40 species. **Baboons:** large size; very short or 'kinked' tail; long, dog-like head; mainly terrestrial; diurnal. **'True' monkeys:** long, straight tail; 800 g–3 kg; most with short hair, a few with long hair; mainly arboreal; diurnal; mostly social.
CHIMPANZEE, BONOBO AND GORILLA *Family Pongidae (pp. 62–67)*
Three species; very large (30–180 kg); no tail; dark colour; social; diurnal.

PANGOLINS Order Pholidota
PANGOLINS *Family Manidae (p. 290)*
Four species; upper parts and sides covered in plate-like scales.

HARES AND RABBITS Order Lagomorpha
HARES AND RABBITS *Family Leporidae (pp. 294–297)*
At least eight species; small size (1–4,5 kg); very long to medium-length ears; well-developed hind limbs; nocturnal; most species solitary.

RODENTS Order Rodentia
GROUND SQUIRRELS *Family Sciuridae (pp. 298–300)*
Five species of ground squirrels; small (500 g–1 kg); long, bushy tail; very short ears; terrestrial; colonial; diurnal.
SPRINGHARE *Family Pedetidae (p. 298)*
Two species; resembles miniature kangaroo; nocturnal.
PORCUPINES *Family Hystricidae (p. 300)*
Three species; 2 – 24 kg; covered in long, banded quills; one species with shorter, unbanded quills; terrestrial; nocturnal.

CARNIVORES Order Carnivora
FOXES, JACKALS AND WILD DOG *Family Canidae (pp. 224–238)*
Twelve species; 1–36 kg; dog-like appearance; long, pointed muzzle; most species mainly nocturnal; terrestrial.

OTTERS, WEASELS, POLECATS AND BADGER *Family Mustelidae (pp. 238–245)*
Ten species; 45 g–18 kg; very variable group; occupy wetland to desert; most nocturnal, some diurnal (otters).

CIVETS, GENETS AND MONGOOSES *Families Viverridae, Nandiniidae and Herpestidae (pp. 246–265)*
At least 36 species have been identified; 220 g–15 kg; a very diverse family; genets, linsang and civets are spotted, blotched and barred, whereas mongooses have a mainly plain coloration; they occupy virtually all habitats and are nocturnal and diurnal; social and solitary.

HYAENAS AND AARDWOLF *Family Hyaenidae (pp. 266–271)*
Four species; 6–80 kg; shoulders stand higher than rump; three species with longish coats, one with short; social and solitary; mainly nocturnal and crepuscular.

CATS *Family Felidae (pp. 272–285)*
Ten species; 1–225 kg; all easily identifiable as cats; short muzzle; all with fully retractile claws except cheetah; social and solitary; mostly nocturnal/crepuscular.

AARDVARK   Order Tubulidentata
AARDVARK *Family Orycteropodidae (p. 288)*
One species; large (up to 70 kg); long, pig-like snout; arched back.

ELEPHANT   Order Proboscidea
ELEPHANT *Family Elephantidae (pp. 220–223)*
Two species, forest and savanna; unmistakable.

HYRAXES   Order Hyracoidea
HYRAXES *Family Procaviidae (p. 286)*
At least five species; two rock-dwelling, three tree-dwelling; small size (2–5 kg); no tail; superficially 'guinea-pig-like'; diurnal and nocturnal.

ODD-TOED UNGULATES   Order Perissodactyla
WILD ASS AND ZEBRAS *Family Equidae (pp. 68–75)*
Four species; three striped black and white, one not; horse-like; social.

RHINOCEROSES *Family Rhinocerotidae (pp. 76–81)*
Two species; very large; two horns on front of head, one above the other.

The Order Whippomorpha includes whales and dolphins.

HIPPOPOTAMUSES   Order Whippomorpha *(pp. 82–87)*
Two species; 160–2 000 kg; partly aquatic; massive head; barrel-shaped body; social and solitary.

EVEN-TOED UNGULATES

PIGS AND HOGS   Order Suiformes *(pp. 88–95)*
Five species; pig-like; medium to large size; social; nocturnal and diurnal.

OTHER EVEN-TOED UNGULATES   Order Ruminantia
GIRAFFE AND OKAPI *Family Giraffidae (pp. 96–101)*

Two species. **Giraffe:** neck and legs greatly elongated; patchwork pattern. **Okapi:** neck and legs partially elongated.

DEER *Family Cervidae (pp. 102–105)*
Two species; males with antlers part of year; unmistakable.

CHEVROTAIN *Family Tragulidae (p. 104)*
One species; up to 13 kg; antelope-like; arched back; no horns; forest; nocturnal.

BUFFALO AND ANTELOPE *Family Bovidae (pp. 106–219)*

Buffalo and 'spiral-horned' antelope *Subfamily Bovinae (Tragelaphinae) (pp. 106–125)*
Nine species; buffalo 'cow-like'; size range giant eland >900 kg, bushbuck >30 kg; tragelaphines have spiralled horns to greater or lesser extent; females of all except eland and bongo lack horns; social to solitary.

Addax, Oryx, Roan and Sable *Subfamily Hippotraginae (pp. 126–133)*
Five species; all five are large in size; both sexes carry well-developed horns; social to highly social.

Waterbuck, Kob, Puku, Lechwe and Reedbuck *Subfamily Reduncinae (pp. 134–146)*
Eight species; large to medium size; most associated with watery or damp habitats, including seasonal floodplains; males have stout, well-ringed horns, in most cases forward-pointing; social.

Grey Rhebok *Subfamily Peleinae (p. 146)*
One species; restricted to South Africa; medium size; males have short, straight, upright horns; social.

Hartebeest, Tsessebe/Topi, Bontebok/Blesbok and Wildebeest *Subfamily Alcelaphinae (pp. 148–161)*
Seven species; back slopes down to rump; long face; medium to large size; social.

Impala *Subfamily Aepycerotinae (p. 162)*
One species; medium size; slender build; males have long lyrate horns; characteristic black hair tuft on hind leg above ankle joint.

Gazelles and Dwarf Antelope *Subfamily Antilopinae (pp. 164–198)*
About 23 species; tiny to medium size (2–80 kg); diverse in appearance, habit and habitat; see species accounts.

Duikers *Subfamily Cephalophinae (pp. 198–215)*
About 16 species; 3–80 kg; all except one forest-dwelling; arched back; tuft of hair between ears; skulking habits.

Goat Antelopes (Goats and Sheep) *Subfamily Caprinae (pp. 216–219)*
Three species; limited distributions; rocky/montane habitats; typical goat and sheep appearances.

KEY TO COLOUR CODING:
Primates
Odd-toed Ungulates
Even-toed Ungulates
Elephants
Carnivores
Hyraxes
Aardvark
Pangolins
Insectivores
Hares and Rabbits
Rodents
Hippopotamuses

ABBREVIATIONS USED IN THIS BOOK:
g = gram
kg = kilogram
cm = centimetre
m = metre
ha = hectare
km^2 = square kilometre
♂ = male
♀ = female
> = more than
< = less than

PRIMATES   Order Primates

Africa is home to at least 60 species of primates, including man, but some of these may in fact only warrant subspecies status, whereas some of the subspecies should perhaps become species in their own right. It is also possible that entirely new species await discovery in the vast forest lands of the Congolean basin. In the following species accounts the larger and more obvious primates are covered. Where species are particularly rare, or occupy rarely frequented areas, they have either been excluded or only briefly mentioned.

POTTO, ANGWANTIBO AND GALAGOS (BUSHBABIES)
Families Lorisidae and Galagidae

■ *Perodicticus potto*
■ *Arctocebus calabarensis* and *A. aureus*
■ Area of overlap

POTTO
Perodicticus potto

Total length 30-50 cm; tail length 5-8 cm; weight 600-1 600 g.
Identification pointers Relatively stocky build; short tail; rounded, short head, superficially bear-like; thick, woolly fur; lowland forest habitat.
Similar species Angwantibo.

A second species of angwantibo is now widely recognized, the Golden Angwantibo (*Arctocebus aureus*). Generally smaller than angwantibo and more reddish-brown in colour. Largely restricted to southern Cameroon, Gabon and Congo, but range not well documented.

DESCRIPTION Small, short-tailed and stoutly built, with a rounded, short-snouted face, small, rounded ears and well-developed hands and feet for grasping branches. Five subspecies are recognized, based primarily on pelage coloration. Fur is thick and woolly and ranges in colour from almost black, greyish-brown to a rich russet-brown, with that on underparts somewhat paler. Size and coloration very variable. The **angwantibo** (*Arctocebus calabarensis*) is smaller and of more slender build, has a pointed snout and larger ears; its pelage colour is usually golden-brown.

DISTRIBUTION Present in the Guinea and Congolean forest blocks, being separated by the Dahomey Gap, and extending eastward into the forests of Uganda and far western Kenya. The angwantibo has a much more limited distribution, within the forests lying between the Congo and Niger rivers.

STATUS Relatively common, although loss of habitat in West Africa has reduced populations. The angwantibos are probably under greater threat because of more restricted distribution and occurrence at lower densities.

HABITAT All are found in tropical primary and secondary forest, and show a preference for areas with dense and tangled undergrowth.

BEHAVIOUR Both the potto and angwantibo are solitary, nocturnal and arboreal, only rarely descending to the ground. The potto has been recorded as occurring in densities of about 12 animals per km^2 but the angwantibo is reported living at much lower densities. In one study female pottos were found to occupy a home range of about 7 ha, and males some 12 ha. The male potto is territorial and although this may also apply to the angwantibo, no evidence is available. When foraging they move slowly and deliberately.

FOOD They include a wide range of food items in their diets, such as invertebrates and fruits, but the angwantibo also includes a high percentage of caterpillars, while the potto takes small mammals, birds and bats on occasion.

REPRODUCTION Young may be dropped at any time of the year but in the few studies undertaken, there is an indication of slight seasonal peaks. A single young is born after a gestation period of 190 days in the potto, and after about 135 days in the angwantibo. There is evidence that a female may give birth twice in a year. Birth weight of the potto is 35 to 50 g and that of the angwantibo up to 30 g.

The potto is a nocturnal animal, and arboreal – only rarely descending to the ground.

The round, short-snouted face and rounded ears of the potto impart a somewhat bear-like appearance.

- ■ *Galago senegalensis* (*Galago moholi* the southern form)
- ■ *Galago alleni*
- ■ *Galago thomasi*
- ■ Area of overlap

Distribution map for *Galago senegalensis*, *Galago moholi* and *Galago gallarum* are combined as actual ranges are not accurately known.

- ■ *Galago demidovii*
- ■ *Galago elegantulus*
- ■ Area of overlap
- ■ Area of overlap (*Galago demidovii* and *Galago inustus*)
- ■ *Galago zanzibaricus*
- ■ Grant's Galago (*Galagoides granti*)

Somali bushbaby (*Galago gallarum*) in Horn of Africa, previously a subspecies of *Galago senegalensis*.

GALAGOS/BUSHBABIES

At least nine, and perhaps as many as 17 species of galago, also known as bushbabies, are recognized, but with a few exceptions, only the experienced field worker can tell them apart. One of the most important identification characters is the call, particularly as opportunities of obtaining clear views of these small primates are rare. The two most frequently encountered species, the bushbaby and the thick-tailed galago, are covered in most detail below, with brief coverage of the other species.

BUSHBABY (SENEGAL GALAGO)
Galago senegalensis

Total length 30-40 cm; tail length 20-25 cm; weight 120-210 g (average 150 g).
Identification pointers Small size, long fluffy tail; large, forward-pointing eyes, short snout; large, thin, highly mobile ears; prodigious jumping ability; arboreal habitat. **Similar species** Other small galago species.

DESCRIPTION Has a fine, woolly, greyish to grey-brown coat, extending on to the well-haired tail. Ears are large, thin and rounded, and extremely mobile. The eyes are very large, forward-pointing and ringed with black, the head is small and rounded, and the snout is short. Although it is not the smallest galago, it is considerably smaller than the thick-tailed galago with which it shares much of its southern range. Other small galagos include the **Zanzibar galago** (*G. {Galagoides} zanzibaricus*), which has a browner colouring and a different call to the bushbaby; the **dwarf galago** (*G. demidovi*), which is the smallest (50 to 90 g) and has darker fur; the **western needle-clawed galago** (*G. elegantulus*), which has reddish dorsal fur and a white-tipped tail; **Allen's galago** (*G. alleni*), which has smoky-grey fur with reddish flanks and may have a white-tipped tail; **Thomas's galago** (*G. thomasi*); and the **eastern needle-clawed galago** (*G. inustus*), which has a very dark coat.

DISTRIBUTION Has the widest distribution of all of the galago species, within a wide range of savanna associations. Most of the other small galago species have limited distributions: the Zanzibar galago along the Kenyan and Tanzanian coasts, the dwarf in tropical rainforests, the western needle-clawed and Allen's in the western Congolean forest block between the Niger and Congo rivers, and Thomas's and the

eastern needle-clawed in forests in the DRC and Uganda.

STATUS Common and widespread. The status of the forest-dwelling species is poorly known but the limited range of the Zanzibar galago makes it vulnerable to habitat changes.

HABITAT Woodland savanna, particularly acacia and riverine associations. The other small galagos live mostly in true forest associations or their margins.

BEHAVIOUR Entirely nocturnal, foraging mainly in trees and only occasionally descending to the ground. Family groups of two to eight individuals sleep together, in self-constructed nests of leaves, tree holes, or in dense vegetation tangles. Group members usually forage alone, or in very loose associations. They are territorial, with groups occupying home ranges of about 3 ha, but this varies according to food availability. Densities of up to 400 individuals per km^2 have been recorded in optimal habitat. In the case of the Zanzibar galago, densities of as many as 150 animals per hectare have been recorded. Their jumping ability is amazing given their small size, and is facilitated by the long, well-developed hind legs. They are very vocal, with a wide range of calls, including low croaks, chittering and grunts. The general behaviour of all of the small galago species is probably similar but has been little studied thus far.

The bushbaby (Galago senegalensis), the southern form of which is now a full species – the South African Galago.

The dwarf galago, or Demidov's: Note the long fluffy tail.

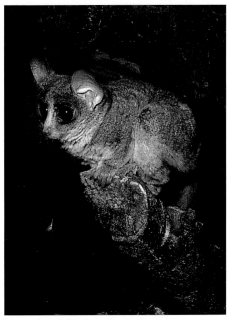

The smallest of all galagos, the dwarf galago.

Thomas's galago is said to associate in groups of 10 or more.

FOOD Gum, or exuding sap of trees, but a wide range of insects are also eaten, which are caught with the hands. All of the small galagos have similar diets but percentages vary: some species take more insects, such as the Zanzibar, but in the case of the western needle-clawed, up to 80% of the diet is made up of gum and resin. All take a small percentage of fruits.

REPRODUCTION One or 2 young are dropped after a gestation of slightly more than 120 days. Birth weight is about 9 g, and young are well haired and have the eyes open. Up to 2 litters a year, usually coinciding with early and later summer in the southern part of range. Some species, such as the dwarf and Zanzibar, give birth to single young. Young are carried by the female when she forages but are left clinging (known as 'parking') to branches while she moves about.

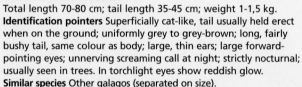

THICK-TAILED (GREATER) GALAGO
Otolemur crassicaudatus
Total length 70-80 cm; tail length 35-45 cm; weight 1-1,5 kg.
Identification pointers Superficially cat-like, tail usually held erect when on the ground; uniformly grey to grey-brown; long, fairly bushy tail, same colour as body; large, thin ears; large forward-pointing eyes; unnerving screaming call at night; strictly nocturnal; usually seen in trees. In torchlight eyes show reddish glow.
Similar species Other galagos (separated on size).

Front

Thick-tailed Galago

DESCRIPTION Considerably larger than the other galago species, but sometimes confused with the bushbaby. Has a superficially cat-like appearance when on the ground, but hindquarters stand higher than shoulder region and the long tail is held high off ground, or erect. Hair of upperparts and tail is fine, woolly and grey-brown (considerable regional variation exists), and underparts lighter in colour. Very large, thin, rounded ears and large forward-pointing eyes, which shine red at night in torchlight. The subspecies *garnetti* is recognized by some authorities as a full species. Some taxonomists recognize as many as four distinct species.

DISTRIBUTION Restricted to the far eastern areas of southern Africa, and extending northward into central and eastern Africa.

STATUS Secure and abundant.

HABITAT Occupy dense, dry woodland and gallery forests. In some montane forests they are present up to altitudes of about 3 500 m.

BEHAVIOUR They are strictly nocturnal, spending the day sleeping in dense vegetation tangles in trees and self-constructed nests. They usually rest together in groups of two to six individuals but foraging is a solitary activity. Each group has a fixed home range, in one area covering some 7 ha, and densities of up to 125 animals per km^2 may be reached. There are several resting sites within a group's home range. Unlike the other galagos, this species does a lot of foraging on the ground. Because of this it is the most frequently observed member of this genus and road casualties are not unusual in areas where it occurs at high densities. The most obvious sign of its presence is a loud screaming call like that of a human baby in distress.

FOOD Fruit and tree gum (resin), particularly that of acacias. They also eat insects, reptiles and birds.

REPRODUCTION Birth times vary according to region; in northern South Africa it falls in November, and in Zimbabwe and Zambia in August and September. Usually 2 young, weighing 50 to 70 g, are born after a gestation period of about 130 days.

Unlike the other galagos, the thick-tailed galago does a lot of foraging on the ground and is therefore frequently observed.

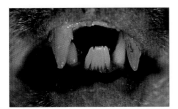

The structure of galago incisors is very similar to that of the Madagascar lemurs.

Skins of the bushbaby (left) and the thick-tailed galago (right).

The widespread thick-tailed galago is the largest of all galagos. It is strictly nocturnal, resting in groups during the day and foraging alone at night.

BABOONS AND MONKEYS
Family Cercopithecidae Subfamily Cercopithecinae

BABOONS
Considerable controversy exists over the status of several baboon 'species'. The hamadryas (*Papio hamadryas*) is a distinct and full species, but the Guinea baboon (*P. papio*), yellow baboon (*P. cynocephalus*), olive baboon (*P. anubis*), and chacma baboon (*P. ursinus*), are probably best treated as races of one species. Other authorities place the baboons as subspecies of the hamadryas. We have not accepted this, although further research may show this to be the case. Some authorities believe the Guinea race to be a western form of the hamadryas. Controversy also surrounds the drill and the mandrill, the rainforest baboons, sometimes given the genus name *Mandrillus* and at others assigned to *Papio*. All have long, dog-like muzzles, particularly well developed in males; shoulders held higher than rump; usually longer hair in shoulder region (mainly males); longish tail with 'broken' appearance, except drill and mandrill which have short stumps. In all cases males are noticeably larger than females.

HAMADRYAS
Papio hamadryas

Total length ♂ 1,5 m ♀ 1,2 m; tail length 60-70 cm; shoulder height 40-60 cm; weight ♂ 20 kg ♀ 10 kg.
Identification pointers Adult males have well-developed silvery-grey cape over shoulders; naked red skin on face and rump; females and young have brown coat.
Similar species Gelada, olive savanna baboon; hybrids between savanna baboon and hamadryas in Ethiopia.

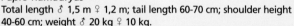

DESCRIPTION Adult males have a well-developed silvery-grey cape, extending down the back and on to the shoulders and chest; cheek hair is also long. Females are smaller and more brown in colour, and lack the cape. Facial and buttock skin is reddish-pink.

DISTRIBUTION Restricted to eastern Ethiopia, northern Somalia, Eritrea, Red Sea hills of Sudan, coastal ranges of south-western Arabia.

STATUS Still occurs in large numbers, despite a reduction in its African range, but expanding in Arabia.

HABITAT Arid and rocky hill country. Although recorded up to 3 300 m in the Simien Mountains of Ethiopia, it occurs most commonly at lower altitudes.

BEHAVIOUR The hamadryas lives in a hierarchial group system (a harem), with a single adult male accompanying between one and three females along with their dependent young. Several of these groups join together in a band averaging 60 individuals. Their home ranges average about 30 km², with the daily distances covered as high as 13 km. They circulate within the range, sleeping on steep cliffs or rocky outcrops, and always within reach of drinking water. In some areas of their range at least, they are seasonal migrants and occupy different areas in the wet and dry seasons.

FOOD Mainly seeds, particularly of grasses, roots and bulbs, other plant parts and probably some animal food, as with other baboons.

REPRODUCTION Little has been recorded but births probably occur throughout the year. A single young is dropped after a gestation period of about 175 days.

The male Hamadryas baboon has a very well-developed cape.

Male hamadryas baboons differ markedly in appearance from the females, the latter being smaller and lacking the cape.

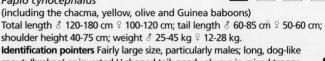

SAVANNA (COMMON) BABOON
Papio cynocephalus
(including the chacma, yellow, olive and Guinea baboons)
Total length ♂ 120-180 cm ♀ 100-120 cm; tail length ♂ 60-85 cm ♀ 50-60 cm;
shoulder height 40-75 cm; weight ♂ 25-45 kg ♀ 12-28 kg.
Identification pointers Fairly large size, particularly males; long, dog-like snout; 'broken' or inverted U-shaped tail; nearly always in mixed troops, but occasionally lone male is seen. **Similar species** Hamadryas, gelada.

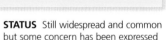

■ *Papio cynocephalus anubis* (olive)
■ *P.c. cynocephalus* (yellow)
■ Area of overlap
▨ *P.c. ursinus* (chacma)
■ Area of overlap
▨ *P.c. papio* (Guinea)

Front

140 mm

Savanna Baboon *(Back)*

DESCRIPTION The fourth largest African primate after the gorilla, chimpanzee and bonobo. Has a relatively slender and long-limbed build, although adult males have powerfully structured shoulders and heads. When standing or walking, shoulders stand higher than the rump. The head has an elongated muzzle, somewhat dog-like in appearance, which is particularly well developed in male baboons, as are their canines. Characteristic is the 'broken'/inverted U-shaped tail, although not so obvious in the Guinea race. Males have a single hard pad of naked skin extending across both buttocks, but the female has one smaller pad on each buttock, which during the menstrual cycle distends enormously into rather unsightly swollen red protuberances. Coat colour is variable but in general that of the chacma baboon is dark grey to grey-brown, the yellow baboon yellowish-brown, the Guinea baboon brown, and the olive baboon olive-greenish. Except for the Guinea baboon which has a brownish-red face, the other three races have naked black muzzles. Males of all races have longer hair on the shoulders but this is most developed in the Guinea and olive baboons.

DISTRIBUTION Has a very wide sub-Saharan distribution, being absent only from central rainforests and true desert. The chacma occurs virtually throughout southern Africa, with the yellow linking with its northern range limits and extending into East Africa and southern Somalia. The olive occurs in western areas of East Africa, northward towards Eritrea and in a belt west to Guinea. The Guinea has the most limited range, being largely restricted to Senegal, Guinea and south-western Mali.

STATUS Still widespread and common but some concern has been expressed for the Guinea race.

HABITAT Primarily different savanna associations but also found in montane areas, dense forest fringes and, in some areas, coastal habitats. They can penetrate arid areas along river courses, provided drinking water is accessible. Large trees or cliffs are a requirement for sleeping out of reach of predators.

BEHAVIOUR Although the Guinea has some behavioural affinities to the hamadryas, the other races are similar in most aspects of their biology. They are highly gregarious and social, living in troops of from 15 to 100 or more individuals. Within a troop all adult males are dominant over the females, a status achieved in their fifth year, but there is a strict order of rank. Only dominant males mate with oestrus females, although subordinate males do mate with young and non-oestrus females. The dominant male determines when the troop will move, and is most closely accompanied by females with infants. Non-breeding females stay close to the subordinate males, sometimes referred to as 'lieutenants', with young and subadult baboons circulating around the edges of the troop. Baboons are very vocal and the bark, or 'bogum', is a common daytime sound.

FOOD Omnivorous, taking a wide range of plants, including flowers, seeds, fruits, resin, bark, leaves, roots and bulbs. Also take a variety of mainly invertebrate animal food, and if the opportunity presents itself, young antelope, hares, mice, birds and reptiles. In agricultural areas they will raid a variety of crops.

Female yellow baboon with infant: Note the latter's pink face and ears.

Savanna baboon (chacma race): Note the sharply angled tail that is characteristic of all 'true' baboons.

Male savanna baboon (yellow race).

Male savanna baboons of the olive race have a large cape.

REPRODUCTION Births take place throughout the year, but there may be slight seasonal peaks in some areas. Female exhibits vastly swollen protuberances in the anal and vaginal region when receptive. The gestation period is about 180 days. At birth the single young has a pink face, and for the first few weeks clings to its mother's chest hairs; as it gains strength it begins to ride on her lower back, often using her tail as a back rest.

GELADA

Theropithecus gelada
Total length ♂ 130 cm ♀ 90 cm; tail length ♂ 55 cm ♀ 40 cm; shoulder height 40-60 cm; weight ♂ 20 kg ♀ 10 kg.
Identification pointers Baboon-like with long black naked muzzle, upward-pointing nostrils set back from tip; naked red patch on chest; well-developed cape of long hair, particularly males; long facial whiskers; limited distribution.
Similar species Olive savanna baboon, hamadryas (separated by bare chest patch and by behaviour).

DESCRIPTION Differs from 'true' baboons, although very baboon-like in appearance. The dark muzzle is elongated and longitudinally ridged but nostrils are set well back from tip and are upturned. Large bare, red patches on the chest are distinctive, as is the mane of long, light to dark brown hair on the neck and shoulders of the cape; this is particularly well developed in adult males.

DISTRIBUTION Ethiopian Highlands at altitudes ranging from 2 000 to 4 400 m.

STATUS Declining, perhaps 600 000 surviving.

HABITAT Montane grasslands.

BEHAVIOUR Believed to be the most terrestrial of all primates. They live in troops, usually referred to as herds, of up to 600 animals but these are loosely structured. Bands of 50 to 250 animals are more stable and made up of two to 30 single-male reproductive units, or harems, with associated all-male groups. Their home ranges overlap and cover from 1 to 10 km^2. Daily distances covered are short and they rarely wander far from the gorge edges, which provide night-time roosts and shelter from predators. Exclusively diurnal, they spend much of their feeding time sitting, shuffling along on their bottoms at regular intervals rather than standing up.

FOOD More than 90% grass (leaves or blades).

REPRODUCTION Breeding is seasonal. A single young is dropped after a gestation period of about 170 days.

MANDRILL

Papio (Mandrillus) sphinx
Total length ♂ 90 cm ♀ 55 cm; tail length 7-10 cm; shoulder height ♂ 60 cm ♀ 45 cm; weight ♂ 30 kg ♀ 10 kg.
Identification pointers Overall body structure/build as baboon; elongated, naked, deeply ridged, brightly coloured face, particularly males with crimson and cobalt-blue; stumpy tail; forest habitat.
Similar species Drill (but ranges do not overlap).

DESCRIPTION Overall build and stature is typical of the baboons but the face is deeply ridged and brightly coloured with red and blue; this is most developed in adult males. The buttock area is also particularly 'dazzling' in males – a combination of scarlet, pink, purple and lilac. Dorsal

Male gelada: Note the chest patch.

Male gelada.

Male mandrill. Females are smaller and lack the bright facial colouring.

pelage is olive-brown, with lighter underparts. A well-developed mane on the head and neck is particularly noticeable in the male. The tail is a short stump.

DISTRIBUTION Restricted to the Gabon forest block between the Sanaga and Congo rivers, and extending little more than 400 km eastward from the coast.

STATUS Are believed to have suffered drastic declines in recent years, through hunting and habitat loss.

HABITAT Tropical rainforest, montane forest, thick secondary forest as well as closed bush country.

BEHAVIOUR Terrestrial and arboreal when foraging, but in the case of the latter they prefer to feed at no more than 5 m above the ground. They are believed to have a flexible social system, living in single-male harem groups of 15 to 50 individuals, but larger temporary groupings of up to 200 have been recorded. Although poorly understood, their complex vocalizations probably serve to maintain contact within the group in the dense habitats they occupy. Their home ranges are believed to cover 30 to 50 km^2.

FOOD Consume a very wide range of plant foods, as well as invertebrates and small vertebrates.

REPRODUCTION Births appear to take place throughout the year, with a single young being dropped after a gestation period of approximately 225 days.

DRILL
Papio (Mandrillus) leucophaeus

E

Total length ♂ about 100 cm ♀ >50 cm; tail length 5-12 cm; shoulder height 45-60 cm; weight ♂ 15-20 kg ♀ 10-15 kg.
Identification pointers Baboon-like build and form; naked black muzzle, face fringed with white hair; males with brightly coloured posterior; high forest habitat.
Similar species Mandrill (but ranges do not overlap).

DESCRIPTION Distinguished by its very short, stubby tail, dog-like naked, ridged black face fringed with white hairs, and in males, bluish-purple naked buttocks. The ears are black and the overall coat colour is greyish-brown with an olive tinge. Females, apart from being smaller, lack the male's brightly coloured posterior.

DISTRIBUTION Restricted to south-eastern Nigeria and western Cameroon, where it does not occur south of the Sanaga River. It may still survive on the island of Bioko in the Gulf of Guinea.

STATUS Endangered.

HABITAT Lowland, coastal and riparian forest associations.

BEHAVIOUR The drill forages both on the ground and in trees. The recorded group sizes of this species range from 14 to almost 200 individuals; as in the case of the mandrill, harem groups of about 20 animals are controlled by a single male and several such groups may associate for varying periods of time. Vocalizations are common and include a loud 'crowing' call. So far no accurate estimate of their home range size has been made but the foraging area is believed to be fairly restricted.

FOOD Similar to that of the mandrill.

REPRODUCTION Births probably occur throughout the year, after a gestation period of about 210 days.

The drill is an endangered species and has a very restricted range in Africa.

The male drill has an entirely black face and is larger than the female.

'TRUE' (TYPICAL) MONKEYS

This is the largest primate family on the African continent and includes at least 35 species, with some having several recognized subspecies, or races. In the following accounts, the more commonly or easily observed species are concentrated upon, but where confusion could arise, others not accorded full accounts are also mentioned. (The term 'true' or 'typical' monkeys refers primarily to those with long tails, although obviously not in the case of the Barbary macaque which has no tail.)

BARBARY MACAQUE
Macaca sylvanus
Total length 55-75 cm; no tail; shoulder height up to 50 cm; weight 6-13 kg (♂ larger than ♀).
Identification pointers Only primate occurring north of the Sahara (restricted to mountains in Morocco and Algeria).
Similar species None.

DESCRIPTION Characterized by a relatively large size, no visible tail, and thick, longish yellow-grey to grey-brown hair. The dense coat is an adaptation to the temperature extremes experienced in the Atlas Mountains. The face is naked and dark flesh coloured. As the Barbary macaque is the only primate occurring in North Africa, it should not be mistaken for any other species.

DISTRIBUTION Once widely distributed in North Africa, it is now restricted to small forest and scrub patches in mountainous terrain in northern Morocco and Algeria, with perhaps 75% of the population surviving in the Middle Atlas range in Morocco. Smaller populations are located in the High Atlas and Rif, Morocco, and Petite Kabylie and Grande Kabylie, Algeria.

STATUS Greatly reduced in range and numbers, with an estimated 12 000 to 23 000 remaining. The main threats include habitat loss and disturbance.

HABITAT Mainly confined to rugged, isolated scrub-covered mountain slopes and gorges and montane forests which are dominated by the cedar (*Cedrus atlantica*) and several oak species, up to an altitude of 3 500 m.

BEHAVIOUR Troops include several adult males, and range in size from seven to 40 individuals, depending largely on conditions, including quality and quantity of available food, level of disturbance and habitat degradation. Home ranges of 25 to 1 200 ha have been recorded.

FOOD Tree fruits, leaves and shoots are important, as well as herbaceous plants, roots, bulbs, and although only making up a small percentage of intake, animal food. Parts of the cedar tree are of great importance at higher altitudes during the severe winter months.

REPRODUCTION Single young of about 400 g are dropped between February and June, after a gestation period of around 210 days.

The Barbary macaque, although it is a true monkey, does not have a visible tail.

The Barbary macaque is the only African primate occurring north of the Sahara.

MANGABEYS

Five (some recognize eight) species are currently recognized, and several distinctive subspecies. They are seldom seen, however, because of the usually dense nature of their forest habitats.

DESCRIPTION All species have slender and somewhat elongated bodies, and long tails often held erect, or curved over the back, when on the move. Snout longer than in other long-tailed monkeys, and pelage colouring is generally dull.

All species similar in size: total length 93-126 cm; tail length 40-80 cm; shoulder height 40-45 cm; weight 5-12 kg (♂ on average larger than ♀).

HABITAT Moist rainforests, but may utilize several forest associations (swamp/gallery types).

BEHAVIOUR Live in multi-male troops of 10 to 40 individuals, with group size varying from species to species and region to region. For example, up to 40 animals have been recorded for the Sanje subspecies of the crested mangabey (average 20 to 25); while troops of the Tana River subspecies (crested) range in size from 13 to 36 individuals but up to 60 have been recorded, involving temporary aggregations of two or more troops. All are extremely agile climbers, although not to the same extent as most of the guenons. The red-capped and crested spend a considerable amount of time on the ground foraging, but the black, grey-cheeked and sooty are principally arboreal foragers. For all species, the home range sizes, which to a large extent are a measure of the quantity and quality of available food, are likely to be small. In the case of the black, it is only 0,5 to 0,7 km² in one area; the grey-cheeked troops in the Kibale Forest of Uganda cover average ranges of 400 ha. All species associate freely with other primates, principally guenons. They are very vocal and their calls are often the first and only indication of their presence; their repertoire includes shrieks, howls and 'whoop-gobbles', and troop members frequently call in chorus.

FOOD Principally fruits and seeds, and also small quantities of leaves. Powerfully developed incisors enable them to include even the hardest seeds. Insects are also eaten, while the grey-cheeked mangabey is known to catch and eat small vertebrates.

REPRODUCTION Evidence indicates that some species and races are seasonal breeders, others non-seasonal. The Tana River race gives birth between November and February. Gestation of the grey-cheeked is up to 180 days, those of other species probably similar.

CRESTED MANGABEY *Cercocebus galeritus*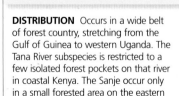
(Sometimes referred to as the agile mangabey. Apart from the two widespread crested mangabey races, two isolated subspecies are recognized – the Tana River (*C. g. galeritus*) and the Sanje (*C. g. sanjei*) – both endangered.) **Identification pointers** Despite its name, a true crest does not occur in any races; overall pelage colour is dirty yellowish-brown, with an olive tinge in some races; white to yellowish underparts. The Tana River race has a fringe of longish hairs around the face. Tail frequently bent forward over the head. **Similar species** Other mangabey and guenon species within range.

DISTRIBUTION Occurs in a wide belt of forest country, stretching from the Gulf of Guinea to western Uganda. The Tana River subspecies is restricted to a few isolated forest pockets on that river in coastal Kenya. The Sanje occur only in a small forested area on the eastern slopes of the Uzungwa Mountains in Tanzania.

STATUS The Congolean forest populations are secure, but the isolated Tana River (fewer than 1 000) and Sanje (about 3 000) groups are endangered.

Crested mangabey. These animals are seldom seen because of the usually dense nature of their forest habitats.

■ *Cercocebus torquatus*
■ *Cercocebus atys*

SOOTY MANGABEY

Cercocebus atys
Identification pointers Pelage overall grey but slightly lighter underparts; facial whiskers have a dark border.
Similar species None.

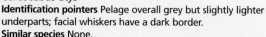

DISTRIBUTION Restricted to forests to the west of the Dahomey Gap in West Africa.

STATUS Still fairly abundant, but loss of habitat significant.

RED-CAPPED MANGABEY

Cercocebus torquatus
(Different races known as the white and the collared mangabey; sooty mangabey now considered full species in its own right).
Identification pointers Upperparts dark smoky-grey, nape and under-parts white, with white-tipped tail; bright chestnut-red on crown.
Similar species Grey-cheeked, crested mangabeys.

DISTRIBUTION East of Nigeria and southward to the Congo River.

STATUS Considered vulnerable but no estimates of population size are available.

■ *Cercocebus albigenia*
■ *Cercocebus aterrimus*

GREY-CHEEKED MANGABEY

Cercocebus albigenia
Identification pointers Overall blackish-brown coat colour; mantle of long hair on shoulders, ranging from pale grey to dark brown in different races; distinctive tuft of stiff hairs above each eye (this characteristic separates it from any other African monkey species). Long-haired tail but hair shortening towards tip; usually held over back and used as 'fifth limb'.
Similar species Black mangabey (but ranges do not overlap).

DISTRIBUTION Northern Congolean forests but not south of Congo River, extending as far east as Uganda.

STATUS Probably secure.

BLACK MANGABEY

Cercocebus aterrimus
Identification pointers As the common name implies, overall pelage colour is black with a glossy sheen; longish, pointed crest on top of head; one race has brown-grey facial whiskers, the other black whiskers. The tail is similar to that of the grey-cheeked mangabey.
Similar species Grey-cheeked mangabey (but ranges do not overlap).

DISTRIBUTION Forests of the central Congo Basin, south of that river and extending marginally into north-eastern Angola.

STATUS Secure, but numbers unknown.

Sooty mangabey

Red-capped mangabey

Grey-cheeked mangabey

Young male black mangabey

CERCOPITHECUS MONKEYS

Although some monkeys in this group are easily observed, there are many forest species that are common but rarely clearly seen. A number of monkeys have distinctive markings and colours but, in the dark undergrowth and canopy of forests, they are difficult and frequently impossible to distinguish. The species that are most likely to be seen are covered in the greatest detail, and the others are dealt with more briefly. The guenons and monkeys usually have the rump slightly higher than the shoulder region, and the tail is never held over the back as in the mangabeys.

VERVET (GREEN) MONKEY
Cercopithecus pygerythrus

Total length ♂ 100-130 cm ♀ 95-110 cm; tail length ♂ 60-75 cm ♀ 48-65 cm; weight ♂ 4-8 (average 5,5) kg ♀ 3,5-5 (average 4) kg.
Identification pointers Typical monkey appearance with long tail; feet and hands darker than rest of usually grizzled-grey coat; most races with black face; more lightly wooded habitat than most monkeys; lives in troops.
Similar species Should not be mistaken for any other monkey.

Front

Back

DESCRIPTION Easily recognizable throughout most of its range but five fairly well-defined groups have been assigned to this species: **callitrix**, lacking the white forehead band and being overall yellowish, from West Africa; **tantalus**, broad white forehead band and prominent upward-pointing facial whiskers, occurs from Ghana to south-western Sudan and Uganda; **grivets**, with very prominent white and fluffy facial whiskers, from Sudan and Ethiopia; **vervets**, with short facial whiskers and forehead band, and typical of eastern to southern Africa; and **Malbrouck**, the only one with a pale flesh-coloured face, occurring in a limited area of southern Congo, Angola and Zambia. Many subspecies and races have been described within these groups but all are readily recognizable as vervet monkeys. The tail is long, and the face short and usually black, with varying amounts of contrasting white fringing hair. Overall body colour is variable but mostly grizzled-grey, and the hair is fairly long and coarse. Underparts are paler and often white, but hands and feet are darker and usually black in most races. The adult male has a distinctive powder-blue scrotum.

DISTRIBUTION The vervet monkey is more widely distributed than any other African monkey, being absent only from desert, high forest and open grassland.

STATUS Common and widespread.

HABITAT Savanna and riverine woodland, and coastal scrub forest.

BEHAVIOUR Lives in troops of up to 20 or more individuals, but most groups tend to be smaller. The formation of large groups is generally associated with an abundant food source or water. They are diurnal and sleep at night in trees or occasionally on cliffs when suitable trees are not available. A clear 'pecking order' or social ranking is well established and maintained in each troop. Foraging takes place in a well-defined home range, with much of the time being spent on the ground. Although not as vocal as the forest-dwelling monkeys, they do have a range of alarm and threat calls.

FOOD A wide range of fruits, flowers, leaves, gum and seeds, and when the opportunity occurs, invertebrates and small vertebrates such as nestling birds.

REPRODUCTION Births may occur at any time of the year but in some areas there is evidence of peaks. After a gestation period of about 210 days, a single young weighing between 300 and 400 g is dropped.

The grivet forms of the vervet monkey have very long facial whiskers and occur mainly in Sudan and Ethiopia.

The West African race of the vervet monkey, sabaeus, has no white around the face and is strongly washed with yellow.

The vervet, or green, monkey has the most extensive distribution of all cercopithecenes and many races are recognized.

The southern race of the vervet monkey: Note the black face and contrasting white fringing hair.

■ *Cercopithecus albogularis*
■ *Cercopithecus nictitans*

BLUE/SYKES'S MONKEY
Cercopithecus albogularis
(Many races have been described but some authorities consider them to be one species, and this latter view is probably more valid.)
Total length ♂ 1,4 m ♀ 1,2 m; tail length ♂ 80 cm ♀ 70 cm;
weight ♂ 8-10 kg ♀ 4-5 kg (some size variation between races but not discernible in the field).
Identification pointers Typical monkey appearance; in most races hair relatively long and dark, especially on hands and feet; long facial whiskers; some races have white throat ruff; forest, woodland associations.
Similar species Other monkeys and guenons within its range.

> Sykes's Monkey is one of the least excitable and aggressive of the "true" monkeys and it is this behaviour that has earned it the name of Gentle Monkey in some regions.

DESCRIPTION This is one of the most frequently observed forest monkeys. Fairly powerfully built, with a straight back and tail held high and in a downward curve when walking. The lower limbs and feet are black in all races but the overall coloration is very variable. The coat is quite long and the hair coarse. Facial whiskers are prominent although their extent differs from race to race, giving the head a larger appearance. A dense and bristly browline is characteristic. Some races have a simple white throat patch whereas others have distinct white neck ruffs, or collars. Dorsal colour in the different races ranges from dark grey-black and bluish-grey, through various shades of brown, to dark golden-yellow. The **putty-nosed guenon** (*C. nictitans*), which some authorities believe to be the same species, replaces the blue in the western Congolean forests and in West Africa. The putty-nosed is similar in size, build and overall coloration to the western forms of the blue monkey, differing only in having a distinctive white patch on the nose. Most have blackish grey underparts but one race, *martini*, from Cameroon, has a white chest.

DISTRIBUTION Restricted to the eastern seaboard and adjacent interior from the Eastern Cape, South Africa, to southern Somalia. They are also present in Ethiopia, on either side of the Great Rift in East Africa and extending into north-central DRC, and in coastal Angola. Many populations are isolated, resulting in the great variation that is seen today. Some of the best locations to observe this species are the St Lucia wetland (South Africa), Mt Kenya and Aberdares (Kenya), and Ngorongoro and Lake Manyara (Tanzania).

STATUS Some races are abundant but others, such as the 'golden' monkey (*C. a. kandti*), found in a limited area of the Virunga Volcanoes, probably number in the low hundreds (endangered).

HABITAT Occupy a wide range of forested and densely vegetated habitats, including lowland and montane forest, swamp forest and also high altitude bamboo thicket. Along the coast they will also utilize low scrub forest, only rarely venturing beyond forest margins. In South Africa they enter commercial plantations but only on feeding forays.

BEHAVIOUR Certain aspects of behaviour vary in the different races but overall it is very similar. They live in troops of up to 30 and 40 individuals but often these are smaller. Most troops are controlled by a single adult male. Much of their time is spent in the trees but they do occasionally forage on the ground and move across clearings. In the tropics they freely associate with other monkeys, guenons and colobus, but are not as excitable as many primates. They are vocal with a range of calls, of which the most obvious is the very loud far-carrying bark, sounding superficially like 'jack', uttered by the males. Calling and their crashing progress through the trees are often the only signs of their presence; however, in some areas

Sykes' monkey photographed on Mount Kenya: Note the white ruff around the neck. Inset: *Blue monkey: Many races of this monkey have been described, this one being from northern South Africa.*

they have become habituated to man and are easy to observe. As with most monkeys they will sun themselves in the early morning but retreat to deep shade during the hottest midday hours. Troop home range size is dictated by many factors, but in one study a troop of the *stuhlmanni* race covered only one tenth to one sixteenth of a square kilometre, and the density in the area was estimated at 200 to 300 individuals per km^2. Behaviour of the putty-nosed is said to be very similar to that of Sykes' monkey.

FOOD Wide range of plants, including fruits, flowers, gum, leaves and seeds. In commercial timber plantations they are reported to debark young trees. They also take insects and have been seen to catch birds and small mammals.

REPRODUCTION In the southern areas of their range young are born during the summer months, but elsewhere, particularly in the equatorial belt, births are aseasonal although peaks may be discernible. A single young weighing about 400 g is dropped after a gestation period of about 220 to 230 days.

DE BRAZZA'S MONKEY
Cercopithecus neglectus

Total length ♂ 110-140 cm ♀ 95-110 cm; tail length 53-85 cm; weight ♂ 5-8 kg ♀ 4-5 kg.
Identification pointers Stout, heavily built; relatively short, thick tail, held arched or hanging down when walking; broad black and reddish bands above eyes; long white beard; white thigh stripe.
Similar species None.

DESCRIPTION One of the forest monkeys most easily identified in the field, with a fairly stocky build and somewhat thickened tail. Overall pelage colour is greeny-grey but a number of markings are clear and contrasting. Apart from the Diana monkey of West Africa, this is the only monkey with a well-developed and pointed white beard. A bright reddish-orange brow stripe, backed by a black band, runs on top of the head. A clear white stripe runs down the outer surface of the thigh. The tail is black.

DISTRIBUTION Patchy range in greater Congo Basin, both north and south of river; isolated populations occur in Uganda, western Kenya (Mt Elgon and Saiwa Swamp) and extreme south-western Ethiopia.

STATUS Secure, although considered endangered in Kenya.

HABITAT Mainly swamp forest but also other montane and lowland associations, including bamboo thickets.

BEHAVIOUR Equally at home feeding on the ground and in the trees. Although troops of between 15 and 35 individuals may be formed, family parties of male, female and offspring, and solitary males are not unusual. Larger troops are led by a single adult male. Although they will flee from danger, freezing is another method used to avoid detection. Unlike most monkey species, they are reported to be good swimmers. On the ground, the males particularly have a somewhat cat-like walk. No detailed study has been made of this monkey. Does not associate readily with other primates, particularly guenons.

FOOD Mixed diet of plant parts, mainly fruits and seeds, as well as insects and other invertebrates.

REPRODUCTION Births apparently take place at any time of year but in some areas at least there are seasonal peaks. A single young weighing about 250 g is dropped after a gestation period of around 182 days.

De Brazza's monkey: Note the white beard and thigh stripe. Unlike many other forest monkeys, this species spends a considerable amount of time foraging on the ground.

De Brazza's monkey: Note the somewhat thickened tail.

De Brazza's monkey with its pointed white beard is very easily identified in the field and should not be confused with any other monkey.

OWL-FACED GUENON *Cercopithecus hamlyni*

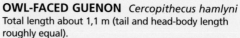

Total length about 1,1 m (tail and head-body length roughly equal).

Identification pointers Medium size; large, rounded face with conspicuous narrow, vertical white band from forehead to upper lip; rest of pelage very dark; occupies dense forest. **Similar species** None.

DESCRIPTION Medium sized, with a large, rounded face clearly marked with a conspicuous narrow vertical white band running from the forehead to the upper lip. The upperparts are dark olive-green and somewhat grizzled, while the underparts and legs are black. The relatively short tail is somewhat thickened and tipped with a black bushy tassel.

DISTRIBUTION Montane and lowland areas in the east-central DRC and marginally in south-western Uganda.

STATUS Considered vulnerable.

HABITAT Montane forest up to 4 600 m altitude, and lowland and bamboo forest.

BEHAVIOUR Live in small troops of fewer than ten individuals, which are led by an adult male. Although they forage in the trees, they also spend a lot of their time on the ground. Nothing else is known of behaviour in the wild. Reports of night activity not reliably confirmed.

FOOD Mixed diet including fruits, leaves and insects.

REPRODUCTION Nothing recorded in the wild.

DIANA MONKEY *Cercopithecus diana*

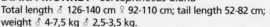
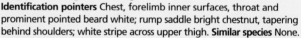

Total length ♂ 126-140 cm ♀ 92-110 cm; tail length 52-82 cm; weight ♂ 4-7,5 kg ♂ 2,5-3,5 kg.

Identification pointers Chest, forelimb inner surfaces, throat and prominent pointed beard white; rump saddle bright chestnut, tapering behind shoulders; white stripe across upper thigh. **Similar species** None.

DESCRIPTION Elegant and beautiful, with distinctive coloration and markings. It is the only monkey in West Africa which has a long, pointed white beard and a white stripe across the upper thigh. The chest, throat, inner forelimbs and a conspicuous brow-band are white, contrasting with the dark grey and black of much of the rest of the body. The tail is black, as are the legs and arms. A reddish-chestnut saddle, at its broadest at the base of the tail, narrows towards the back of the shoulders. The inner sides of the hind legs are reddish or creamy-white.

DISTRIBUTION Restricted to the Guinea high forest of West Africa.

STATUS Vulnerable because of limited range, habitat loss and meat hunting.

HABITAT Mainly high canopy forest,

but also secondary, riverine and semi-deciduous forest types. Most time spent in upper canopy but also in dense understory.

BEHAVIOUR Diurnal, and almost entirely arboreal, rarely descending to the ground. A typical troop consists of an adult male, six to eight adult females and dependent offspring, with group sizes of 15 to 40 individuals having been recorded. Each group is believed to defend a territory, and home ranges of 189 ha are known, which is large for a forest monkey. They associate freely with other monkey species.

FOOD Fruits, oil-rich seeds and invertebrates are most important.

REPRODUCTION No information available from the wild.

The race *roloway* is sometimes considered to be a species in its own right.

Owl-faced guenon. Inset: *Note the conspicuous white band running from the forehead to the upper lip.*

The Diana monkey is easy to distinguish by its long white beard and contrasting black face.

Apart from De Brazza's monkey, the Diana monkey is the only monkey with a well-developed and pointed beard.

- ■ *Cercopithecus l'hoesti*
- ■ *Cercopithecus preussi*

L'HOEST'S GUENON *Cercopithecus l'hoesti*

Total length about 1,1-1,5 m; tail length 48-80 cm; weight 3-8 kg (♂ larger than ♀).
Identification pointers Overall dark and black; reddish infusion on back; strongly contrasting long white cheek fringe; tail tip hooked.
Similar species Blue monkey races in areas of range overlap.

DESCRIPTION Very dark with strongly contrasting white cheek and throat hair. Most of the body is covered in very dark to black hair, although the back may be variously infused with reddish-brown. The closely related (some believe them to be the same species) Preuss's guenon (*C. preussi*) of south-eastern Nigeria and adjacent areas of Cameroon, has grey facial whiskers but retains the white throat.

DISTRIBUTION North-eastern Congo and the montane and hill country of western Uganda where they occupy large home ranges.

STATUS Considered vulnerable because of limited range. Preuss's may be endangered.

HABITAT Mainly montane forest; also recorded from lowland rain- and gallery forests, and well-wooded mountain slopes.

BEHAVIOUR Forage in trees, undergrowth and on the ground. They run in one-male troops ranging in size from 10 to 17 animals. Troops in western Ugandan forests are recorded as utilizing home ranges covering about 10 km², which is large for forest guenons. Mix freely with other guenons and colobuses.

FOOD Wide variety of plant foods but fruits are very important. Will raid crops.

REPRODUCTION No record in the wild but breeding appears to be seasonal.

Also called the dwarf guenon. Some believe that northern and southern populations constitute separate species.

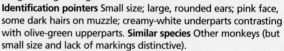

TALAPOIN *Miopithecus talapoin*

Total length ♂ 66-93 cm ♀ 50-82 cm; tail length 26-53 cm; weight 800 g ♂ 2 kg.
Identification pointers Small size; large, rounded ears; pink face, some dark hairs on muzzle; creamy-white underparts contrasting with olive-green upperparts. **Similar species** Other monkeys (but small size and lack of markings distinctive).

DESCRIPTION By far the smallest African 'true' monkey, without any striking markings or coloration. The face is dirty pink, with dark hairs on the muzzle, and the ears are large, rounded and prominent. Upperparts are olive-green with an infusion of straw-yellow, contrasting with paler underparts.

DISTRIBUTION North and south of the Congo River, extending from Cameroon in the north to well into Angola in the south. There appear to be three discrete populations but it is likely that they are linked with one another.

STATUS Apparently common.

HABITAT Lowland swamp and coastal forests, including mangroves.

BEHAVIOUR Normally run in troops of 10 to 20 individuals, although larger troops of up to 80 animals are on record. Smaller troops are believed to be made up of family units, within which there appears to be no strict 'pecking order'. They mix with other monkeys, particularly the mona monkey and moustached guenons. Although they are primarily arboreal, they are reported to be capable swimmers. They move rapidly through the trees and are extremely agile, and generally difficult to observe.

L'Hoest's guenon. Inset: *Young talapoin: This is Africa's smallest 'true' monkey.*

FOOD Wide range of fruits (including cultivated varieties), seeds, nuts, flowers, buds and leaves; will also take insects on occasion.

REPRODUCTION The only 'true' monkey in which the female undergoes genital swelling during the oestral cycle when she is sexually receptive. Apparently a seasonal breeder, and young, weighing about 160 g each, are dropped between November and March. The gestation period is about 190 days.

■ *Cercopithecus mona*
■ *Cercopithecus solatus*
■ *Cercopithecus salongo*

■ *Cercopithecus pogonias*
■ *Cercopithecus sclateri*

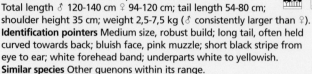

MONA MONKEY *Cercopithecus mona*

Total length ♂ 120-140 cm ♀ 94-120 cm; tail length 54-80 cm; shoulder height 35 cm; weight 2,5-7,5 kg (♂ consistently larger than ♀).
Identification pointers Medium size, robust build; long tail, often held curved towards back; bluish face, pink muzzle; short black stripe from eye to ear; white forehead band; underparts white to yellowish.
Similar species Other guenons within its range.

DESCRIPTION Several races are recognized and some authorities believe certain ones should be afforded full species status. In general, the face is slate-blue with a contrasting flesh-coloured muzzle. A greyish-white (varying in different races) band on the forehead separates the face from the darker crown, and a black stripe runs from the eye to the ear. The crown and shoulders are olive-green grizzled, but the rump region is darker and the underparts white. The outer surface of the arms is black, and the tail is dark above and white to yellow below. There may be pale ear tufts. In general, facial coloration is diagnostic, although the colour of shoulders, back and rump varies in different races.

DISTRIBUTION Two separate extensive populations, one centred on the forests of the Congo Basin and extending marginally into East Africa and Angola, the other occurring in a broad belt from Senegal to Cameroon.

STATUS In general secure, but some localized races may be threatened.

HABITAT Lowland rain- and gallery forests.

BEHAVIOUR Its name is derived from the moaning contact call of the female. They form fairly large troops containing one or more adult males, and will freely mix and feed with other monkeys. There is apparently no strict hierarchy within the troop. They are largely arboreal but do come to the ground occasionally.

FOOD Very wide variety of plants and plant parts, and also invertebrates.

REPRODUCTION A single young is born after a gestation period of about 180 days. Although in some areas young appear to be dropped at any time of year, there is some evidence of seasonality.

The **crowned guenon** (*C. pogonias*) is assigned by some to the **mona** group of races. It is similar in size and has relatively minor colour differences, with the brow-line forming a slight crest (hence the name) and the underparts and rump being yellow. There is no nose spot. They only occur on the north bank of the Congo River, from the Gulf of Guinea to the north-central DRC. All aspects of their biology are similar to those of the mona. Three additional species that have very localized distributions, and are unlikely to be seen by anyone other than the very determined naturalist, are the **sun-tailed guenon** (*C. solatus*), which takes its name from its bright orange tail and is restricted to a large forest block in central Gabon; the **Salongo guenon** (*C. salongo*), which is only known at this stage from the Wamba Forest in the north-central DRC; and **Sclater's guenon** (*C. sclateri*) found in a small area of south-eastern Nigeria. All four are relatively recent discoveries and none has been studied in the wild.

The common name of the mona monkey is derived from the moaning contact call of the female.

ALLEN'S SWAMP MONKEY *Allenopithecus nigroviridis*

Total length 85-105 cm; tail length 45-55 cm; weight 2,5-5 kg
(♀ only slightly smaller than ♂).
Identification pointers Stocky build; relatively short tail; upperparts dark olive-green, underparts off-white; red patch under tail; no other distinguishing features.
Similar species Mona monkey, where ranges overlap.

DESCRIPTION A rather nondescript, medium-sized monkey with stocky build and proportionately short tail. Head is round, with a prominent muzzle. No distinguishing features or markings, other than a reddish patch under the tail. Upperparts dark olive-green with some grizzling; underparts are usually dirty-white.

DISTRIBUTION Almost entirely restricted to the northern DRC, on both banks of Congo River.

STATUS Apparently declined (poorly known).

HABITAT Swamp and associated forests.

BEHAVIOUR Variously reported as occurring in small family troops, each with one adult male, and in larger multi-male bands. Forages readily on the ground, as well as in the trees. Swims well.

FOOD Wide variety of fruit and other plant parts; also insects and other invertebrates. They also raid crops (manioc).

REPRODUCTION Nothing known in the wild.

PATAS MONKEY
Erythrocebus patas

Total length ♂ 1,1-1,6 m ♀ 1-1,5 m; tail length 50-74 cm; weight 4-13 kg (♂ consistently larger than ♀).
Identification pointers Long legs; slender body, 'greyhound' appearance; coat brick-red to yellowish, underparts paler; white moustache and nose patch contrasting with dark face; only 'true' monkey on open savanna. **Similar species** None.

DESCRIPTION Large, slender and long-legged. Adult males have a brick-red coat that contrasts with the pale to white underparts; females and young have more dull straw-coloured to russet-grey upperparts. The (variable) black and white facial markings are distinctive.

DISTRIBUTION Occurs throughout the savannas of West Africa, from Senegal eastward to Ethiopia.

STATUS Not threatened.

HABITAT Dry savannas and rocky areas, but avoiding dense cover.

BEHAVIOUR The most terrestrial of the primates, apart from baboons and the gelada. They range over open and lightly wooded savanna country and are able to run at great speeds. Virtually all foraging takes place on the ground but they sleep in trees and use them as vantage points to watch for predators. Although small troops averaging 15 individuals are usual, in East Africa as many as 50 individuals are seen; up to 100 have been recorded in West Africa but these may constitute temporary groupings. Each troop has a dominant female and one adult male, and a very clear 'pecking order' is maintained. They frequently stand on the hind legs to scan over long grass. Unlike forest monkeys, patas cover very large home ranges of 80 km^2 or more.

FOOD Very wide range of plant and animal food, the latter primarily insects.

REPRODUCTION Breeding is seasonal. A single young is dropped after gestation of 170 days.

The patas monkey is the only 'true' monkey that occupies the open savanna plains. The male spends a large part of his time on watch for potential danger, and may use a tree or termite mound as a lookout post. Inset: Allen's swamp monkey

'SPOT-NOSED' GUENONS

The 'spot-nosed' monkeys are a complex of species and races that in general are difficult to identify in the field, but all are closely related. They are frequently labelled as belonging to the *cephus* group. The species most likely to be encountered is the red-tailed guenon, which has an extensive distribution in central Africa, extending as far east as Uganda and western Kenya. All species are capable of moving very rapidly through trees; most mix frequently with other primates.

HABITAT All species occur in tropical rainforest, although the red-tailed is also found in secondary and riparian forest in some parts of its range.

BEHAVIOUR All are predominantly arboreal, seldom descending to the ground. They are all strictly diurnal, and live in troops usually numbering 10 to 25 individuals, although smaller and larger numbers are not unusual. They mix readily with other monkeys, guenons, mangabeys and colobuses (studied in most detail for the red-tailed in the Kibale Forest, Uganda). All appear to occupy fixed home ranges and in at least some instances troops defend a territory against bands of the same species.

In the few studies undertaken, it appears that a troop has a single dominant male, and a strict 'pecking order' is followed. Visual and vocal communications are very important and each species has a distinctive repertoire of calls.

FOOD All take a broad spectrum of plant species, including most parts such as fruits, seeds and flowers, as well as insects, other invertebrates and possibly small vertebrates.

REPRODUCTION A single young can be dropped at any time of year, although there is evidence of seasonal peaks in some areas; however, little information is available.

MOUSTACHED GUENON
Cercopithecus cephus

Total length ♂ 1,2-1,6 m ♀ 1,1-1,3 m; tail length 70-95 cm; weight 3-5 kg.
Identification pointers Similar in overall appearance to red-tailed guenon, but grey underparts; blue face, white stripe on upper lip (hence name).
Similar species Red-tailed guenon marginally in east of range.

DISTRIBUTION Southern Cameroon, Gabon, Democratic Republic of Congo and extends marginally into northern Angola.

STATUS Apparently secure, despite limited distribution.

RED-EARED GUENON
Cercopithecus erythrotis

E

Total length ♂ 100-130 cm ♀ 86-110 cm; tail length 45-77 cm; weight 2,2-4,2 kg.
Identification pointers Similar to red-tailed guenon; nose spot brick-orange or white; cheek patches yellow or cream; tail entirely red, or red at base and white towards the tip; one race has reddish-brown ears, another has white ears. **Similar species** None in range.

DISTRIBUTION Restricted to a small area of southern Nigeria and adjoining Cameroon, as well as the island of Bioko.

STATUS Endangered.

The moustached guenon is distinguished by its white upper lip.

RED-BELLIED (WHITE-THROATED) GUENON

E

Cercopithecus erythrogaster
(Virtually no data on measurements available but seems on average slightly smaller than other 'spot-nosed' monkeys.)
Identification pointers Nose spot white or more commonly black; facial whiskers white, no black stripe; tail greenish above, white below and no red; chest and belly reddish-brown or grey; crown yellow, contrasting with dark face. **Similar species** None in range.

DISTRIBUTION Restricted to a small area between the Niger River delta and the Benin Gap of West Africa.

STATUS Endangered.

RED-TAILED GUENON

Cercopithecus ascanius
Total length ♂ 100-150 cm ♀ 85-130 cm; tail length 55-90 cm; weight 1,8->6 kg (considerable regional variation, but ♂ consistently larger than ♀).
Identification pointers Relatively small size; middle to tip of tail rufous-red; nose usually white but can be pale brown or black; cheeks white with black stripe; underparts usually white and dorsal coat dark greenish-olive with a reddish infusion. Several races are recognized but most cannot be separated in the field.
Similar species Moustached guenon in far west of range.

DISTRIBUTION Central Africa, particularly the DRC, and eastward to western Kenya. The forests of Uganda, such as Kibale, offer the best viewing possibilities.

STATUS Common.

(LESSER) SPOT-NOSED GUENON

Cercopithecus petaurista
Total length ♂ 100-120 cm ♀ 95-110 cm; tail length 60-68 cm; weight 2-3,5 kg.
Identification pointers White nose spot; cheek fur white, black stripe running below ear; underparts white, including ventral tail surface; dorsal tail surface olive-brown, as rest of body.
Similar species Putty-nosed guenon.

DISTRIBUTION Restricted to the forests of West Africa beyond the Dahomey Gap.

STATUS Relatively common.

Red-bellied guenon

Red-tailed guenon (race schmidti)

Moustached guenon

(Lesser) spot-nosed guenon

Front

Back

THE COLOBUS GROUP Subfamily Colobinae

If taxonomic problems exist within many of the 'true' monkeys and guenons, the colobuses are a nightmare. Some species are distinct and easy to recognize while others, particularly the red colobus (superspecies *badius*), have been split into numerous races, subspecies and species on relatively minor grounds. A very simplified field guide is therefore offered for this group. Most are relatively large, somewhat robust in appearance but of slender build, with a long tail, in the case of the black and white colobuses, well haired and, with the exception of the olive and black species, are distinctively marked. Although not a visible field character, the thumbs are absent, which is a feature unique to the colobus.

OLIVE (VAN BENEDEN'S) COLOBUS *Procolobus verus*

Total length 1–1,4 m; tail length 57–64 cm; weight 3–5 kg.
Identification pointers Small, round head; dull olive-green upperparts; grey underparts; no clear markings; male with slight crest on middle of crown. **Similar species** None.

DESCRIPTION The smallest colobus. Olive-green with greyish underparts. No pelage markings apart from two fairly obvious grey patches on the forehead.

DISTRIBUTION Restricted to the forests of West Africa, from Sierra Leone to Nigeria.

STATUS Rare, but abundant in parts of range.

HABITAT Mainly lowland rainforest, preferring the areas of the dense understory.

BEHAVIOUR Primarily arboreal, extremely shy and retiring, and therefore seldom seen. Although a preference is shown for the forest understory, they frequently associate with *Cercopithecus* species and will then move and forage through the canopy. Troop sizes range from six to 20 individuals, with an average of 10. Individuals disperse when foraging.

FOOD Primarily young leaves but also small quantities of fruits and seeds.

REPRODUCTION Virtually nothing known. Apparently the only African monkey whose female carries the infant in her mouth.

BLACK (SATANIC) COLOBUS
Colobus satanas

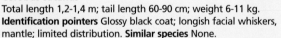

Total length 1,2–1,4 m; tail length 60–90 cm; weight 6–11 kg.
Identification pointers Glossy black coat; longish facial whiskers, mantle; limited distribution. **Similar species** None.

DESCRIPTION Large, heavy build, with an entirely glossy black coat. Hair around the face and shoulders longer than elsewhere, but tail hair relatively short.

DISTRIBUTION Restricted to the forests centred around Gabon and southern Cameroon, and on the island of Bioko.

STATUS Endangered.

HABITAT A range of forest types but mainly coastal evergreen, primary, montane and swamp forests. They are absent from secondary forests.

BEHAVIOUR Arboreal, and live in small troops of 6 to 15 individuals, including one or more adult males. Troop home ranges vary from 70 ha in coastal forests to 180 ha in forests in the interior.

FOOD Young leaves and seeds.

REPRODUCTION Nothing recorded.

The colobus is unique in that it has no thumbs. The individual shown here is an Angolan black and white colobus.

Front

Back

RED COLOBUSES

The red colobus monkey is broadly divided into five species, all generally grouped under the 'superspecies' *badius*. All are generally recognizable as red colobuses but there is much variation in colour and markings. They all have fairly large bodies, long limbs and proportionally small heads and reddish, chestnut, or orange-brown fur is present to a greater or lesser extent. The back slopes down from the rump to the shoulders and has a slightly arched appearance. Should not be confused with any other primate within its range.

Total length ♂ 100-150 cm ♀ 90-140 cm; tail length ♂ 55-80 cm ♀ 42-80 cm; weight ♂ 9-13 kg ♀ 7-9 kg.

HABITAT All truly arboreal, rarely coming to the ground except to cross clearings. Reds spend most of their time in the canopy and higher reaches of the forest strata. A range of forest types are occupied by the different races, including lowland rainforest, gallery forests, mangrove and montane forest. Very occasionally they will venture into dense savanna woodland (e.g. Temminck's in far West Africa).

BEHAVIOUR Group size is variable in the different races but in general ranges from 25 to 50 individuals, although can be as low as four to six. Each group is accompanied by one or more adult males, with multi-male groups being most common. In most races males and females may move between groups on reaching maturity but in some only females leave the birth troop. Home range size is very variable, being largely dependent on food quality, but in general averages from 9 to 35 ha, with considerable overlap between troops. Reds mingle freely with several other monkey species, particularly in food trees. Although quite vocal, they are probably less so than the black and white colobus group.

FOOD Some 80% or more of their food is made up of leaves, primarily young growth, for which they have a highly developed digestive system. Fruits, flowers and other plant parts make up the remainder.

REPRODUCTION Red colobus monkeys are poorly known in the wild, but at least some races appear to be seasonal breeders.

■ *Procolobus rufomitratus*
  tholloni
■ *P.r. foai*
■ *P.r. oustaleti*
■ *P.r. tephrosceles*
□ *P.r. ellioti*
□ *P.r. rufomitratus*

CENTRAL/EASTERN RED COLOBUS
Procolobus rufomitratus

(includes the subspecies Oustalet's, Elliot's, Foa, Thollon's, Uganda and Tana River colobus, and several others not clearly defined)
Identification pointers Most variable of all in colour spread but easily recognizable as 'red colobus'. Crown colour varies from black to rufous and yellow in different races; most forms have reddish to reddish-brown coloration on upperparts and paler underparts.

DISTRIBUTION In a relatively narrow belt on both sides of the Congo River, and then through western Uganda (best sighting location Kibale Forest) into western Tanzania along Lake Tanganyika. An isolated population is located in the riparian forest of lower Tana River in Kenya.

STATUS Little is known about the forms occurring in the DRC but the Uganda red (*P. r. tephrosceles*) is threatened by habitat loss and hunting, and the Tana River race (*P. r. rufomitratus*) is on the verge of extinction, with possibly fewer than 300 surviving.

Some 80 per cent of the food of the red colobus is made up of leaves, primarily young growth, for which they have a highly developed digestive system. The individual shown here is a Zanzibar red colobus.

The red-capped form of the eastern red colobus, tephrosceles, *photographed in the Kibale Forest, Uganda. Most individuals are black dorsally with the remainder of the body being deep red.*

■ *Procolobus kirkii*
■ *Procolobus gordonorum*

■ *Procolobus badius badius*
■ *Procolobus badius waldroni*
▨ *Procolobus badius temmincki*
▨ *Procolobus pennanti pennanti*
□ *Procolobus pennanti bouvieri*
□ *Procolobus pennanti preussi*
■ *Procolobus p. epieni*

Front

Back

GORDON'S RED COLOBUS *Procolobus gordonorum*
Identification pointers Recognizable as a red colobus.

DISTRIBUTION Occupies the southern and eastern forested slopes of the Uzungwa Mountains in south-central Tanzania. The most viable population is located in the Magombero Forest.

STATUS Endangered.

ZANZIBAR RED COLOBUS *Procolobus kirkii*
Identification pointers Long-haired white brow-line; white cheeks, underparts and hind limbs; black on shoulders, with red on rest of back; pale tail; restricted distribution.

DISTRIBUTION Only occurs on the island of Unguja, Zanzibar.

STATUS About 1 500 animals remaining.

WESTERN RED COLOBUS *Procolobus badius*
(includes the subspecies Miss Waldron's bay, Temminck's and the Bay colobus)
Identification pointers Dark face, pale around eyes; whiskers shades of red or orange; no crest in central crown area; dorsal pelage glossy black to dark grey; sides, underparts, legs and arms reddish-brown to orange – very distinctive. Buttocks and area partly down back of legs white – extent variable.

DISTRIBUTION Occurs from Senegal to western Ghana.

STATUS Endangered to vulnerable.

PENNANT'S RED COLOBUS *Procolobus pennanti*
(includes the subspecies Pennant's, Preuss's and Bouvier's colobus)
Identification pointers Typical red colobus form and overall appearance; colour extremely variable; blackish colour always present on shoulders, with remaining parts being to a greater, or lesser, extent red, reddish-brown to yellowish-brown; underparts yellowish-brown, grey or white.

DISTRIBUTION Forest patches west of the Congo River.

STATUS Endangered.

THE BLACK AND WHITE (PIED) COLOBUS GROUP
As with the red colobus group, the black and white, or pied, colobus monkeys are all readily recognizable as belonging to this assemblage. General form and structure are the same but races are based primarily on the extent and length of the white hair on a black background, as well as the colour and bushiness of the tail. They can be broadly divided into three groups, the western or *polykomos* group, the Angolan *angolensis* and the Abyssinian or guereza *abyssinicus*.
Total length 1,1-1,6 m; tail length 65-90 cm; weight 9-23 kg (♀ is only slightly smaller than ♂).

The Zanzibar red colobus occurs only on the island of Unguja, Zanzibar. About 1 500 animals remain today.

Zanzibar red colobus, photographed in the Jozani Forest, Unguja, Zanzibar.

The red-capped form of the eastern red colobus, tephrosceles, photographed in the Kibale Forest, Uganda. Most individuals are black Temminck's red colobus, a subspecies of the western red colobus (badius group).

HABITAT Spend much of their time in the upper canopy and middle sector of the forest trees. They occupy forests from sea level to montane reaches exceeding 3 000 m. Many forest types are occupied, as well as dense woodland and riparian habitats penetrating otherwise unsuitable areas.

BEHAVIOUR Highly arboreal, only coming to the ground to cross clearings. They live in troops of 10 to 25 individuals, and occasionally more, with one or more adult males. Each troop occupies a relatively small home range of about 15 ha but it varies according to food availability and quality. Troops are territorial but in optimal habitat, density is high. This is one of the easiest monkeys to observe in areas where they are not disturbed. They frequently bask on exposed branches in the mornings, looking like giant 'blossoms' decorating the trees.

A characteristic call is a far-carrying deep croak uttered by both males and females; calling is done primarily from the sleeping trees, then after having moved to the feeding sites, and again at sunset. Aggression is minimal when compared to the guenons.

FOOD Almost entirely leaves, principally young growth, but also small quantities of lichen, fruits, seeds and insects.

REPRODUCTION Apparently non-seasonal breeders but in areas where food supply fluctuates there may be seasonal peaks. A single, all-white young weighing about 450 g is dropped after a gestation period of about 180 days (literature records differ by up to 40 days). The youngsters take on adult colouring at between two and three months of age.

■ *Colobus polykomos*
■ *Colobus vellerosus*

WESTERN BLACK AND WHITE COLOBUS
Colobus polykomos

Identification pointers Overall relatively long, black, glossy coat; facial whiskers and front chest region greyish-white; short-haired tail entirely white. **Geoffroy's black and white colobus** (*C. vellerosus*) is sometimes recognized as a full species, and differs in having long but 'neat' white facial whiskers and beard, while the thighs have extensive patches of white hair.

DISTRIBUTION Limited to the far western forests of West Africa. Geoffroy's occurs from the Ivory Coast to the Niger River.

STATUS Not threatened.

GUEREZA (ABYSSINIAN) BLACK AND WHITE COLOBUS *Colobus guereza (abyssinicus)*

Identification pointers Overall black; mantle of long white hair around sides and lower back; tail black to grizzled towards base, then white and bushy, the extent varying in different races but all easily recognizable; facial whiskers and short beard white. Infants totally white. This is the species most frequently seen by visitors to East Africa, specifically to Lake Nakuru, Mt Kenya, Aberdares, Ngorongoro and Mt Meru.

DISTRIBUTION From Gulf of Guinea eastward, north of Congo River, to Lake Victoria. Separate populations in south-western Kenya and central Ethiopia.

STATUS Not threatened but greatly reduced in some areas.

The western black and white colobus is restricted to the western forests of West Africa.

The newborn young of the guereza are pure white with pink faces, and look very different from the adults.

Guereza, photographed at Lake Nakuru, Kenya: Note the very bushy tail.

ANGOLA BLACK AND WHITE COLOBUS

Colobus angolensis
Identification pointers Black, glossy coat; white hair patches of variable length on shoulders; tail black, white or both and has bushy tip in some races; white facial whiskers long and erect.

DISTRIBUTION Extensive in the Congo Basin, with an isolated population occurring from south-eastern Kenya into Tanzania, to the north of Lake Nyasa (Malawi).

STATUS Not threatened generally.

MAN-LIKE APES   Family Pongidae
There are three members of the **Pongidae** family in Africa, the **chimpanzee** with three races, the **gorilla** of which also three races are recognized, and the **bonobo**. All are characterized by their large size, absence of a tail and mainly black coloration.

CHIMPANZEE   *Pan troglodytes*
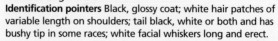
Total length ♂ 75-95 cm ♀ 65-85 cm; standing height about 1 m; weight 30-55 kg (♂ generally heavier than ♀).
Identification pointers Human-like appearance; fur, skin generally black; facial skin pink, black or mottled with both; does not occur south of Congo River. **Similar species** None. Also called Robust Chimpanzee.

■ *Pan troglodytes schweinfurthi*
■ *Pan troglodytes troglodytes*
■ *Pan troglodytes verus*

Sometimes referred to as the Common or Robust Chimpanzee, to separate it from the Bonobo, often erroneously called the Pygmy Chimpanzee.

Back

A fourth subspecies, *Pan t. vellerosus* sometimes recognized from Nigeria.

DESCRIPTION Quite heavily built but much lighter than gorilla; easy to tell apart in areas where both species occur. The limbs are long but the legs are considerably shorter than the arms, and when walking the back slopes down to the rump. Top of the head and body are usually well covered in black hair but older animals may be bald. Skin colour in adults is generally black but facial colour may be black or pink, or mottled with both. Youngsters often have a tuft of longish white hair on the rump. Although three subspecies are recognized, the western (*verus*), central (*troglodytes*) and the eastern chimpanzee (*schweinfurthi*), differences between them are minimal.

DISTRIBUTION West African populations are highly fragmented, occurring in south-western Ghana, Ivory Coast, Liberia, Sierra Leone, Guinea and south-western Mali. The central and eastern populations are more or less continuous. Populations on the north-eastern shores of Lake Tanganyika and in the forest reserves of Uganda offer the best opportunities of observing this species in the wild.

STATUS Fewer than 200 000 animals remain, western population estimated at only 17 000. Threatened by habitat loss and hunting, particularly in West Africa.

HABITAT Has the widest habitat tolerance of the three man-like apes, occupying or utilizing a range of forest and woodland types. In some areas they live in savanna woodland or in more open savanna types where they can easily retreat to small evergreen forest patches, usually located in gorges and gullies. They are equally at home at sea level and at altitudes of about 3 000 m. The principal limiting factors appear to be access to water and trees suitable for sleeping.

BEHAVIOUR Probably the most studied primate, both in the wild and in captivity, with most studies in the wild having taken place on the north-eastern

Angola black and white colobus with young: Note the white hair patches on the shoulders of the adult.

Bonds between a chimpanzee mother and her offspring usually endure throughout her life.

The faces and ears of adult chimpanzees are usually black.

shore of Lake Tanganyika and at three locations in West Africa. Chimpanzees live in loose communities of 15 to over 100 individuals, but averaging some 35 animals, with each community occupying a home range of 10 to 50 km^2. They forage on the ground and in trees, in small groups rarely numbering more than six animals and often a female and her dependent offspring. Males nearly always remain within the community into which they were born, but females, on reaching maturity, usually disperse and join neighbouring communities. Males frequently travel through the community's home range in groups and patrol the boundaries. Migratory communities have also been recorded, particularly in savanna habitats, and home ranges may cover between 200 and 400 km^2.

FOOD Very varied diet including many different plant parts, and invertebrates and vertebrates which may be opportunistically or deliberately hunted, including young antelope, small duikers, monkeys and guenons, and also birds and their eggs.

REPRODUCTION They are promiscuous and a female in oestrus will mate with several different males. High-ranking males compete with each other for the right to mate with a female as she approaches ovulation. A single young is usual, but occasionally twins are born. Breeding is non-seasonal. A young chimpanzee passes through a five-year period of infancy during which it is entirely reliant on its mother. Years of development closely follow those of a human child. Links and bonds between a mother and her offspring usually endure throughout her life. The gestation period is about 240 days and birth weight 1,5 to 2 kg.

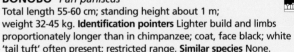

BONOBO *Pan paniscus*
Total length 55-60 cm; standing height about 1 m; weight 32-45 kg. **Identification pointers** Lighter build and limbs proportionately longer than in chimpanzee; coat, face black; white 'tail tuft' often present; restricted range. **Similar species** None.

DESCRIPTION Originally called the 'pygmy chimpanzee' but, although having a more slender build than the chimpanzee, there is little difference in overall size between the two. The head of the bonobo is proportionately smaller and the face flatter and always black, although the lips are pink. The white 'tail tuft' present in infants is often retained in adulthood.

DISTRIBUTION Restricted to the central forests of the Congo Basin, south of the Congo River.

STATUS Uncertain, but possibly 20 000.

HABITAT Primary and secondary forest, as well as seasonally flooded swamp forest.

BEHAVIOUR Live in groups of 30 to 80 individuals but up to 120 have been recorded. Small subgroups, usually of males and females, forage over the home range and all live in loose association. Compared to the chimpanzee they are relatively peaceful and tranquil and sex ratios are approximately equal. Females are up to eight times more available to males for mating than their chimp counterparts, thus reducing conflict over copulation rights. Sexual intercourse is frequent and acts as a stabilizing influence in the community. Males remain within their birth group for life but females join other groups on reaching maturity. They spend about 30% of the day feeding, foraging both on the ground and in the trees, with most arboreal feeding taking place during the cooler morning and late afternoon hours. They sleep in self-constructed nests well above the forest floor.

FOOD As varied as that of the chimpanzee but fruit usually makes up the bulk of their daily intake.

REPRODUCTION Young are born at any time of year, and weigh about 1,5 kg; gestation period is about 240 days. Young is dependent on its mother until it reaches maturity.

Back

Young chimpanzees usually have pinkish faces and ears and a tuft of white hair on the rump.

The years of development of the young chimpanzee closely follow those of the human child.

The head of the bonobo is proportionately smaller and the face flatter than that of the chimpanzee.

- Gorilla gorilla gorilla
- Gorilla gorilla graueri
- Gorilla gorilla berengei

Front

Back

Cross River, Nigeria, population sometimes separate subspecies, *G. g. diehli.*

A small, isolated population of mountain gorillas survives in the Bwindi Forest of western Uganda.

GORILLA *Gorilla gorilla*

Standing height ♂ about 1,7 m ♀ about 1,5 m; weight ♂ 140-180 kg ♀ 70-100 kg.

Identification pointers Very large size; entirely black except adult males with silver-coloured 'saddle' and western populations with reddish-chestnut on crown; much larger than chimpanzee.

Similar species Chimpanzee (separated on size).

DESCRIPTION Largest of the primates with a massive build, powerful muscle structure, large head with low forehead and small ears. The arms are longer than the legs, and the back slopes down from the shoulders to the rump. The belly is large, with the appearance of a 'beer paunch'. The coat is black to greyish-black and adult males have a broad, whitish-silver 'saddle' on the back, its extent varying in the different races. Three races, or subspecies, are currently recognized: the western lowland (gorilla), the eastern lowland (graueri) and the mountain gorilla (berengei). The western lowland has quite short hair which frequently has a brownish tinge, particularly on top of the head. The 'saddle' of the adult male extends from the shoulders on to the rump and thighs. The eastern lowland has a pure black coat and the male's 'saddle' is restricted to the back. The mountain race is marginally larger than the two lowland forms and the black hair is longer.

DISTRIBUTION The western lowland has the widest distribution, covering southern Cameroon, Gabon and the Congo. The eastern lowland population centre lies more than 1 200 km to the east in east-central DRC. The mountain race is entirely restricted to a part of the Virunga range, straddling the DRC/Ugandan/Rwandan borders.

STATUS Up to 45 000 western lowland gorillas are estimated to survive, but fewer than 5 000 eastern lowland animals, and a mere 600 mountain gorillas remain.

HABITAT Show a marked preference for forest margins, secondary forest, vegetated clearings and riverine forest. Occur seasonally in primary forest. The mountain gorilla utilizes bamboo thickets occasionally, and has been recorded as high as 3 400 m. The western race makes extensive use of swamp forest.

BEHAVIOUR Live in groups of two to a recorded maximum of 37 individuals; the western lowland lives in smaller groups averaging five members and the eastern race in groups averaging nine. Each group is dominated by an adult 'silverback' male, and includes several adult females and immature animals up to the age of about eight years. Both males and females leave birth group on reaching maturity, females joining lone males or small groups, while males remain alone until they can attract females and hold their own groups. They move from the night resting sites quite late, feeding for about two hours in the morning and a further three or four hours in the afternoon. Females and young construct sleeping nests in trees but the heavy males usually bed down on the ground. Groups occupy home ranges of 5 to 35 km², with those of western race being most extensive. There is evidence of some seasonal movements, related to food availability and preferences. Their daily group movements rarely cover more than one kilometre but greater distances are undertaken by western populations.

FOOD The eastern populations are primarily folivorous, taking a wide range of herb, shrub and vine leaves, as well as pith. In the west, fruits are much more significant. The western lowland race also include some animal food in their diet. Termites are harvested after the gorilla has swiped off the top of a mound with its hand – an indication of its strength.

REPRODUCTION Young may be born at any time of the year. A single infant of about 2 kg is dropped after gestation of 260 days.

Male western lowland gorilla. The western race readily wades through streams and pools, often to harvest aquatic plants.

Male mountain gorilla. All three gorilla races are hunted for their meat.

Female mountain gorillas: Note the shaggy black coat and longer hair – an adaptation to their high altitude home. As a result of serious habitat loss, only 600 of these animals survive today.

ODD-TOED UNGULATES Order Perissodactyla

■ *Equus asinus africanus*
■ *Equus asinus somaliensis*

Front

95 mm

Back

African Wild Ass

WILD ASS AND ZEBRAS
Family Equidae

AFRICAN WILD ASS
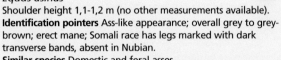

Equus asinus
Shoulder height 1,1-1,2 m (no other measurements available).
Identification pointers Ass-like appearance; overall grey to grey-brown; erect mane; Somali race has legs marked with dark transverse bands, absent in Nubian.
Similar species Domestic and feral asses.

E

DESCRIPTION Has a typical ass-like (donkey) appearance, with a relatively large head and long, pointed ears. Two subspecies are recognized by some authorities, the Nubian wild ass (*E. a. africanus*), and Somali wild ass (*E. a. somaliensis*), based on minor, variable colour differences. The overall body colour of the Nubian is grey to greyish-buff and it has no dark markings on the legs; the pelage of the Somali tends to be infused with more pale brown and the dark transverse leg markings are distinctive. The body hair is short with the exception of the erect mane and the tail. It has been suggested, however, that these characteristics are not consistent in the two races and that no subspecies should be recognized.

DISTRIBUTION Previously occurred from the Saharan Atlas in Morocco, south and eastward to the Horn of Africa region. Current populations are restricted to southern Eritrea and to Ethiopia, from the Danakil Desert, along the Awash River and extending into Ogaden, marginally into Djibouti and into northern Somalia east to the Nogal Valley.

STATUS Endangered, with less than 2 000 animals surviving, and possibly only a few hundred following recent warfare and drought within their range, and confusion with sightings of feral asses. Because of mixed characteristics it is feared that the Nubian race has interbred with feral asses to such an extent that it could well be extinct. Apart from hybridization problems, hunting is an ongoing threat to the continued survival of this species.

HABITAT Occupies arid, rugged hill country and desert plains.

BEHAVIOUR Very little field work has been done on this species but it is known that adult males defend territories of between 5 and 10 km², with females associating with the territorial males and other females. Otherwise they form unstable herds of up to 50 individuals, including the young. They are said to be very agile, spending the daylight hours in more rugged terrain and descending at night to feed in the inter-hill valleys; this is probably influenced by the human and domestic stock pressure throughout their range. Territorial males deposit their droppings in middens of more than 1m², scattered around the perimeter of the territory. Although access to drinking water is essential, up to three days may pass between visits to water points.

FOOD Favours grazing but browses readily.

REPRODUCTION Mares give birth for the first time at about four years of age; a single foal is dropped after a gestation period of between 330 and 365 days.

Wild ass (Somali race). Inset: *Note the black banding on the lower legs.*

MOUNTAIN ZEBRA
Equus zebra

- ■ *Equus zebra zebra*
- ■ *Equus zebra hartmannae*

100 mm

Mountain Zebra

CAPE MOUNTAIN ZEBRA
Equus zebra zebra

   E

HARTMANN'S MOUNTAIN ZEBRA
Equus zebra hartmannae

Cape subsp.: shoulder height 1,3 m; tail 40 cm; weight 250-260 kg.
Hartmann's subsp.: shoulder height 1,5 m; tail 40 cm; weight 250-350 kg.
Identification pointers Black and white stripes, no shadow stripes; legs striped to hoofs; grid-iron pattern on rump; dewlap on throat.
Similar species Plains zebra in north-western Namibia, and on game farms in southern Africa where both species have been introduced.

DESCRIPTION Hartmann's is slightly larger than Cape and has minor striping variations on the rump, but otherwise the two are very similar, being white with black stripes, with legs striped to the hooves, and white underparts. Shadow stripes are never present, as in some races of the plains zebra, but a distinctive 'grid-iron' pattern of transverse black stripes is present on the rump above the tail. The tip of the muzzle is black, blending into orange-brown. The erect mane runs from the top of the head to the withers and a dewlap is present on the throat. The dewlap and the rump pattern are only found on this species.

DISTRIBUTION The Cape race once occurred widely in mountain ranges south of the Gariep (Orange) River (South Africa) but it is now restricted to some 20 widely scattered populations in conservation areas. Hartmann's is restricted to the western montane escarpment, on the Namib fringe, through the length of Namibia and marginally into extreme south-western Angola. Naturally occurring populations are increasingly scattered and fragmented, with animals having been introduced on to South African game farms and reserves outside their natural range. It is generally believed that mountain zebra occurred within historical times in a continuous belt from south-western Angola to the Eastern Cape, South Africa.

STATUS Less than 1 200 individuals of the Cape race survive and although secure in several well-managed national parks and reserves, such low numbers hold great survival risks. An estimated 7 000 Hartmann's survive, down from about 16 400 in 1972.

HABITAT Rugged mountainous areas and adjacent flats and plains. Previously greater use was probably made of grassed plains, particularly during rains.

BEHAVIOUR Adult stallions form small harem groups of usually four or five mares with their accompanying young. In the case of Hartmann's, temporary congregations of 40 or more individuals may be observed, particularly at areas of good grazing or at water-points. This may have applied to the Cape race in the past but small, isolated and confined populations do not allow for it. Non-harem stallions form bachelor groups, which may include young mares and weaned foals of both sexes. Territories are apparently not held but harem stallions defend their mares against potential competing stallions while tolerating submissive males.

FOOD Predominantly grazers, but will browse on occasion.

REPRODUCTION A single foal is dropped after a gestation period of about a year.

Cape mountain zebra: Mountain zebras have no shadow stripes, striping does not extend onto the belly, and a small dewlap develops on the throat. Inset: Skin showing the 'grid-iron' patterning on the rump of the mountain zebra.

Hartmann's mountain zebra is very similar to the Cape race but is slightly larger and has a slightly different rump pattern. Inset: The distinctive patterning on the rump and tail is diagnostic of both subspecies.

Front

103 mm

Back

Grevy's Zebra

GREVY'S ZEBRA
Equus grevyi
Total length 3,2-3,5 m; tail length 75 cm; shoulder height 1,5 m; weight 350-430 kg.

Identification pointers Narrow black striping on white background, no shadow stripes; white underparts; broad dark stripe along spine; larger than plains zebra.
Similar species Plains zebra, where ranges overlap.

E

DESCRIPTION The largest zebra species, characterized by very narrow black striping, without shadow stripes laid over the white stripes. A distinct black stripe runs from the tail along the length of the spine, and on the rump this is flanked by white. The belly is white but the legs are densely striped. The head is large with long mule-like ears and a long, erect mane extending from the head to the withers.

DISTRIBUTION Previously occurred throughout Kenya east of Lake Turkana and the Great Rift Valley and to the north of Mount Kenya, and still largely within this area, but in greatly reduced numbers and fragmented populations. Now mainly restricted to conservation areas, principally Samburu, Shaba and Buffalo Springs National Reserves, Kenya. Also occurs in three small areas in Ethiopia, north-east of Awash National Park, the Sarite Plain and vicinity of Lake Chew Bahar, but extinct in Somalia.

STATUS Considered endangered because of steady declines (as much as 90% since the 1960s); fewer than 1 500 survive in Ethiopia and slightly more than 4 000 in Kenya. In the past they were hunted extensively for their skins, but competition for grazing and water with domestic stock pose the major problem today. Given the present circumstances it has been estimated that this species could become extinct within the next 50 years.

HABITAT Semi-desert plains, and dry open woodland savanna on flats and in broken hill country.

BEHAVIOUR Adult stallions establish territories, marked with piles of dung, which they actively defend against incursions by other stallions, although nursery herds (mares and foals) pass through them freely. During very dry periods stallions may temporarily abandon their territories, returning when conditions are more favourable. Herds of mixed sex and age-group are most frequently sighted during the dry season. Because of the arid nature of their favoured habitats they roam over vast home ranges, even exceeding 10 000 km^2. Breeding stallions establish core territories as large as 12 km^2 close to a water source. This species is able to withstand drought conditions better than the plains zebra, but must drink every two to five days.

FOOD Predominantly grazers although up to 30% of their diet may be made up of browse.

REPRODUCTION Births occur at any time of the year, peaking at the onset of the rainy season. Recorded gestation periods lie between 387 and 428 days, a single foal being dropped at term.

Grevy's zebra. Inset: *Note the narrow stripes and the black vertebral stripe.*

PLAINS ZEBRA *Equus quagga/burchellii*

(including Grant's zebra (E. b. boehmi), the Upper Zambezi zebra (E. b. zambeziensis), Crawshay's zebra (E. b. crawshayi), Chapman's zebra (E. b. chapmanni), and the Damara zebra (E. b. antiquorum). Total length 2,3-3 m; tail length 43-56 cm; shoulder height 1,3 m; weight 290-340 kg. **Identification pointers** Stocky and pony-like; black and white stripes, some races with, others without, shadow stripes superimposed on white stripes; stripes extend on to underparts; no dewlap. **Similar species** Hartmann's zebra in north-western Namibia, Grevy's in Kenya.

Plains Zebra

90 mm

Recent taxonomic thinking places this zebra as *Equus quagga* in southern Africa, but elsewhere it is still called *Equus burchellii*. The now extinct quagga is believed to have been only a race, or subspecies of the plains zebra.

DESCRIPTION The most widespread and abundant of Africa's wild horses, showing considerable variation in patterning with five extant subspecies being recognized (or seven by some authorities). Animals in southern Africa are generally characterized by having shadow stripes overlaid on the white stripes but these are absent in central and East African races. Within any population, however, the striping is variable and certain populations are hybrids of two distinct races, this being pronounced in parts of Zimbabwe, Namibia and Botswana. The shadow stripes are most pronounced towards the rump. The mane is long, erect and alternately black and white, coinciding with the neck stripes. The tail is short-haired towards the base but then long-haired. The ears are comparatively shorter than those of other zebra species.

DISTRIBUTION Occur widely in eastern and southern Africa, with the largest concentrations, exceeding half a million, being centred on Kenya and northern Tanzania, while game reserves and private farms in Namibia, South Africa and Zimbabwe also hold substantial numbers. Grant's zebra occurs throughout East Africa and the Horn of Africa, and in the Upper Zambezi in the DRC, Angola and western Zambia; Crawshay's zebra occurs in northern Mozambique, in Malawi and in eastern Zambia, Chapman's zebra in southern Mozambique, and the Damara zebra in Namibia and South Africa.

STATUS Current population of all races combined is in the vicinity of 700 000, but numbers are in decline in at least seven range countries. They are hunted for their meat and the attractive skins.

HABITAT Mainly open woodland and grassland savanna, from the coastal plain up to altitudes of 4000 m.

BEHAVIOUR Run in small family herds, consisting of an adult stallion, mares and their accompanying young, usually averaging four to six animals. Although much larger herds are frequently seen, these only stay together for short periods and the family units retain their integrity. Males will fight viciously to retain, or gain, tenure over mares. Stallions without breeding units join together in bachelor herds, or run alone. They frequently mix with other herding species, such as blue wildebeest, topi and gazelles. Movements are generally dictated by conditions, with some populations being relatively sedentary and others undergoing substantial seasonal migrations, for example in the Serengeti/Ngorongoro/Mara ecosystem in East Africa. Their barking 'kwa-ha-ha' is one of the distinctive calls of the African savannas. They are heavily preyed upon by lions, spotted hyaenas and wild dogs wherever their ranges coincide. Access to water is an essential requirement and they usually drink every day.

FOOD Grazers, but do browse on occasion.

REPRODUCTION A single foal weighing between 30 and 35 kg dropped after a gestation period of about 375 days. Foaling usually coincides with the onset of the rainy season when there is an abundance of grass.

Plains zebra from northern Namibia. Note the shadow stripes characteristic of the southern races, and the striping that extends onto the belly. Plains zebra frequently mix with other herding species, such as blue wildebeest, topi and gazelles.

The ears of the plains zebra are comparatively shorter than those of the other zebra species.

Rump patterning of plains zebra from Kenya: Note that there are no shadow stripes.

RHINOCEROSES
Family Rhicocerotidae

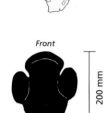

HOOK-LIPPED (BLACK) RHINOCEROS
Diceros bicornis

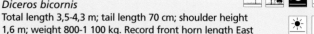

Total length 3,5-4,3 m; tail length 70 cm; shoulder height 1,6 m; weight 800-1 100 kg. Record front horn length East Africa 1,2 m; South Africa 1,05 m.

Identification pointers Large size, no hump on neck, pointed upper lip; two horns on face; head held well above the ground; shrub, tree habitat.

Similar species Square-lipped rhinoceros.

Front

200 mm

Back

Black Rhino

DESCRIPTION Most commonly called the black rhinoceros, but 'hook-lipped' is more appropriate and less confusing, referring to the pointed, triangular-shaped prehensile upper lip. Usual skin colour is dark grey but this generally takes on the colour of local mud and dust as they are frequent wallowers. There is no raised hump on the neck as in the square-lipped, and the head is noticeably shorter and carried higher from the ground. Two horns, composed of matted, hair-like filaments, are located on the face, one behind the other, with the front horn usually being longer. The horns are attached to the skin and not to the bone. The tail is naked except towards the tip and body hair is very sparse, except for a fringe of black hair around the edge of the ear. Four subspecies are currently recognized but cannot be separated in the field, except on the basis of distribution.

DISTRIBUTION Once occurred virtually throughout southern, central and eastern Africa wherever habitat was suitable. Since the 1960s the range has shrunk dramatically and today, tiny, isolated populations are all that remain, virtually all of which are located in conservation areas, primarily in Kenya, Namibia, South Africa, Zimbabwe and Tanzania. The most northerly surviving population is located in Cameroon.

STATUS One of Africa's largest mammals, which has undergone catastrophic declines in numbers and range over the past three decades. At the turn of the 20th century,

there were as many as one million animals, but by 1984 fewer than 9 000 were estimated to survive and today only slightly more than 2 500 remain. Although some were lost due to rapidly expanding human populations, the vast majority have been slaughtered for their horns, used in the production of traditional medicines in the Far East and for carving into dagger handles for the tribesmen of the Arabian Peninsula, particularly in Yemen and Oman. Given present circumstances, the best chances for survival lie in small, intensively patrolled and managed sanctuaries, with satellite populations being established in countries such as Australia and the USA.

HABITAT Requires areas with shrubs and trees, usually to a height of 4 m, to provide both food and shade. Water is a requirement but in more arid areas animals may only drink every three to five days if considerable distances have to be covered. Occupies areas of relatively high rainfall, as well as arid regions, and although generally absent from true forest it does occur in some forest margins and riparian woodland.

BEHAVIOUR Solitary, although groups may gather temporarily at waterholes and locations with mineral-rich soils. Bulls and cows only consort briefly to mate, and the single calf may accompany the cow for between two and four years, until the cow's next pregnancy, or birth of the next calf. They live in established home ranges, but these may overlap with

The head of the hook-lipped, or black, rhinoceros is noticeably shorter and held higher from the ground than that of the square-lipped, or white, rhinoceros.

The triangular prehensile upper lip of the hook-lipped rhinoceros is ideally suited for browsing selected shoots.

those of others in a population. Bulls do, however, establish a dominance hierarchy, particularly in areas of fairly high density, through fighting, which also occurs in competition for cows in oestrus. Home range sizes vary according to the abundance and quality of food, and access to water. Their ranges vary from 0,5 km^2 to more than 500 km^2 and generally the larger the home range, the more arid the area. Feeding takes place during the cooler daylight hours but also at night, and the hotter midday period is usually spent in shade. In dry areas considerable distances may lie between home ranges and surface water, and movements between these are usually linear, rarely involving detours. Dung is deposited in midden areas or at random through the home range, with several individuals using the same sites, and this is kicked vigorously with the hind feet leaving distinct grooves in the ground. This probably serves some marking function not yet properly understood; urine squirting probably also plays a role. The dung balls of the two rhino species are distinguished by the content which reflects their differing diets, those of the square-lipped consisting of relatively fine plant fibres, and those of the hook-lipped containing more coarse, woody material.

FOOD The pointed upper lip is used to grasp leaves and twigs, which are either snapped off or cut through by the cheek-teeth. The horns are used to break off branches and twigs that are out of reach of the mouth. Browse forms the bulk of the diet but they are selective feeders. In most areas green grass is taken in small quantities but in some localities, such as in the Ngorongoro Crater, grass forms an important component of the diet.

REPRODUCTION Calves, weighing about 40 kg, are dropped at any time of the year, after a gestation period of some 450 days. The calf is able to walk and suckle within three hours of birth, and walks beside or behind the mother, in contrast to the calf of the square-lipped rhinoceros which walks ahead of the female.

SQUARE-LIPPED (WHITE) RHINOCEROS
Ceratotherium simum

Total length 4,5-4,8 m; tail length 1 m; shoulder height 1,8 m; weight ♂ 2 000-2 300 kg ♀ 1 400-1 600 kg. Record front horn length South Africa 1,58 m.
Identification pointers Large size; broad, square muzzle, large head carried low; hump on neck, large pointed ears, two horns on face.
Similar species Hook-lipped rhinoceros (separated on size).

DESCRIPTION The square-lipped rhinoceros is also known as the white rhinoceros, despite being grey or taking on the colour of local dust and mud in which it frequently wallows. It is noticeably larger than the hook-lipped rhinoceros, has a large, distinctive hump on the neck and the long, heavy head is usually carried only a few centimetres from the ground. Its name is derived from the broad, squared-off muzzle adapted for grazing. Of the two horns on the face the front one is usually the longer. The ears are large and pointed. Two subspecies are recognized, *C. s. simum* from southern Africa, and *C. s. cottoni* from eastern Africa, but differences between them are minimal.

DISTRIBUTION Once widely distributed in Africa's grassed savannas, it is now limited to isolated pockets. The southern subspecies was restricted to the Umfolozi Game Reserve (KwaZulu-Natal) at the beginning of the 20th century but has now been widely distributed to reserves and private farms throughout its former range. Reintroduced populations in Botswana have been

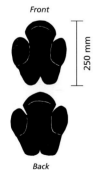

Front

250 mm

Back

White Rhino

A young hooked-lipped, or black, rhinoceros

The square-lipped, or white, rhinoceros is noticeably larger than the hook-lipped rhinoceros and has a large hump on the neck. The long, heavy head is usually carried only a few centimetres from the ground.

poached to the verge of extinction and in Zimbabwe they are under severe pressure. By far the majority are located in South Africa. The northern race (*cottoni*) is now only present in the Garamba National Park, in the savanna country of north-eastern DRC (<10 animals), and a possible remnant population may survive in adjacent areas of the Sudan. Visitors to Kenya may observe square-lipped rhinos at Lake Nakuru National Park and Solio Ranch, the founder stock of these populations being of the southern race.

STATUS The total population of the northern subspecies is estimated at less than 10, of which all known are located in Garamba. In 1958 it was estimated that at least 1 000 rhinoceroses roamed that reserve, with a similar number in southern Sudan, while previously they also occurred on the grassed savannas of the Central African Republic and Uganda. Some 7 500 of the southern subspecies survive in South Africa, with the largest 'herd' in the Kruger National Park, followed by that of the Umfolozi/Hluhluwe complex, while substantial numbers are also located on numerous game farms and private nature reserves.

HABITAT Shows a distinct preference for areas of short-grass savanna, with access to thick bush cover for shade, and water for drinking and wallowing. Favoured habitats are usually those of mixed grass/open woodland associations.

BEHAVIOUR More social than the hook-lipped, with typical groupings consisting of a territorial bull, subordinate bulls, cows and their accompanying young. Territorial bulls usually only move out of their area if they do not have direct access to water, leaving every three or four days to drink. These movements are generally linear with little detour, and the same paths are used. Other bulls are generally tolerant of a male intruder if he shows subordinate behaviour. The territories are quite small – one study showed less than 3 km^2 – but the size is dictated by the quality and abundance of food. Cows occupy home ranges of between 6 and 20 km^2 that can overlap the territories of several bulls. Although fights over territories are usually avoided, severe conflicts do occur, particularly when a bull is in the company of an oestrus cow. Bulls mark their territories with large dung middens located around the perimeter as well as within it, which may involve scuffing with the hind feet after defecation. The spraying of urine also has a territorial marking function. Most feeding takes place during the cooler daylight hours and at night, with shade being sought during the hotter midday hours. Despite their cumbersome appearance they can attain a speed of 40 km per hour when under stress. Eyesight is poor but the senses of hearing and smell are acute. Generally more tolerant of human presence than the hook-lipped, but approaches to these animals on foot should be made with caution as there have been several human fatalities following charges.

FOOD Selective grazers, showing a distinct preference for short grass species.

REPRODUCTION After a gestation period of about 480 days, a single calf weighing some 40 kg is dropped. The cow moves away from the group to give birth, remaining apart for several days. The calf walks in front of the mother. Calves can be dropped at any time of the year but in KwaZulu-Natal there are peaks in March and July. A calf remains with the cow for two to three years after birth.

Square-lipped, or white, rhinoceros cow with large calf.

The broad mouth of the square-lipped rhinoceros is adapted for grazing.

HIPPOPOTAMUSES Order Whippomorpha

HIPPOPOTAMUSES
Family Hippopotamidae

COMMON HIPPOPOTAMUS

Hippopotamus amphibius
Total length 3,4-4,2 m; tail length 35-50 cm; shoulder height 1,5 m; weight
♂ 1 000- >2 000 kg ♀ 1 000-1 700 kg.
Identification pointers Large, barrel-shaped body with short, thick legs;
massive head with broad muzzle; most daylight hours spent
in, or close to, water. **Similar species** Pygmy hippopotamus.

■ *High concentration area*
□ *Total distribution area*

Front

250 mm

Back

Hippopotamus

DESCRIPTION Very large and barrel-shaped, with smooth, hairless skin that is greyish-black in colour with a pink tinge at the skin folds and around the eyes, ears and mouth. Patchy pink pigmentation is not unusual elsewhere on the body, particularly on the feet and the lower legs. The underparts are pinkish-grey. Very young calves are generally paler in colour than adults. The legs are short and stocky, with four-toed feet which leave a characteristic track. The head is massive, with a very broad muzzle and an impressive array of tusk-like canines and incisors. The short, flattened tail has a tuft of black bristles at the tip. When they are in the water, usually only the eyes, nostrils and the tiny rounded ears are visible.

DISTRIBUTION This 'keystone' species of Africa's waterways once occurred in most of the rivers, lakes and swamps and even some inshore coastal habitats such as the waters around the Bijagos Archipelago of Guinea Bissau. Most of the larger populations now occur in protected conservation areas, with distribution restricted to the south of the Sahelian belt, excluding the Horn of Africa. Densities tend to be low in the equatorial forest belt where grazing possibilities are limited.

STATUS The latest estimate indicates that less than 150 000 animals survive, which is a considerable decline over the past 50 years. In some areas they are hunted for

their meat, although in others this practice is considered taboo and the animals are then left unmolested. They are also hunted for their ivory, increasingly so since the ban on the commercial trading of elephant ivory. Zambia is believed to have the largest 'national herd', of which some 20 000 live along the Luangwa River in the north of the country. There are also large populations in Uganda, although there have been serious declines as a result of poaching, particularly in the DRC in recent years. They are currently known to occur in 34 countries but are believed to be declining in 18 of these.

HABITAT Sufficient water to allow for complete submergence is a requirement, and a preference is shown for permanent waters with sandy substrates. Access to adequate grazing is also essential but these animals will move several kilometres away from water-bodies to reach suitable feeding areas.

BEHAVIOUR Semi-aquatic, spending most of the daylight hours in water, but emerging frequently to bask on sand- and mudbanks and on occasion to feed, particularly on overcast, cool days and in areas where they are not disturbed. They emerge at night to move to the grazing grounds, which may be a few 100 metres to several kilometres away (distances of up to 30 km have been recorded), depending largely on the quantity and quality of grazing and the size of the population. They normally live in

The common hippopotamus frequently basks on sand- and mud-banks during the day.

These animals feed mainly at night and will often travel several kilometres away from their daytime aquatic retreats to reach their grazing grounds.

herds, or schools, of between 10 and 15 individuals, although larger groups and solitary bulls are not uncommon. In areas of high density, such as the Luangwa River Valley, herds of 30 or more animals are common. In areas subjected to human disturbance hippopotamuses are secretive and will usually lie low in waters with dense, fringing vegetation cover, but elsewhere they are easily observed. Schools are usually dominated by an adult bull, which holds tenure over a number of cows and their young of different ages. Dominant bulls vigorously defend their herds against intruding bulls and vicious fights can ensue. Territories in the water are very narrow but broaden towards the grazing grounds. Territorial defence is greatest in and close to the water but of little consequence in feeding areas. Dominant bulls mark their territories on land by scattering dung with vigorous sideways flicking of the tail on to bushes, tall grass clumps and rocks; many of these marking sites serve an orientation function. Herds disperse when feeding, only retaining their integrity when in the water. Fixed pathways to and from feeding grounds are used and these are characterized by a 'tram-line' trail, consisting of two parallel tracks separated by a slightly raised centre ridge.

Adults can remain submerged for as long as six minutes and can move rapidly underwater by running along the bottom. When lying in the sun, or otherwise on dry land, skin glands secrete a reddish fluid that acts as a skin lubricant and moisturizer to protect against desiccation, although unknowing observers often mistake this for blood. Deep roaring grunts and snorts are frequently uttered, particularly at the water, and serve as herd communication or, in bulls, as a warning to potential rivals; this, along with the call of the fish eagle, is one of Africa's most typical and evocative sounds.

The hippopotamus is considered by many to be Africa's most dangerous mammal, as attacks almost invariably result in death for the unfortunate who provokes, wittingly or unwittingly, one of these animals. Getting between a hippopotamus and water, and provoking a solitary bull or cow with a young calf, can be particularly dangerous.

FOOD Grazes selectively, consuming only about 40 kg each night. A preference is shown for shorter grasses but taller and coarser grasses are eaten, particularly during the dry season or at times of shortage. Areas with high densities of hippopotamuses are often heavily overgrazed, particularly close to the water, with erosion often resulting.

REPRODUCTION Mating takes place in the water and usually coincides with the dry season. The gestation period is between 225 and 257 days, and a single calf weighing around 30 kg (range 25 to 55 kg) is born. Cows give birth on land, usually in dense cover such as reedbeds, rejoining the herd after about two weeks but frequently maintaining some distance for considerably longer. The birth season is usually associated with the rainy season, with a single peak in southern Africa and a double peak in East Africa.

The common hippopotamus has an impressive array of tusk-like canines and incisors. It is considered by many to be Africa's most dangerous mammal, as attacks invariably result in death.

These animals are semi-aquatic, spending most of the daylight hours in water.

PYGMY HIPPOPOTAMUS

Hexoprotodon liberiensis

Total length 1,6-2 m; tail length 15-20 cm; shoulder height 70-90 cm; weight 160-275 kg.

Identification pointers Small 'replica' of common hippo; less protruding eyes; well-separated toes; restricted to forest habitats in West Africa.
Similar species Common hippopotamus, particularly the young.

DESCRIPTION Small size and great similarity to the common hippopotamus makes this species easy to identify. The skin is greenish-black in colour, with slightly paler underparts and is pinkish-brown around the lips and throat. The ears are tiny and rounded and the muzzle is broad, but the head is proportionately smaller than that of its large relative.

DISTRIBUTION Restricted to a few areas in Liberia (where the greatest number are believed to be centred), the Ivory Coast, Sierra Leone and Guinea, with an apparently isolated population in the delta of the Niger River, Nigeria (a separate subspecies – *heslopi*). Its occurrence in Guinea Bissau is doubtful.

STATUS Increasingly rare and fragmented as a result of habitat loss and hunting; possibly only 5 000 animals survive but the nature of their habitat makes accurate counting impossible.

HABITAT Dense lowland forests and swamp forests, in close association with water-bodies such as rivers, streams, swampy areas and wallows.

BEHAVIOUR Given the dense and inhospitable nature (to man) of its chosen habitats, very little work has been done in the wild. They are usually solitary, or occur in pairs or in a pair accompanied by a single young. Most activity takes place at night. During the day they lie hidden in swamps, other waters, or under overhanging river banks, and on occasion amongst dense vegetation. Well-defined pathways are created through the vegetation and these are marked at numerous places along their length by dung scattered by vigorous flicking of the short, flattened tail. The pygmy hippopotamus does not spend as much time in water as its larger cousin but is still dependent on it. Home ranges are small, given the abundance and availability of food in the forests, and it is probable that males, and possibly pairs, defend a territory.

FOOD A much more varied vegetarian diet than the common hippo, including leaves, roots, tubers and fallen fruits. Grass is taken but is usually in limited supply in tropical lowland forests.

REPRODUCTION A single calf is born after a gestation period of approximately 188 days (range 180 to 210 days), weighing between 5 and 7 kg. There appears to be no specific birth season and young are born in dense cover on land.

Unlike its larger relative, the pygmy hippopotamus is mainly solitary.

This hippopotamus does not spend as much time in water as the common hippopotamus does but is still dependent on it.

EVEN-TOED UNGULATES
PIGS AND HOGS   Order Suiformes

PIGS AND HOGS
Family Suidae

COMMON WARTHOG *Phacochoerus africanus*
(Recent thinking has placed the common warthog as *P. africanus*
and the Somali warthog as *P. aethiopicus*; however, in the field the two
cannot be separated as differences relate to dentition and the skull).
Total length 1,3-1,8 m; tail length 45 cm; shoulder height 60-70 cm; weight
♂ 60-105 kg ♀ 45-70 kg (adult ♂ consistently larger than ♀).
Identification pointers Pig-like appearance; grey skin, sparsely haired except
for long mane on neck and back; wart-like lumps on face; curved, upward-
pointing tusks; thin tail with dark-haired tip, held erect when running.
Similar species Bushpig, red river hog and giant forest hog.

45 mm

Warthog

DESCRIPTION Africa's most frequently observed wild pig. Overall body colour is grey with a sparse covering of bristle-like hairs, and a mane of long erectile hair along the neck and back that varies in colour from straw-brown to black. Normally the mane lies flat but when an animal is under stress it is raised. Tufts of pale-coloured whiskers lie along sides of the face and are particularly pronounced in young animals. When running, the thin, dark-tipped tail is held erect (other African pigs run with the tail held down). The flattened snout is typically pig-like, and prominent wart-like protuberances on the face are characteristic. The male has two pairs of these 'warts' and the sow one pair, those of the boar being larger. The canine teeth develop into long, curved tusks, particularly large in the males, and are formidable weapons. Ears are pointed but do not carry tufts at the tips. Piglets are pale grey and lack body striping.

DISTRIBUTION Distributed throughout the savannas and semi-arid areas of sub-Saharan Africa. Naturally occurring populations are absent from much of the south and west of southern Africa and the tropical Guinea-Congolean lowland forests. The Somali warthog is apparently restricted to parts of the Horn of Africa and north-eastern Kenya.

STATUS Abundant, reaching high densities in areas of optimal habitat (e.g. Lake Nakuru National Park, Kenya, and Umfolozi/Hluhluwe, South Africa) but they have undergone serious declines in the Sahel zone due to drastic habitat changes, and are believed to be extinct in Mali and Niger. Heavily hunted in non-Muslim areas for their meat.

HABITAT Open grass and woodland savannas, from low to high rainfall areas and from sea-level to about 3 000 m.

BEHAVIOUR Predominantly diurnal but they sometimes feed at night. Under most circumstances they retreat to burrows, self-excavated or dug by such species as aardvark and porcupine, and make frequent use of road culverts when available. Adult females, usually one to three, and their accompanying young, form sounders. Boars, on reaching maturity at about two years, usually leave the birth sounder and form loose bachelor groups, or live a solitary existence. Sexually active boars usually move freely and alone, unless with an oestrus sow. Territories are not formed but boars will contest for breeding rights. Heavily preyed upon by carnivores such as lion, leopard, cheetah and to a lesser extent wild dog. A study in Zimbabwe found sounder home ranges to cover from 64 to 374 ha; this varies considerably according to habitat conditions and seasonal differences.

FOOD Grass and grass roots form the bulk of the diet and grazing usually takes place in a kneeling position. Occasionally they also browse, take dropped fruits,

The warthog is Africa's most frequently observed wild pig. It is apparently not as water dependent as are other African pigs but drinks and wallows regularly when water is available.

Warthog with young

The male warthog has two pairs of warts on its face.

and excavate bulbs, corms and succulent roots with the snout.

REPRODUCTION Breed throughout the year in the equatorial belt but show distinct birthing peaks where there are clearly separated wet and dry seasons. Litter sizes range from 1 to 8 piglets, weighing from 480 to 850 g. Weaning takes place from nine weeks to as much as five months.

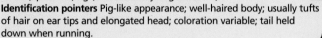

BUSHPIG *Potamochoerus larvatus*
Southern African specimens: Total length 1,3-1,7 m; tail length 38 cm; shoulder height 55-88 cm; weight 46-82 (up to 115) kg (♂ consistently larger than ♀).
Identification pointers Pig-like appearance; well-haired body; usually tufts of hair on ear tips and elongated head; coloration variable; tail held down when running.
Similar species Warthog, red river hog and giant forest hog.

55 mm

Bushpig

DESCRIPTION Body is well covered with long, bristle-like hair varying in colour from light reddish-brown to brown, grey-brown and almost black. The long head may have a white facial mask and ear-tufts. A mane of longer, paler coloured hair extends from the back of the neck to the shoulders. When running the tail is always held vertically downwards. Piglets are dark brown with distinct longitudinal pale stripes along body.

DISTRIBUTION An isolated population is located on the coastal plain and adjacent interior of southern South Africa; scattered and localized populations occur in Angola. Distribution is extensive in East Africa and the north-east of southern Africa wherever there is suitable habitat.

STATUS Still abundant and widespread throughout much of its range although habitat modification and hunting have fragmented populations in some regions, notably in southern Africa. In some areas it is hunted for its meat and is treated as a problem animal where it feeds on crops.

HABITAT Occupies a wide range of habitats from sea-level to altitudes of 4 000 m but dense cover is a requirement.

BEHAVIOUR Predominantly nocturnal, but in areas of low human disturbance and during cooler periods, foraging during the day is not unusual. Sounder size appears to vary from region to region, but ranges from one to 15, with most sounders comprising a dominant boar and sow and their young. Bachelor groups, of short duration, are also formed and solitary pigs, mainly boars, are not unusual. In one study undertaken in the forests of the southern coastal plain of South Africa, the average distance moved by sounders was 3 km (range 0,5 to 5,8 km) and the average home range sizes were 7,2 km². There is evidence that the dominant boar and sow in each sounder actively defend a resource territory and that the boar takes an active part in the rearing and defence of the piglets.

FOOD A true omnivore, although vegetable matter makes up an important part of the diet. They use their flat, hardened snouts to uproot rhizomes, bulbs and tubers, and such sites take on the appearance of miniature ploughed fields. They also browse and feed on fallen fruits and fungi. Animal food makes up an important portion of diet.

REPRODUCTION Births appear to be seasonal but this may be less defined within the equatorial belt. Litters are mainly dropped towards the end of the dry season, or at the beginning of the rains. Some 75% of births in the southern coastal belt of South Africa occur between September and November. The gestation period is about 120 days, and the average litter size is 2 to 4 piglets (but a maximum of 8 has been recorded). Birth weights average 750 g.

Bushpigs are very variable in colour and hair cover, and some develop extremely hairy coats. The incisors may extend beyond the lips but never to the same extent as in the warthog or giant forest hog.

Bushpig: Note the mane of pale hair and the tufted tail tip.

RED RIVER HOG
Potamochoerus porcus
(There has been considerable controversy over the taxonomic standing of this pig but it is now generally held to be a distinct species, standing apart from the closely related bushpig. Measurements similar to bushpig.)
Identification pointers Overall structure and build similar to bushpig; pelage colour bright brick-red; short vertebral crest of white bristles and long white hair tassels on ear tips; prominent white facial whiskers.
Similar species Bushpig, giant forest hog (separated on body colour).

DESCRIPTION Overall build and form is similar to that of the bushpig but pelage colour is brick-red with a contrasting white vertebral stripe and short mane, facial whiskers and long ear tassels. Although variable, body hair length is generally shorter than that of the bushpig.

DISTRIBUTION Restricted to the Congolean forest block and adjacent areas, extending through the forests of West Africa to southern Senegal.

STATUS Still quite abundant but fragmentation of the West African forests has had detrimental effects.

HABITAT Occurs in most forest types through its range and some well-wooded savanna woodland associations, but rarely encountered far from substantial cover.

BEHAVIOUR Believed to be mainly nocturnal, although in undisturbed areas they probably forage during the day. Sounder sizes of between one and 15 (average 10) have been recorded. In Guinea and eastern DRC, groups of 30 to 60 animals have been recorded.

FOOD Probably similar to that of the bushpig.

REPRODUCTION Believed to be a seasonal breeder.

EURASIAN WILD PIG *Sus scrofa algira*
Total length 1,2-1,5 m; tail 15-21 cm; shoulder height 70-90 cm; weight 60-130 kg (♂ consistently larger than ♀).
Identification pointers Large, typical pig-like appearance; long head with no facial warts; dense, longish hair, which is grizzled brownish, to brown-grey. **Similar species** None within range.

DESCRIPTION Large and well-haired, with a long head and no facial warts. Overall pelage colour is grizzled brown, becoming greyer with age, and similar coloured facial bristles. Tusks are relatively short but in adults protrude beyond the lips. Piglets are dark brown with distinctive yellowish-brown longitudinal stripes.

DISTRIBUTION Once occurred along entire length of North African Mediterranean seaboard.

STATUS The Islamic nature of its North African range ensures that it is rarely hunted.

HABITAT Mostly oak and other forests and scrub; small, isolated thickets also utilized.

BEHAVIOUR Most activity takes place during early morning and late afternoon hours but may be nocturnal where disturbance levels are high, or during summer heat. Live in sounders of between six and 20 individuals; larger units occasionally form. Sounders normally consist of one or more adult sows and their most recent litters. Boars tend to retain loose contact with one or more sow groups.

FOOD Omnivorous, taking a wide range of plant and animal food.

REPRODUCTION Litter size variable, with 4 to 10 young. Gestation period is about 112 days. Young weaned at about three months.

Front

50 mm

Eurasian Wild Pig

The red river hog is closely related to the bushpig.

Eurasian wild boar showing winter coat. Inset: *Eurasian wild boar showing summer coat.*

GIANT FOREST HOG
Hylochoerus meinertzhageni

Total length 1,6-2,5 m; tail 30-45 cm; shoulder height 85->100 cm; weight 130->235 kg (♂ considerably larger than ♀; there is an east-west cline in size, with the largest animals occurring in the East African highlands and the smallest in West Africa).

Identification pointers Massive size, powerful build; covered with coarse, black hair; large head, with large protrusions below eyes and prominent tusks in boar. **Similar species** Bushpig in east of range, red river hog elsewhere (separated on coloration and size).

DESCRIPTION The largest wild pig in the world, with weights of up to 275 kg having been recorded. The grey-brown skin is fairly well covered by long, coarse, bristle-like hairs, with longer hair on the neck and back. The head is elongated and massive, with a typical pig-like snout and large swollen protrusions below the eyes and tusks, or tushes, especially in the case of adult boars. The tail is long, thin and tufted and never held erect. Piglets are paler in colour than the adults but have no markings. Three subspecies are recognized, the largest being H. m. meinertzhageni of East Africa and the smallest H. m. ivoriensis of West Africa, with H. m. rimator occupying the tropical lowland forests of northern Central Africa.

DISTRIBUTION A tropical species, the West and Central African populations being separated by the Dahomey Gap. They do not occur south of the Congo River but form a near continuous belt from the Gulf of Guinea in the west to the western Rift Valley lakes in the east. H. m. meinertzhageni occurs in the vicinity of the lakes, becoming patchy further eastward; usually associated with montane forests. An isolated population occurs in south-western Ethiopia. Two of the best viewing locations are the Queen Elizabeth National Park, Uganda, and Virunga National Park, DRC.

STATUS Because of rather restricted distribution and occurrence at low densities there is some concern for its long-term future, particularly in West Africa.

HABITAT Occupies a wide range of forest types, from sea level to altitudes of up to 3 800 m, as well as associated dense thickets and woodland. They readily enter open grassland where adequate thicket cover is available and where water is accessible.

BEHAVIOUR Although shy and largely nocturnal in some areas, they emerge to feed during daylight hours, particularly on cooler overcast days. They live in sounders of six to 14 individuals (average 10), led by a dominant boar, but one or two additional adult boars may be present, and two or more adult sows with their accompanying young. The home ranges of these sounders are believed to average about 10 km^2 but this will vary according to local conditions. Each group territory includes regularly used resting sites, a network of paths, a water-hole and mineral licks with communal latrine sites. According to a study undertaken in the eastern DRC, a sounder may cover 8 to 12 km each day/night, and about 10 hours per day are spent feeding.

FOOD Predominantly grazers but they also take large quantities of forbs, and animal food on occasion. Feeding is selective, with different plant species being taken during different months.

REPRODUCTION Although litters may be dropped at any time of the year, at least in the eastern DRC there are two birth peaks: from January to March, and from July to September. After a gestation period of about 151 days a litter of 2 to 4 piglets is dropped, although higher litter sizes have been recorded. As with the bushpig and red river hog sows, farrowing takes place in a nest of tall grasses or under a pile of branches.

Giant forest hogs are frequent visitors to water and mud wallows.

Giant forest hog boar grazing in an open forest glade.

RUMINANTS Order Ruminantia

GIRAFFE AND OKAPI
Family Giraffidae

GIRAFFE
Giraffa camelopardalis

♂ Total length 4,6-5,7 m; tail length 96-150 cm; shoulder height 2,6-3,5 m; height to top of head 3,9-5,2 m; weight 970-1 400 kg;
♀ Total length <5 m; tail length 75-90 cm; shoulder height 2-3 m; height to top of head 3,7-4,7 m; weight 700-950 kg.
Identification pointers Unmistakable; huge height, and back sloping down from shoulders to rump; 'patchwork' pattern.
Similar species None.

■ *Giraffa camelopardalis giraffa*
■ *G. c. rothschildi*
▨ *G. c. tippelskirchi*
☐ *G. c. reticulata*
▨ *G. c. camelopardalis*
☐ *G. c. antiquorum*
▨ *G. c. peralta*
■ *G. c. thornicrofti*

Front

180 mm

Giraffe

DESCRIPTION The name giraffe is derived from the Arabic word 'xirapha' which translates as 'one who walks swiftly'. This, the world's tallest mammal, has a very long neck and legs, and its body is covered with a beautiful lattice pattern consisting of large, irregularly shaded patches separated by networks of light-coloured bands. The colour and structure of the patterning is very variable but several subspecies can be recognized based on distinctive regional differences. Depending on the taxonomic criteria followed, there are perhaps eight different subspecies, although there are areas of range overlap which make race distinction difficult. Giraffe subspecies are the **West African** (*G. c. peralta*), **Kordofan** (*G. c. antiquorum*), **Nubian** (*G. c. camelopardalis*), **reticulated** (*G. c. reticulata*), **Rothschild's** or **Baringo** (*G. c. rothschildi*), **Maasai** or **Kenyan** (*G. c. tippelskirchi*), **Thornicroft's** (*G. c. thornicrofti*) and the **southern** (*G. c. giraffa*); in south-western Africa the **Angolan** (*G. c. angolensis*) is sometimes separated from the southern. In general, old bulls tend to be darker in colour than the females or young, this being most marked in the southern subspecies. Both sexes carry one pair of short bony horns on the top of the head but in the northern races, particularly in the adult bulls, additional horns are often present.

DISTRIBUTION Giraffes once had a more or less continuous distribution throughout the savannas of sub-Saharan Africa, wherever there were suitable food trees. Today, they are still widely distributed but the populations have become greatly fragmented, particularly in West and southern Africa.

STATUS Although still abundant in numerous savanna conservation areas, particularly in southern and East Africa, these animals have disappeared from many regions within their former range through habitat loss, including total tree destruction in many savanna areas. They are also hunted for their meat, tough hides and tails – the latter being used as fly whisks and the tail hairs for plaiting bracelets! Some races, such as the southern, Maasai and reticulated giraffes, still survive in substantial numbers, but the West African, Nubian and Rothschild's have declined drastically. Thornicroft's is restricted to the Luangwa Valley in Zambia, but is under no threat at present. It is unlikely that giraffes will survive outside parks and reserves in the long term.

HABITAT Dry savanna woodland, particularly in areas dominated by *Acacia*, *Commiphora*, *Combretum* as well as *Terminalia* species. They also occur in semi-desert country, such as the Kaokoland in Namibia. Access to drinking water, for which they will move considerable distances, is an essential requirement.

BEHAVIOUR Giraffes do not establish defended territories but occupy large home ranges of 20 to

Reticulated giraffe

Maasai, or Kenyan, giraffe

Southern giraffe

Rothschild's, or Baringo, giraffe

>120 km^2, the size depending on food availability and abundance. Ranges of mature bulls average smaller than those of cows but young bulls range widely. Although they usually run in herds of four to 30 individuals, these groupings are relatively unstable and there is considerable movement between herds. The only stable unit is that of cow and calf, with adult bulls spending much of their time alone, only consorting temporarily with oestrus cows. A complex dominance hierarchy exists amongst bulls which obviates territory formation, and aggression is minimal, with dominant bulls in a particular area having priority access to oestrus females. Young bulls have developed an elaborate ritualized fight called 'necking', that helps to establish dominance. Although young cows frequently remain within the home ranges of their mothers, young bulls disperse from their birth range when they are between three and four years of age. They feed both at night and during the day but activity is greatly reduced during the hottest hours. Although the giraffe appears to walk in 'slow motion', the pacing walk is amazingly rapid and involves swinging the two legs on the same side of the body forward at almost the same time. Other species that walk in this manner, all being long-legged and having long necks, are the okapi, gerenuk and camel. When the giraffe is moving at a full gallop, speeds of up to 60 km per hour may be reached.

FOOD Almost exclusively browsers, the adult bulls consume a daily average of 66 kg and the cows 58 kg – a small quantity given the size of the animal. The long neck and legs give access to food out of the reach of most other species; also, feeding competition between the sexes is reduced because the male can feed with the head vertically stretched while the female keeps the head horizontal. Most of the diet is made up of tree leaves, flowers, shoots and to a lesser extent pods, which are stripped off by the articulate 45 cm-long tongue and by the lips. On occasion they also feed on grass, particularly during its early growth stages.

REPRODUCTION A single calf, averaging 100 kg, is dropped after a gestation period of about 450 days. The newly born calf can stand and walk within an hour of birth but remains isolated for between one and three weeks. Giraffe cows do not drop their calves at random within their home range but birthings are concentrated in traditional calving grounds. One explanation for this behaviour is that the concentration of births facilitates the forming of similar age calf groups or, as they are sometimes called, creches. Detailed knowledge of the calving area may also hold some advantages of survival against predators. Research indicates that a giraffe cow will return to the same area to drop her calf each time. Calves join the 'creches' at some one to two weeks after birth. Although cows move away from these 'nursery groups' to feed, the females are protective and will defend the young against attacks by predators. Despite their large size, giraffes, particularly young animals, frequently fall prey to lions and to a lesser extent to spotted hyaenas and leopards.

Giraffes are particularly vulnerable to predators when drinking.

Giraffes 'necking' in an effort to establish dominance.

Juvenile Maasai, or Kenyan, giraffe

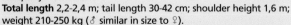

OKAPI

Okapia johnstoni

Total length 2,2-2,4 m; tail length 30-42 cm; shoulder height 1,6 m; weight 210-250 kg (♂ similar in size to ♀).

Identification pointers Superficially giraffe-like appearance; elongated neck, longish limbs, two bony horns on top of head of male only; distinctive white striping on legs, extending on to rump.

Similar species None.

Front

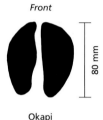

80 mm

Okapi

DESCRIPTION Often referred to as the 'forest giraffe', having an elongated neck and long legs, but not comparable. Pelage is soft and velvety, and overall rich chocolate-brown in colour, with a distinct reddish or purplish gloss. Upperparts of the legs and rump are conspicuously marked with dark brown and white transverse stripes, and serve as superb agents of camouflage. Only the male carries the short, hair-covered bony horns. As in the giraffe, the tongue is very long (about 35 cm).

DISTRIBUTION Has a very limited distribution, being restricted to the tropical lowland rain- forests of the northern DRC, between the Oubangi and Uele rivers in the west and north, almost to the Uganda border and the Semliki River in the east.

STATUS Probably still secure, at least in parts of their range, but no estimates of population size are available. They are known to have become extinct in some areas, presumably as a result of hunting and habitat destruction. They apparently occurred in western Ugandan forests but are now extinct there, and have probably also disappeared from most of the forested areas in North Kivu Province, DRC. They were first revealed to the scientific fraternity in 1901.

HABITAT Entirely restricted to tropical lowland forest but showing specific preferences for certain forest types and not uniformly distributed; for example in areas dominated by the tree *Gilbertiodendron dewevrei*, densities are very low, and in other areas that are seemingly ideal they are absent. Secondary forest, clearings and glades provide the most suitable feeding areas, but closed high-canopy forest with minimal ground cover is unsuitable.

BEHAVIOUR Only one detailed study has been undertaken, in the Ituri Forest in the north-east of its range. They are mainly diurnal and because of the great abundance of available food, home ranges and distances moved each day are relatively small. Within the Ituri the established home ranges cover from 1,9 to 10,5 km^2 but the situation elsewhere is not known. Males have the larger ranges and wander more widely than the females, those of the latter averaging 3 to 5 km^2; subadults of both sexes have the smallest home ranges. They live a mainly solitary existence but loosely associated groups seem to occur, particularly in areas of high density. Indications are that males may be territorial to some extent. Apart from hunting by man, evidence indicates that the leopard is a significant predator, with even adult animals being killed.

FOOD Almost exclusively browsers, with virtually all food being taken in the forest understory. In the Ituri more than 100 browsed plant species have been identified, with a number of plants being deliberately avoided. Fruits and fungi are taken on rare occasions but are apparently not of great significance. Captive animals readily make use of mineral licks and forest hunters maintain that they lick at bat dropping accumulations in tree hollows.

REPRODUCTION A single calf is born after a gestation period of 421 to 457 days, and no birth season is apparent. Males will fight aggressively over an oestrus female. This includes neck fighting and butting with the horns. Calves remain hidden in the undergrowth for several weeks after birth. Under captive conditions calves are weaned at six months.

The okapi occurs only in the tropical lowland forests of the northern DRC.

The rump patterning of the okapi is very distinctive.

DEER
Family Cervidae

BARBARY RED DEER
Cervus elaphus barbarus

E

Total length ♂ 1,4-1,5 m ♀ 1,05-1,15 m; tail length 15 cm; shoulder height ♂ 1,12 m ♀ 90-110 cm; weight ♂ 150-220 kg ♀ 100-150 kg.
Identification pointers Deer-like; stags large, multi-branched antlers for part of year; winter coat dark brown, faint spotting; summer coat lighter, brighter, spotting more obvious.
Similar species None.

Front

75 mm

Back

Barbary Red Deer

DESCRIPTION Subspecies *C.e. barbarus* is smaller than races occurring in Europe, but is nevertheless a large deer. The winter coat is dark brown with faint white spotting, while the summer coat is more yellowish- to reddish-brown and the spotting is clearer. A dark grey dorsal stripe runs from the neck to about two-thirds of the length of the back and there is a paler coloured rump patch. The underparts are fawnish. Only the stags carry the multi-branched antlers that are shed and regrown each year.

DISTRIBUTION Once widespread in suitable habitat in northern Algeria and Tunisia but now restricted to extreme north-western Tunisia and adjacent areas of north-eastern Algeria. Red deer in Morocco are descendants of animals introduced from Spain, therefore a different race.

STATUS About 2 000 animals survive in Algeria and the same number in Tunisia, having recovered from a severe reduction around 1960.

HABITAT Relatively wide habitat tolerance but mainly found in forest and open bush cover, usually in association with hill country. In the

past seasonal movements were undertaken but these are now greatly limited.

BEHAVIOUR For most of the year stags and hinds live in separate herds, with each sex normally living in groups of eight to 20. Hind herds are quite cohesive but those of stags are much more loosely associated and older stags frequently spend much of their time alone. However, during the rut, taking place from September to the end of October, a mature stag moves into an area occupied by a herd of hinds, and although the dominant hind continues to control the herd, the stag tries to keep other stags away. During this time the stags give impressive roaring displays, often sufficient to keep rivals at bay, but if this and dramatic posturing does not work, severe fighting may occur.

FOOD Browse and graze, including a wide range of plants and plant parts and tree bark, fungi, moss and lichens.

REPRODUCTION A single fawn is dropped after a gestation period of about 235 days; remains hidden in dense plant cover for the first two to three weeks after birth.

Antler

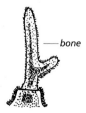

—— bone

Horn

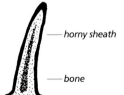

—— horny sheath

—— bone

Diagram showing basic differences between antler and horn structure.

Barbary red deer stag with antlers in velvet – a skin covering present during antler growth and development.

The barbary red deer hind is smaller than the stag and has no antlers.

EUROPEAN FALLOW DEER   *Cervus dama (introduced)*

Total length 1,4-1,7 m; tail length 15-20 cm; shoulder height 90 cm; weight ♂ 95 kg ♀ 35-50 kg.
Identification pointers Males branched antlers much of year; distinct white spotting; largely restricted to enclosed farms in South Africa. **Similar species** None.

Front

65 mm

Back

Fallow Deer

DESCRIPTION Variable in colour and patterning; summer coat is a rich yellowish-fawn with bold white spotting and a white flank stripe. Underside of the tail and surrounding area is white and underparts and inner leg surfaces are dirty white to grey-fawn. Winter coat has longer hair and is darker and duller. Stags carry multi-branched antlers.

DISTRIBUTION Introduced from European stock on to private game farms in South Africa.

STATUS Several thousand.

HABITAT Open woodland, scrub and grassland.

BEHAVIOUR Although generally considered a herding species, the basic social unit is in fact the individual, or hind and accompanying fawn. Hinds and stags remain separated for much of the year, when females and young may move in loose 'nursery herds'. Stags enter the nursery herd home ranges during the rut, when loose aggregations form.

FOOD Principally browsers but readily take grass, and also tree bark and fungi.

REPRODUCTION A single fawn, occasionally twins, dropped in summer months. Gestation 225 to 240 days; birth weight about 3 kg.

CHEVROTAIN   Family Tragulidae

WATER CHEVROTAIN
Hyemoschus aquaticus
Total length 80-95 cm; tail length 10-14 cm; shoulder height 30-40 cm; weight 8-13 kg (♂ smaller than ♀, weighing about 20% less).
Identification pointers Very small, antelope-like; hunched back, small head with short, rounded ears; no horns, males have long upper canines; dark reddish-brown, distinct pale markings; paler underparts. **Similar species** Some small forest duikers, royal antelope (*Neotragus pygmaeus*), Bates's pygmy antelope (*N. batesi*) (separated on appearance).

DESCRIPTION Small size and distinct paler spotting arranged in lines and striping on a reddish-brown coat are distinctive. Has broad, clearly defined dark and white bands on throat. Horns absent in both sexes. Long upper canines of males protrude outside mouth. Relatively short legs. Closely related to deer and pigs.

DISTRIBUTION See map.

STATUS Probably fairly secure.

HABITAT Lowland tropical forests, wherever there are swampy areas and streams.

BEHAVIOUR In Gabon it was found female home ranges are 13 to 14 ha, with little or no overlap. Males occupy 20 to 30 ha ranges that may overlap those of two females. Occurred at densities of 7,7 to 28 individuals per km^2 in Gabon.

FOOD Mostly fallen tree fruits and foliage. They apparently scavenge from dead animal material; have been recorded catching and eating insects and crabs.

REPRODUCTION Gestation period from 120 to 180 days. A single young born at any time of year, and weaned within three months.

For much of the year, fallow deer stags carry multi-branched antlers, which are shed and then regrow. This individual has regrowing antlers.

Fallow deer are often kept on farms for decorative purposes, and for trophy and meat hunting.

Fallow deer hind: Note the distinct spotting and the white underside of the tail.

BUFFALO AND ANTELOPE
Family Bovidae

BUFFALO
Subfamily Bovinae: Tribe Bovini

■ *Syncerus caffer caffer*
■ *Syncerus caffer nanus*
■ Area of overlap

Front

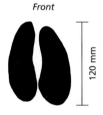

120 mm

Buffalo

AFRICAN BUFFALO *Syncerus caffer*

(Two distinct subspecies are recognized, the savanna buffalo (*S. c. caffer*) and the red, or forest, buffalo (*S. c. nanus*), the latter being somewhat smaller.)
Savanna: Total length 3,2-4,4 m; tail length >70 cm; shoulder height 1,4 m; weight ♂ 700 kg ♀ 550 kg. Forest: Total length 2,9 m; tail length 70 cm; shoulder height 1-1,2 m; weight ♂ 320 kg ♀ 260 kg. (Both species - consistently larger than ♀). Record horn length southern Africa (Zimbabwe) 124,8 cm.
Identification pointers Cattle-like appearance; large size, heavy build; savanna race massive horns and overall dark brown to black colour; forest race smaller horns and reddish-brown coat.
Similar species Domestic cattle, domesticated Asian buffalo.

DESCRIPTION Africa's only wild cattle species, easily separated from domestic cattle. The savanna is massive and heavily built, with relatively short, stocky legs. Ears are large, fringed with hair, and hang below massive horns. The forest (red) is more lightly built and smaller, overall colour reddish to dark red-brown, tending to be darker on legs and head. Horns considerably smaller and lighter, curving outward, backwards and upwards; bulls lack the heavy boss. Ears large with distinctive tassels at tips. Hair is longer overall. Hybridization does occur between the two races.

DISTRIBUTION Very wide sub-Saharan distribution; savanna and lowland equatorial forests.

STATUS Both races occur in considerable numbers but have decreased in many areas, both from hunting and diseases.

HABITAT Savanna race prefers open woodland savanna, with abundant food grasses and drinking water. It also occupies areas of montane forest (eg. the Aberdares and Mount Kenya) in East Africa, but usually leaves cover to graze in clearings. The forest race occupies more closed habitats, in lowland as well as highland forests.

BEHAVIOUR A highly gregarious, herding animal. Savanna runs in herds of several score to several thousands; large herds split into smaller groups, rejoining the main body later. Bachelor herds frequently encountered apart from main herd. Solitary bulls, often older, not unusual. Within herds, of mixed sex and age, adult bulls maintain a dominance hierarchy. Cows also establish a hierarchial system amongst themselves. Savanna herds occupy clearly defined home ranges, which rarely overlap, in contrast to the forest race whose ranges overlap considerably. Most feeding takes place at night. Usually drink in the early morning and late afternoon, lying up in the shade in the heat of day. Forest race moves in much smaller herds, usually 20 or fewer individuals.

FOOD Predominantly grazers, showing a marked preference for grasses that grow in dense swards ('buffalo pastures'). In marshy areas, particularly during the dry season, they feed on reeds and other aquatic plants. Both races include a percentage of browse in their diet.

REPRODUCTION Seasonal breeders, but less pronounced in the forest where food supply is more constant. The majority of savanna calves are born in wet/warm seasons. Gestation period is about 340 days, with calf averaging 40 kg at birth. Cow remains within, or in close proximity to herd when giving birth, and the calf is able to keep up within a few hours.

Savanna buffalo bull: Note the massive horns (particularly large in the bull) which form a heavy boss where they meet. Buffalo have an awesome record for attacking and killing humans, especially when wounded by arrow or gunshot.

Red, or forest, buffalo cow

Savanna buffalo cow

ELAND, BONGO, KUDU, NYALA, SITATUNGA AND BUSHBUCK (SPIRAL-HORNED ANTELOPE)
Subfamily Tragelaphinae; Tribe Tragelaphini

GIANT (LORD DERBY'S) ELAND
Tragelaphus (Taurotragus) derbianus

Total length ♂ 3,6-4,4 m ♀ >2,7 m; tail length 55-78 (maximum 90) cm; shoulder height ♂ 1,5-1,8 m ♀ 1,5 m; weight ♂ 450-907 kg ♀ 450 kg. Horn length ♂ maximum 1,23 m, ♀ shorter.
Identification pointers Contender for Africa's largest antelope (see common eland); generally more 'brightly coloured' than common eland, distinctive white body striping; both sexes have long, shallow spiralled horns.
Similar species Common eland (but ranges do not overlap).

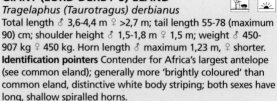

DESCRIPTION Extremely large and somewhat ox-like, with raised shoulder hump and clearly defined dewlap on the throat, which is particularly well developed in bulls. Both sexes carry horns, those of bulls being particularly large, with the spiral more open than in the common eland. The ears are also markedly larger and more conspicuous than those of the other species. Bulls never develop to the same extent the bristly mat of hair on the upper face. Overall pelage colour is chestnut to reddish-brown, with 12 to 15 vertical white stripes on each side. Two races are recognized, the western *derbianus* which is most reddish and has 15 stripes, and the eastern *gigas* which is more sandy in colour and usually has only 12 vertical stripes. Older animals of both races become greyer with age, particularly on the neck and forequarters. Usually a white chevron connects the eyes, white spots are present on the cheek and a black stripe extends down the spine.

DISTRIBUTION Once occurred in a more or less continuous belt across the West African and north Central African woodland savannas from Senegal to northern Uganda. Populations are now highly fragmented, particularly those of the western. The eastern remains viable only in parts of the Central African Republic and possibly southern Sudan.

STATUS Because of its large size it is frequently hunted for meat and this, with habitat changes, particularly in the Sahel, has greatly reduced populations. The western is considered to be endangered; with probably less than 1 200 surviving. Although more abundant with about 15 000 animals surviving, the eastern is also seriously threatened.

HABITAT More restricted in habitat requirements than the common eland, favouring more densely wooded savanna areas but absent from true forest. Apparently the extensive areas of *Isoberlinea* woodland are often favoured. Access to drinking water is essential.

BEHAVIOUR They are more tied to woodland than the common eland and although seasonal movements may be undertaken, they are generally more sedentary. Movements appear to be seasonally linked, and are probably to ensure a more reliable food supply. Herds are generally smaller than those of other species, with fewer than 25 individuals being most common and between 50 and 60 apparently the maximum. Most feeding takes place at night, possibly to avoid hunting pressure. They are generally shy and retiring.

FOOD Even more strict browsers than the common eland, and showing a marked preference for feeding from the *Isoberlinia* tree, with branches being brought within reach by thrashing of the horns. On occasion they have been recorded grazing on freshly burnt areas showing new green plant growth.

REPRODUCTION A single calf, weighing 23 to 35 kg, is dropped after a gestation period of up to 285 days.

Giant eland cows showing the distinctive white striping on the body.

Giant eland bull: Note the dewlap on the throat and the long, shallowly spiralled horns.

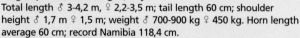

COMMON ELAND
Tragelaphus (Taurotragus) oryx

Total length ♂ 3-4,2 m, ♀ 2,2-3,5 m; tail length 60 cm; shoulder height ♂ 1,7 m ♀ 1,5 m; weight ♂ 700-900 kg ♀ 450 kg. Horn length average 60 cm; record Namibia 118,4 cm.

Identification pointers Very large; ox-like appearance; fawn to tawny-grey overall coloration; adult bulls have very pronounced dewlap on throat and a forehead hair-tuft; both sexes have straight, shallowly spiralled horns.

Similar species Giant eland (but ranges do not overlap).

Front

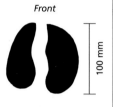

100 mm

Eland

DESCRIPTION The largest living antelope along with the giant eland. Older bulls develop a large pendulous dewlap on the throat and a distinctive mat of fairly long, coarse dark hair on the forehead. A short dark mane runs down the back of the neck of both sexes. Both carry shallowly spiralled horns, with those of the bull more robust and distinctly ridged along their length. Overall body colour usually fawn or tawny, with forequarters in particular turning blue-grey with age. Some white vertical striping may be present on sides, but never as pronounced as in giant eland. There is no white chevron between the eyes, nor white facial spots. The relatively long tail is tipped with a tuft of black hair. Ears are quite large, but not as well developed as those of the giant eland.

DISTRIBUTION Formerly occurred throughout the savannas and savanna woodlands of southern, Central and East Africa but has become extinct in many areas and reduced in others, although it is present in many conservation areas.

STATUS No accurate estimates have been made, but there are probably somewhat more than 150 000 animals surviving.

HABITAT Occupies most savanna and open woodland associations, from semi-desert to relatively high rainfall areas, and coastal plains to montane regions; they have been recorded at natural mineral deposits at 5 000 m on Mount Kilimanjaro.

BEHAVIOUR Normally form herds of from 25 to 60 animals but on occasion congregations of 1 000 or more individuals occur, particularly during the onset and through the course of rains. Highly nomadic in most parts of their range but some populations appear to be more or less sedentary. Although not clearly understood, it appears that the more nomadic herds occur in more arid areas, probably because of the need to move between food sources. Home ranges are generally large, covering 1 500 km² for mixed herds in one East African study but only 25 to 100 km² for the adult bulls. Bulls establish a hierarchy which determines breeding rights. Cows also develop a hierarchial system which establishes factors such as access to feeding sites and position within herd. Active both diurnally and nocturnally, they spend more time feeding at night during summer. On the move they make a distinct clicking sound, believed to be produced by two halves of the hoof knocking against each other when the foot is raised, or by movement of the carpal bones or knee joint. This far-carrying sound is often the only sign of their presence.

FOOD Predominantly browsers but they also graze, particularly green grass. They also actively dig for bulbs, tubers and roots, and eat wild fruits, especially those of ground creeping cucurbits.

REPRODUCTION Dominant bulls mate with receptive cows and after a gestation period of approximately 270 days a single calf weighing between 22 and 36 kg is dropped. Growth is rapid and a mass of 450 kg can be reached by the end of the first year of life; this makes them a potentially important meat-producer on game ranches. The calf remains hidden in bush cover for about the first two weeks. Births may take place at any time of the year.

Common eland bull: Note the large dewlap on the throat and the mat of fairly long, coarse dark hair on the forehead. Despite their massive size, eland are prodigious jumpers, easily clearing heights of two metres and more from a standing position.

Common eland cows and young bulls. Eland are hunted for their meat and hides, and attempts are being made in Russia to domesticate herds for commercial production.

BONGO
Tragelaphus (Boocercus) euryceros
Total length 2,5-2,6 m; tail length 25-28 cm; shoulder height 1,25 m;
weight ♂ 300 kg ♀ 240 kg. Horn length 60-100 cm.
Identification pointers Large, stocky antelope; bright chestnut-red
pelage, distinct white striping; stout, shallowly spiralled horns;
dense forest habitat.
Similar species Bushbuck (distinguished on size).

Front

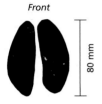

80 mm

Bongo

DESCRIPTION Relatively large and stocky, and generally bright chestnut-red in colour, though darker in males, with between 10 and 16 distinct narrow, vertical white stripes on each side, extending from the shoulders to the rump. There is a white chevron between the eyes and usually two distinct white spots on the side of the face, a white band across the lower throat and contrasting white and black marks on the legs. An alternately dark brown and white crest extends from the shoulders to the rump. The tail is tufted at the tip and both sexes carry heavy, smooth and openly spiralled horns. Although standing out when in the open, it is superbly camouflaged when within its forested habitat.

DISTRIBUTION Extensively distributed in the Congolean lowland forests, with more fragmented populations occurring in the Guinean forests of West Africa and in a few isolated montane forests in Kenya, such as the Aberdares and Mount Kenya.

STATUS It is probably still abundant within the large expanse of Congolean forests but in West Africa it is known to have undergone serious declines throughout much of its range. However, the fact that it is able to survive in secondary forest growth holds out hope for its survival in that region. The isolated pockets in Kenya seem to have mixed prospects, with those on Mount Kenya probably being secure but those (along with the giant forest hog) in the Aberdares having undergone a drastic decline following the introduction of lions; as the latter population was the largest in Kenya, this decline could have

serious consequences. It is unlikely that many more than 500 animals survive in Kenya, and elsewhere numbers are unknown.

HABITAT Occur in dense forest, including both lowland and highland areas. In East African montane areas they also live in extensive bamboo thickets fringed by forest. They are able to survive in areas of secondary forest in some areas, and are perhaps more adaptable than is generally believed.

BEHAVIOUR Little research has been undertaken but it is generally believed that adult bulls are predominantly solitary while cows and calves form loosely associated nursery herds. At least in the Aberdares it has been suggested that home ranges extend over 120 to 300 km² and some bulls may even cover larger areas. In lowland tropical forests home ranges are probably considerably smaller. Territorial behaviour is apparently absent and bulls move through the ranges of more than one nursery herd. Most bull-on-bull interactions involve elaborate displays and posturing, and direct combat is rare.

FOOD Browsers, feeding from a wide range of plants, including bamboo, various creepers and herbaceous plants, tree foliage and apparently also fungi.

REPRODUCTION Mating and birth periods have seasonal peaks in the extreme east of their range, but it appears (and requires confirmation) that births can take place at any time of the year elsewhere. A single calf is born after a gestation period of about 284 days.

Young bongo cow showing distinct white body striping.

Bongo bull: Note the stout, white-tipped horns and large ears.

Horn development

9 months

14 – 17 months

17 – 21 months

24 months

30⁺ months

bull in prime

(after C.D. Simpson, 1966)

GREATER KUDU
Tragelaphus strepsiceros

Total length 2,3-2,9 m; tail length 43 cm; shoulder height 1,4-1,55 m; weight ♂ 250 kg ♀ 180 kg. Horn length average 120 cm, record along curve – Mozambique 187,6 cm.

Identification pointers Large; long legs and shoulder hump; six to 10 vertical white stripes on grey-brown sides; large, rounded ears; tail dark above, white below and bushy; bull carries long, spiral horns.
Similar species Lesser kudu, eland (distinguished on size).

DESCRIPTION Large and elegant, with long, slender legs and a characteristic maned hump on the shoulders. Overall pelage colour is grey-brown to rufous, with the neck usually greyer than the rest of the body; this is most pronounced in older bulls. Six to 10 clearly defined vertical white stripes are present on each side and there is a distinct white chevron between the eyes, with several white cheek spots. Both sexes have a long-haired mane on the neck but in the bulls this extends to beyond the shoulders; bulls also have a fringe of long hair on the throat and lower neck. The tail is bushy, dark above and white below, and may have a dark tip. When they run, the tail is usually raised vertically. The ears are very large and rounded, clearly showing the pink interior skin. Only the bull carries horns, which are long and deeply spiralled. Young closely resemble cows.

DISTRIBUTION The only large antelope to have expanded its range in recent times, most markedly in South Africa. They occur widely in southern Africa, but distribution is more patchy in eastern Africa with an apparently isolated population in adjoining areas of Chad, Central African Republic and Sudan.

STATUS Relatively abundant in parts of southern and south Central Africa but increasingly uncommon northward into East Africa.

HABITAT Woodland savanna associations, but extending into more arid areas where there are thickets which provide cover and adequate food supplies. It avoids open grassland and forest but has been able to penetrate the open, interior plains in southern Africa and elsewhere by moving along wooded watercourses. In many areas it shows a marked preference for *Acacia* woodland and broken hill country.

BEHAVIOUR Gregarious, although herds are generally small and usually average between three and 10 individuals. Larger herds, up to 30 animals, are occasionally seen but these are temporary groupings. The usual herd consists of cows and their young, and may also be accompanied by an adult bull. Bulls normally only associate with the nursery herds during the rut but may mix freely at any time of the year. Bulls may be solitary, or form temporary loose bachelor herds. Nearly all research on this species has been undertaken in southern Africa but is probably applicable elsewhere. Home ranges of nursery herds vary in size from 1 to 25 km² depending on food quality and availability; the smallest range sizes were recorded in the Eastern Cape, South Africa, where suitable food plants are abundant. Bulls occupy larger home ranges, up to 50 km² in extent. In conservation areas they are most active during the coolest daylight hours but in areas of disturbance, such as on farms, they are predominantly nocturnal. There is also some seasonal variation in times of activity with more time spent feeding at night during the hottest months. They are always highly alert to danger and will flee readily if disturbed. In common with the eland, they have prodigious jumping skills and are able to clear a two-metre fence with ease. Like other tragelaphine species, they give vent to a harsh, barking cough which carries over considerable distances.

Greater kudu calf

The greater kudu bull has long, spiralled horns.

Greater kudu cows lack horns and are smaller than the bulls.

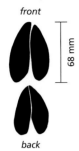

front

68 mm

back

Greater Kudu

FOOD They are predominantly browsers, although grass is also included in the diet, particularly when fresh, green growth is available. They take a very wide range of species, showing a preference for leaves and shoots but also eating seed pods, particularly of the *Acacia*. In some areas, and frequently seasonally influenced, large quantities of non-woody plants may be eaten. They are also able to eat a number of plant species that have toxic sap and are avoided by most other herbivores. In a number of agricultural areas they are considered to be a pest as they feed readily on a number of crop plants, including alfalfa (lucerne). During long periods of drought they will also eat tree bark, scraping it off with their lower incisors.

REPRODUCTION Calves may be dropped at any time of the year, but most births coincide with the rainy season(s). A single calf is born after a gestation period of about 270 days and weighs an average 16 kg. The calf may remain hidden for up to two to three months after birth but the mother rejoins the other females, only returning for it to suckle.

LESSER KUDU
Tragelaphus imberbis

Total length 1,85-2,05 m; tail length 25-30 cm; shoulder height 1 m; weight ♂ 100 kg ♀ 62 kg. Horn length (♂ only) along curve average 75 cm.
Identification pointers Medium size; body form similar to greater kudu; overall greyish-brown, numerous vertical white stripes, two large white patches on throat; sleek, with short hair; only male carries widely spiralled horns.
Similar species Greater kudu, bushbuck (separated on size).

DESCRIPTION Arguably the most attractive of all Africa's medium-sized antelope, with overall greyish-brown coloration and up to 15 narrow, vertical white stripes down the sides of the body. There are two very distinctive white markings on the throat and the inner legs and a white area just above the hoofs. The lower legs are orange-brown in colour. They are lightly built with slender legs, a slightly raised shoulder region and large, prominent ears. Only the ram carries horns and these are long and widely spiralled.

DISTRIBUTION Restricted to eastern Africa, from south-central Tanzania and north-eastern Uganda, to north-eastern Ethiopia in the north.

STATUS Possibly fewer than 40 000 animals survive and outside conservation areas they can be considered to be threatened as a result of habitat destruction and hunting for meat.

HABITAT Shows a distinct preference for areas dominated by *Acacia* woodland and dense scrub, mostly in regions of fairly low rainfall. They avoid open country and rarely move far from cover.

BEHAVIOUR Occupy fixed home ranges and may live a predominantly solitary life, in pairs, or in small groups of ewes and their young. No territorial activity is exhibited by either sex. Most activity takes place at night and in cooler daylight hours. Adult rams occupy home ranges averaging 2 to 3 km²; ewes about 1,8 km². Subadults, trying to establish ranges, cover the largest distances. Adult rams may live in fairly close proximity to each other, but rarely interact and generally avoid contact.

FOOD A wide dietary range, dominated by browse species and including leaves, flowers, fruits and seed pods. Also recorded to feed on succulents, while grass is important during the rainy season. Very selective in species of grass taken, and of the growth stage.

REPRODUCTION Lambs may be seen at any time of the year, but there are distinct birth peaks during the rains. A single calf, weighing about 7 kg, is born after a gestation period of some 220 days.

Lesser kudu ram showing the white body striping and widely spiralled horns.

The lesser kudu ewe is smaller than the ram and has no horns. Both sexes have white markings on the throat and inner legs.

MOUNTAIN NYALA
Tragelaphus buxtoni

Total length 2-2,8 m; tail length 25 cm; shoulder height up to 1,35 m; weight ♂ 300 kg (maximum) ♀ 150-200 kg.

Identification pointers Large, similar to greater kudu; overall dark-greyish, white markings of variable intensity; bulls with open spiralled horns.

Similar species Greater kudu.

DESCRIPTION Large, with a shaggy greyish-brown coat and four poorly defined vertical white stripes on each side. There is a white chevron between the eyes, two white patches on the throat and two white spots on each cheek. A brown and white mane extends down the neck and on to the back. The tail is bushy and dark above but white below. Only males carry the open spiralled horns, which may reach up to 1,2 m in length. The males are larger than the females, but otherwise both sexes are similar in coloration and overall appearance. In many ways they look more like the greater kudu than like the nyala (*Tragelaphus angasi*) of southern Africa, and should perhaps more correctly be called mountain kudus.

DISTRIBUTION Restricted to a very limited highland area of east-central Ethiopia, between the Harerghe and Bale mountains from 3 000 to 4 200 m above sea-level.

STATUS First discovered by the scientific world in 1908 and described in 1910. Because of their very limited distributional range they are vulnerable to disturbance, hunting and outbreaks of disease. Given their relative inaccessibility, no accurate population estimate is available but it is probably between 2 000 and 4 000 animals, more likely closer to the lower figure. It is estimated that about 1 400 animals are located in the Bale Mountains National Park. In the past the range was almost certainly more extensive within the Ethiopian Highlands than it is today.

HABITAT Occupies areas of mixed woodland, montane heath and moorland above 3 000 m, and denser vegetation structures during the dry season. A small, isolated population occurs at Wondo Genet, Ethiopia, at about 1 800 m, clearly indicating that they were more widespread in the past.

BEHAVIOUR Live in small herds of up to 15 individuals, although much larger temporary aggregations of up to 96 have been recorded. Herds may consist of cows and calves, or small groups of younger bachelors, with the latter generally of a transitory nature. The older bulls are usually solitary. No territorial behaviour is evident, although a dominance hierarchy exists amongst males. Most activity takes place at night, particularly in areas with high disturbance levels, but some also occurs during the cooler daylight hours. Population densities vary from 1,5 to 6,9 animals per km^2. Some local movement takes place, and is largely dictated by the different seasons, with denser habitats being utilized to a much greater extent during the dry season.

FOOD Browsers, feeding on a range of herbaceous plants, bushes and leaves from lower tree branches. Grass is occasionally taken, particularly during the rains.

REPRODUCTION About 70% of births take place towards the end of the rainy season, and cows drop a single calf. Information on the gestation period and birth weight is not available as yet.

Mountain nyala bull and cow photographed in the Bale Mountains, Ethiopia. Inset: *Mountain nyala cow: Note the white patches on the throat.*

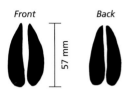

Front   *Back*

57 mm

Nyala

Horn development

9 months

12 months

18 months

30 months

54 months

(after J.L. Anderson, 1986)

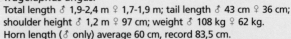

NYALA
Tragelaphus angasi

Total length ♂ 1,9-2,4 m ♀ 1,7-1,9 m; tail length ♂ 43 cm ♀ 36 cm; shoulder height ♂ 1,2 m ♀ 97 cm; weight ♂ 108 kg ♀ 62 kg. Horn length (♂ only) average 60 cm, record 83,5 cm.

Identification pointers Ram slate-grey overall, long mane along full length of back, long fringe hanging below underbelly from throat to between hind legs; lower legs rufous or yellow-brown; eight to 14 vertical white stripes on sides; tail bushy, white below; horns spiralled. Ewe smaller; yellow-brown to chestnut in colour, up to 18 vertical white stripes on sides; lacks horns.

Similar species Bushbuck, sitatunga.

DESCRIPTION Lies approximately between greater kudu and bushbuck in size. Sexes are markedly different and the uninformed could be forgiven for thinking they were different species. The ram has a fringe of long hair hanging from the underparts from just behind the chin to between the hind legs, and a mane of hair extending from the back of the head to the rump. The mane ordinarily lies flat but is raised during certain behavioural interactions, e.g. when two rams meet. The rump and upperparts of the hind legs are covered with long hair. There are eight to 14 narrow white vertical stripes on each side, which become less distinct with age. Overall background colour is slate-grey to dark brown with the lower legs rufous to yellow-brown. A shallow V-shaped white chevron runs between the eyes and there are two or three white spots on each cheek. The ewe is much smaller and lacks the long shaggy hair of the ram; overall body colour is yellow-brown or chestnut, with up to 18 vertical white lines on the sides of the body. Only the rams carry the slightly spiralled horns, which are tipped with whitish-yellow.

DISTRIBUTION Occurs patchily in the north-eastern parts of southern Africa, and also in southern Malawi.

STATUS Fairly abundant, although scattered in southern Mozambique and eastern South Africa. The Malawian range is limited, and in southern Zimbabwe extended periods of drought have reduced populations.

HABITAT Restricted to dry savanna woodland and along watercourses, and although it may feed in adjacent open areas, it never moves far from cover.

BEHAVIOUR Rams do not hold territories but appear to rely on displays, which include raising the neck mane and walking very slowly and with stiff legs, to establish dominance hierarchies. They are commonly seen in groups, nursery herds of ewes and fawns, or bachelor groups, but solitary rams are also encountered. The group composition is fluid and continuously changing, with nursery groups somewhat more stable. Larger groupings are usually associated with water points and flushes of fresh vegetation growth. Home range sizes vary from 0,65 to almost 4 km^2.

FOOD Mixed browsers and grazers, with browse most frequently taken but grass being more important during the rains.

REPRODUCTION A single fawn, closely resembling the ewe and weighing 4,2 to 5,5 kg, is born at any time of year, after a gestation period of about 220 days. There are, however, two birth peaks, from August to December and a lesser one in May. The fawn remains hidden in vegetation for the first two weeks of its life.

Nyala ram: Note the long, shaggy coat and the shallowly spiralled horns.

Nyala ewes and young look very different from the adult rams.

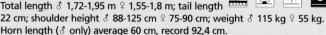

SITATUNGA *Tragelaphus spekei*
Total length ♂ 1,72-1,95 m ♀ 1,55-1,8 m; tail length 22 cm; shoulder height ♂ 88-125 cm ♀ 75-90 cm; weight ♂ 115 kg ♀ 55 kg. Horn length (♂ only) average 60 cm, record 92,4 cm.
Identification pointers Semi-aquatic habitat; hindquarters higher than shoulders; fairly long, shaggy coat; extremely long, slender hooves diagnostic. **Similar species** Nyala, bushbuck (separated on habitat).

Front

80 mm

Sitatunga

DESCRIPTION Several subspecies of the sitatunga have been described, based mainly on body coloration and the extent of white markings, although even within these races there is considerable variation. In the western race *gratus*, the rams are dark brown with abundant white markings and the ewes reddish-brown; the southern race *selousi* is dull greyish-brown and has minimal white markings, while the ewes are similar but tending to be slightly more brightly coloured; *spekei* rams are grey-brown with faint striping and the ewes are bright chestnut. The hair texture also varies in the races, from smooth and silky to coarse. Adult rams are larger than ewes and the coat is long-haired and shaggy, particularly in the former. Both sexes have a white chevron between the eyes and white cheek spots are usually present. The tail is dark above and white below. The hoofs are unique, reaching a length of 18 cm and splaying widely to allow walking on mud and floating vegetation mats. Only the rams carry the long, lightly spiralled horns, which closely resemble those of the nyala (but habitat requirements separate these species).

DISTRIBUTION The distribution centre lies in the lowland basin of Central Africa, with outlying and fragmented populations in West, East and southern Africa. Because of its very distinctive habitat requirements, distribution is very patchy.

STATUS Still abundant in the core distribution area but the other populations are extremely fragmented and many will disappear within the next 20 years. The greatest concern is for those in West Africa where most populations are considered to be endangered, while the northern-most population, around Lake Chad, is also unlikely to survive. It is also endangered in Kenya.

HABITAT Dense reedbeds and well-vegetated aquatic environments are essential but occasionally they move away from these habitats to feed in woodland fringes. The latter, however, is largely dependent on the level of disturbance and probably the number of large predators present.

BEHAVIOUR The common grouping consists of an adult ram with several ewes and their young, averaging six individuals. Solitary animals, particularly rams, are not unusual and mixed groups of subadult animals are also seen. Most activity takes place during the day, although during the midday hours they lie up in dense cover on trampled mats of reeds. Night feeding also takes place and its importance is probably greatest in areas of heavier human disturbance. When disturbed or threatened, they will readily take to deep water, and also do so when moving between feeding sites. The abundance and richness of their food allows them to make use of small home ranges.

FOOD They eat papyrus and other reeds, as well as aquatic grasses and dryland and floodplain grasses. On occasion they will browse.

REPRODUCTION A single fawn is dropped after a gestation period of about 220 days, with indications of seasonal peaks. Mating, at least in some areas, coincides with the driest times when they are more concentrated and have closer contact. The young remain hidden for several weeks, when they often join with others of the same age. The bond between the mother and fawn is apparently quite weak.

Sitatunga ram, northern race (spekei): Note the shaggy coat and white markings.

Sitatunga ewe: The northern races (spekei) are more clearly marked than the southern forms.

Sitatunga ram, southern race, in water

Sitatunga ram: The southern race has very few white markings and is greyish-brown in colour.

Bushbuck

44 mm

BUSHBUCK
Tragelaphus scriptus

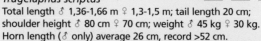

Total length ♂ 1,36-1,66 m ♀ 1,3-1,5 m; tail length 20 cm;
shoulder height ♂ 80 cm ♀ 70 cm; weight ♂ 45 kg ♀ 30 kg.
Horn length (♂ only) average 26 cm, record >52 cm.
Identification pointers Vertical white stripes and spots on sides, but
variations in pelage colour, extent and clarity of markings in different
races; short, bushy tail, dark above, white below; ram carries short,
almost straight horns with slight spiral and ridge.
Similar species Nyala, sitatunga.

DESCRIPTION As many as 29 subspecies have been described; there are considerable variations in colour and markings, both regionally and even within specific populations. General coat colouring ranges from almost black to reddish-yellow; white markings are very abundant and prominent in some races but barely discernible in others. The most northerly and western forms fall within the so-called 'harnessed bushbuck' group, which are generally chestnut to reddish with very clear markings. Eastern forms are usually browner in colour and most white lines are broken down into a series of spots, while the southernmost animals tend to be darker, with poorly defined white markings. Within these broad race distributions there are pockets of differently coloured animals, including the almost black *meneliki* and *powelli* found in Ethiopia. Although rarely present, a white chevron between the eyes can occur, and there are two large, distinct white patches on the throat. A crest, or mane, of longer hair extends down the back of the ram, which is raised during threat and other displays. The bushy tail is dark above, white below and may be raised by displaying rams, or raised by both sexes when in flight.

DISTRIBUTION The most widely distributed of the African tragelaphines, with an extensive sub-Saharan range, but absent from much of western and central southern Africa, the Congolean forest block and the Horn of Africa.

STATUS Still widespread and abundant but habitat changes and hunting have reduced some populations and possibly caused several local extinctions.

HABITAT Riverine woodland and bush cover associated with, or close to, water, from sea-level to montane habitats. It often emerges onto adjacent open areas to feed but never wanders far from cover.

BEHAVIOUR Generally solitary, but pairs and small, loosely knit groups of ewes and lambs are commonly observed. May reach amazingly high densities, with up to 26 animals per km². Size of home ranges varies considerably, records range from 0,25 to 6 km² and possibly higher. Home ranges overlap considerably but each adult usually has a restricted area in which it lies up. Whether or not there is some seasonal variation in home range largely depends on water permanence and abundance and quality of food. Males exhibit an age hierarchy, but territoriality is apparently absent. Ewes in oestrus are closely attended by dominant rams, only being displaced by higher ranking rams in the area. Predominantly nocturnal but also frequently feed and are active in the late afternoon and the cool, early morning hours.

FOOD Predominantly browsers, they take mainly leaves but will also eat shoots, flowers, fruits and grass. In some areas they cause considerable damage to agricultural crops.

REPRODUCTION A single fawn of 3,5 to 4,5 kg is dropped after a gestation period of about 180 days. For the first few months of life (up to four) young lie up in dense cover before moving around with mothers. Births are recorded for all months of the year but in some regions there are definite peaks, apparently associated with the rainy season.

Bushbuck ram, Zambezi Valley. Bushbuck are very variable in colour.

Bushbuck ewe, Zambezi Valley

Bushbuck ewe, Eastern Cape, South Africa

Bushbuck ram, Eastern Cape, South Africa

ADDAX, ORYX, ROAN AND SABLE
Subfamily Hippotraginae; Tribe Hippotragini

Some populations certainly extinct

Front

96 mm

Back

Addax

ADDAX
Addax nasomaculatus

Total length 1,7-2,2 m; tail length 25-35 cm; shoulder height average 1 m; weight 80-120 kg (♂ heavier than ♀).
Identification pointers Fairly large, heavy build; overall smoky-grey, paler on rump, underparts and legs; white chevron on face; mat of brown hair on forehead; both sexes have long, spiralled horns.
Similar species Scimitar-horned oryx.

DESCRIPTION Fairly large and heavily built, with enlarged hoofs to facilitate movement across the sandy substrates it inhabits. Overall body colour smoky-grey with paler to white rump, underparts and legs; a distinct white chevron crosses the face below the eyes. A mat of coarse dark brown hair is located on forehead of both sexes, and both carry long, diverging and spiralled horns, with those of females being more slender.

DISTRIBUTION Once ranged widely in the northern limits of the Sahel, extending into the Sahara. Tiny remnant populations in Mauritania, Mali, Niger and Chad.

STATUS Less than 250 animals survive in the wild, although more than this number are in captivity.

HABITAT Survives under extremely harsh conditions: sand dunes and on gravel plains.

BEHAVIOUR Previously formed herds of up to 20 individuals but today generally much smaller; migratory herds of hundreds are now just a memory. Move great distances following new plant growth that emerges after the scarce rain showers; do not need access to drinking water. Herd home ranges may extend up to several thousand square kilometres.

FOOD Diet dominated by grasses but also feeds on shoots and leaves of Acacias, shrubs and various herbaceous plants.

REPRODUCTION A single calf dropped after gestation of 257 to 264 days; weighs 4,8 to 7 kg. Births may be linked to rainy seasons.

SCIMITAR-HORNED ORYX *Oryx dammah*
Shoulder height 1,2 m; weight 200 kg.
Identification pointers Relatively large size, stocky build; long, curved horns; body colour white/dirty white, neck and chest chestnut, rump and back legs paler brown; tail horse-like. **Similar species** Addax.

Front   *Back*

89 mm

Scimitar-horned Oryx

DESCRIPTION Large and powerfully built, characterized by both sexes carrying long horns that sweep backwards in a curve, with those of female more slender. Body coloration dominated by white to dirty white, with brown to chestnut hair on neck and chest, paler brown markings on rump and back legs. The extent of brown varies but the face is always predominantly white with a broad brown blaze. Tail well haired and horse-like.

DISTRIBUTION Probably extinct in central Chad with possible tiny outliers in Niger and on border between Burkina Faso and Mali. Occurred widely in Sahel belt, and into Sahara Desert.

STATUS Probably extinct in the wild.

HABITAT Semi-desert country, penetrating true desert in search of fresh grazing.

BEHAVIOUR Formerly lived in herds of 20 to 40 animals; when moving

Addax cow: Note the white chevron below the eyes.

Addax cow: Both sexes carry long, spiralled horns.

Although large numbers are held in captivity, the scimitar-horned oryx is seriously endangered and is probably extinct as a wild ranging species.

in search of pastures formed vast herds of hundreds. No territories are defended, and frequent nomadic movements occur. Independent of drinking water.

FOOD Mainly grazers, but browse

frequently taken; numerous herbaceous plants.

REPRODUCTION A single calf of about 15 kg born after 242 to 256 days. In Niger births have been recorded throughout the year.

ORYX/BEISA/GEMSBOK *Oryx gazella*

Total length 1,98-2,16 m; tail length 46 cm; shoulder height 1,2 m; weight ♂ 240 kg ♀ 210 kg. Horn length average 85 cm, record Kalahari 125,1 cm.
Identification pointers Large size, short heavy neck; distinctive black markings, particularly face; horse-like tail; long, rapier-shaped horns both sexes.
Similar species Roan antelope (distinguished by horns, body markings).

■ *Oryx gazella gazella*
■ *Oryx gazella callotis*
▨ *Oryx gazella beisa*

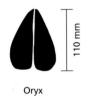

110 mm

Oryx

Some authorities believe there are two distinct Beisa Oryx species.

DESCRIPTION Large and heavily built, with a short, thick neck. Both sexes carry long, almost straight, transversely ridged, rapier-like horns, with those of the bull being shorter and more robust. Overall body colour is greyish-fawn in southern form to sandy-fawn in northern races, with distinctive black and white facial markings. The southern subspecies *gazella* is most extensively marked with black, having a broad side stripe separating upperparts from white underparts and patches on upper legs and top of rump; the lower part of legs are paler to white. In the northern subspecies, *beisa* and *callotis*, the black stripe on the sides is narrower. All have long, horse-like tails, particularly well developed in *gazella*. Subspecies *callotis* is distinguished by long tufts of hair growing from tips of ears. Calves are plain fawn; lack black body markings.

DISTRIBUTION Southern subspecies has an extensive distribution in western, central and north-western southern Africa. Subspecies *beisa* is widespread but populations are fragmented in north-eastern Africa. Subspecies *callotis* has the most limited distribution, overlapping the Kenyan and Tanzanian border in east.

STATUS All races have seen range and population declines. All in conservation areas.

HABITAT Show a marked preference for dry, open country but also occur in light woodland, open grass

savanna and in the case of the southern race, in sand dune country. Water is not essential.

BEHAVIOUR Gregarious, usually forming herds of up to 30 individuals; larger, mostly temporary herds numbering several hundred animals frequently encountered, usually associated with nomadic movements to fresh grazing grounds. There is some regional and seasonal variation in herd size and composition: these may be mixed, consisting of bulls, cows and young, or herds of cows and young; solitary bulls commonly encountered. A territorial bull rounds up mixed or nursery herds into his territory, and then has sole mating rights with receptive cows. Evidence indicates that bulls establish territories from five to seven years of age and in one part of the range of *gazella*, these averaged 7,6 km^2. In the south-western Kalahari Desert, territories averaged 25,7 km^2, whereas female home ranges averaged about 1 430 km^2. Territories may be held for up to three years.

FOOD Predominantly grazers but also browse; taking wild fruits like cucurbits, and tree pods, mainly from *Acacias*.

REPRODUCTION Single calf born after some 264 days, usually during rainy season, but also at any time of year. Calf remains hidden during day, may move at night with mother to a new site. Calves generally join the herd at three to six weeks.

The southern subspecies gazella, *or gemsbok, is the most extensively marked with black. The oryx has several physiological adaptations, including specialized blood cooling mechanisms in the head that allow for survival under harsh arid conditions.*

Note the ear tufts of the northern subspecies callotis, *known as the fringe-eared beisa.*

The northern subspecies beisa: *Note that the black stripe on the sides is narrower than that of the southern oryx.*

Roan Antelope

ROAN ANTELOPE
Hippotragus equinus

Total length 2,26-2,89 m; tail length 54 cm; shoulder height 1,1-1,5 m; weight 220-300 kg (♂ heavier than ♀). Horn length ♂ average 75 cm, record southern race (*equinus*) 99,06 cm.

Identification pointers Large; overall greyish-brown, West African with reddish tinge; black and white facial markings; heavily ridged, swept-back, curved horns; long, narrow, pointed ears with tufts.

Similar species Sable antelope (separated on coloration), oryx.

DESCRIPTION In Africa the roan is surpassed in size only by the two eland species. It has a somewhat horse-like appearance, and is powerfully built with a short, thick neck. A distinct erect mane runs from between the ears to just beyond the shoulders. The long, narrow ears are tipped with a tassel of hair. The tail is long and tufted. The overall body colour is greyish-brown, with West African animals in particular usually having a more reddish tinge and other races being based on other slight pelage colour variations (some five have been described on this basis). The face is distinctly marked with black and white, giving a somewhat 'clown-like' appearance. Both sexes carry back-curved and heavily ringed horns, but those of the cow are lighter and shorter.

DISTRIBUTION Predominantly the savannas to the north, south and east of the lowland tropical forest zone but outliers extend into northern and north-eastern southern Africa, and in a narrow tongue northward towards the Red Sea to the west of the Ethiopian Highlands.

STATUS Numbers and range depleted but still abundant, with more than 150 000 animals present in about 30 countries.

HABITAT Requires open or lightly wooded grassland with medium to tall grass and access to water. Areas with short grass are avoided.

BEHAVIOUR Herds usually number between five and 12 individuals, with each unit normally led by an adult bull. On occasion larger herds of up to 80 animals are recorded but these might not be stable and involve temporary gatherings close to water or favoured food supply. Herds consisting of adult cows and young occupy fixed home ranges which are defended by dominant bulls, who drive off intruding bulls. Unlike most other territorial antelope, the dominant bull is not defending a piece of ground but the nursery herd over which he has control. Herd range size is variable, being largely dictated by quality of food and access to water; up to 100 km² has been recorded. The actual herd is usually led by a cow that establishes dominance over the other animals. This cow selects feeding and resting locations. The territorial bull is also responsible for inseminating receptive cows. At two years of age bulls are driven away from the herd by the dominant bull and these form small bachelor herds. At five to six years of age bulls leave the bachelor groups to live solitary lives, or to take over control of nursery herds. Although most activity (including feeding) takes place during the day, nocturnal movement is not unusual, particularly in areas of high human disturbance.

FOOD Predominantly grazers, which select medium to long grasses.

REPRODUCTION After a gestation period of some 280 days, a single calf weighing on average 16 to 18 kg is dropped. Births may occur at any time of year but distinct birth peaks are discernible in parts of range. Shortly before parturition the cow moves away from the herd and remains in cover until the birth; she remains close to the calf for the first few days but then rejoins the herd only returning for the calf to suckle in the early morning and late afternoon. At about two weeks the calf joins the herd. Calf body colour is a rich rufous-brown and facial markings are clearly evident.

Roan antelope bull. Inset: *Roan antelope cow. These animals have a horse-like appearance, hence the scientific name.*

115 mm

Sable Antelope

SABLE ANTELOPE
Hippotragus niger

Total length 2,3-2,56 m; tail length 50 cm; shoulder height 1,35 m; weight 180-270 (average 230) kg. Horn length ♂ average 102 cm, record South Africa 127,6 cm; Angola 164,7 cm.
Identification pointers Large; black and white facial markings; black, dark brown or chestnut upperparts; white underparts; long, curved, transversely ridged horns; no ear tufts.
Similar species Roan antelope (separated on coloration).

DESCRIPTION Large and very distinct, with clear sexual dimorphism in the overall body coloration. Adult bulls are overall pitch black with sharply contrasting white underparts, whereas cows and subadults are usually reddish-brown to chestnut in colour but also with pure white underparts. Both sexes have distinctive black and white facial markings. The face is mainly white, with a broad black blaze from forehead to nose and a black stripe from below the eye almost to the muzzle. An erect and fairly long mane extends from the top of the neck to just beyond the shoulders. The ears are long, narrow and pointed but lack the ear tuft present in the roan. They carry some of the most magnificent horns of any African antelope, particularly the bull, sweeping backwards with a pronounced curve, and deeply ringed with transverse ridges. The longest horns recorded are from the so-called giant sable (*H. n. variani*) of north-western Angola. Calves are uniform reddish-fawn with white underparts and facial markings.

DISTRIBUTION The most important population centres in Zimbabwe, Zambia and Tanzania. A small, isolated population is located in the Shimba Hills in extreme south-eastern Kenya; the 'giant' race is only found in north-western Angola. In South Africa, the populations are restricted to reserves and game farms.

STATUS Nowhere abundant but probably more than 30 000 occur in Tanzania, with lower numbers elsewhere. The 'giant' is threatened with extinction.

HABITAT Usually found in association with dry, open woodland with medium to tall grass. They avoid dense woodland and short grass savanna but drinking water is essential.

BEHAVIOUR Live in herds averaging 10 to 30 individuals but larger temporary groupings are occasionally observed, usually in favourable feeding locations or at water. Territorial bulls establish territories that overlap the home ranges of one or more nursery herds of cows and young animals. The home ranges of the nursery herds are stable and fixed and in studies undertaken in different parts of their range, averaged only 0,2 to 0,4 km². During the rutting season territorial bulls try to hold the nursery herds within their territories. An adult cow establishes leadership over a nursery herd and usually directs movement to feeding and resting areas. Young bulls join bachelor herds until their fifth or sixth year, when they move away to establish their own territories. Territorial bulls use display to intimidate intruding bulls and, if this fails, serious fighting can result. Most activity takes place in the early morning and late afternoon hours.

FOOD Predominantly grazers but during the dry season they browse on occasion.

REPRODUCTION Seasonal breeders, with animals in the southern parts of the range usually dropping calves between January and March. The single reddish-brown calf, weighing between 13 and 18 kg, is born following a gestation period of about 270 days. The cow leaves the herd to give birth and the calf remains hidden for several weeks, with the female returning to suckle the calf once or twice each day. After each suckling period the calf moves to a new hiding-place, thereby reducing the risk of being found by predators.

Sable antelope in a mixed herd. These animals were photographed in the Shimba Hills, Kenya, where that country's only population is located.

Sable antelope bull testing a cow for readiness to mate. Note the colour dimorphism between the sexes.

WATERBUCK, KOB, PUKU, LECHWE AND REEDBUCK
Subfamily Reduncinae; Tribe Reduncini

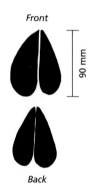

■ *Kobus ellipsiprymnus defassa*
■ *Kobus ellipsiprymnus*
  ellipsiprymnus

Front

90 mm

Back

Waterbuck

WATERBUCK
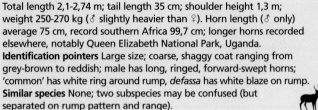
Kobus ellipsiprymnus
Total length 2,1-2,74 m; tail length 35 cm; shoulder height 1,3 m;
weight 250-270 kg (♂ slightly heavier than ♀). Horn length (♂ only)
average 75 cm, record southern Africa 99,7 cm; longer horns recorded
elsewhere, notably Queen Elizabeth National Park, Uganda.
Identification pointers Large size; coarse, shaggy coat ranging from
grey-brown to reddish; male has long, ringed, forward-swept horns;
'common' has white ring around rump, *defassa* has white blaze on rump.
Similar species None; two subspecies may be confused (but
separated on rump pattern and range).

DESCRIPTION Two groups
are recognized, the common,
ellipsiprymnus, and the defassa,
defassa; they have a similar build and
form but differ in pelage colouring and
markings. They are large and robust,
with coarse, shaggy coats. Hair on
the neck and throat is usually longer
but not in all cases. Ears are short and
rounded, white on the inside and black
on the tips. White markings, of lesser
or greater intensity, are located on the
throat, around the nose and mouth
and above the eyes. In the common
the overall body colour is usually grey-
brown, with either grey or brown being
dominant, and a broad white ring
encircles the rump; the forehead hairs
are often chestnut in colour. Defassa
are usually more reddish in colour,
although in some populations they are
more grey-brown, and the rump has a
broad white patch. Only the bulls carry
the long, heavily ridged, forward-swept
horns. Some authorities believe that
the two subspecies groups should be
afforded full species status but in areas
of range overlap the common and
the defassa hybridize; in these cases a
number of intermediate forms develop
but rump patterns vary.

DISTRIBUTION The common occurs in
south-eastern Africa, with East African
populations occurring almost entirely
to the east of the Great Rift Valley. The
defassa is restricted almost entirely to
the west of the Great Rift Valley but
then occurs in a broad belt westward
from Ethiopia to Senegal. Populations
of both species in East Africa are patchy
and fragmented, but overlap in a few

locations in Kenya and Tanzania and in
parts of Zambia.

STATUS Both races still abundant in
a number of areas, with particularly
high densities at a few locations; e.g.
the highest known concentration is
that of defassa in the Lake Nakuru
National Park in Kenya. Probably in
excess of 150 000 animals survive
and both races are well represented
in conservation areas.

HABITAT Befitting the name, they
are always associated with water,
preferring areas with reed beds or
tall grass as well as woodland. Open
grassland adjacent to cover is usually
utilized for grazing.

BEHAVIOUR Gregarious and occur
in small herds numbering five to 10
individuals but up to 30 is not unusual
in optimum habitat. Adult bulls
establish territories through which
nursery herds of cows and calves
move freely, but during the rut bulls
try to hold cows for mating. Younger
bulls form bachelor herds, but these
are relatively unstable, at least in
some areas. Bulls establish their own
territories at five or six years of age
and once established, these are very
stable and held until the bull's position
is usurped by another animal. Territories
are exclusive and range in size from
about 0,5 to 2,8 km². In some locations
at least, herd sizes have been found
to be a function of season, with larger
herds noted in the wet season and
smaller ones when food abundance is
more limited. An experienced tracker

Defassa waterbuck bull: Note the solid white rump patch. Inset: *Defassa waterbuck cows*

Common waterbuck bull and cows: The broad, white ring encircling the rump is diagnostic.

can usually identify the presence of waterbuck by their strong musky scent.

FOOD Mainly grazers but browse occasionally.

REPRODUCTION A single calf is usual but there appears to be a higher incidence of twins than in other antelopes, although this is nevertheless rare. Gestation is about 280 days and a newborn calf weighs approximately 13 kg. The calf remains hidden for the first three to four weeks of life, only then beginning to follow the mother to join the herd.

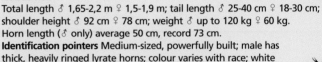

KOB
Kobus kob

Total length ♂ 1,65-2,2 m ♀ 1,5-1,9 m; tail length ♂ 25-40 cm ♀ 18-30 cm; shoulder height ♂ 92 cm ♀ 78 cm; weight ♂ up to 120 kg ♀ 60 kg.
Horn length (♂ only) average 50 cm, record 73 cm.
Identification pointers Medium-sized, powerfully built; male has thick, heavily ringed lyrate horns; colour varies with race; white markings always present. **Similar species** Subspecies.

■ *Kobus kob kob*
■ *Kobus kob thomasi*
□ Area of overlap
■ *Kobus kob leucotis*
■ Area of overlap

DESCRIPTION The male is a robust, powerfully necked animal, carrying heavy, laterally ridged, lyrate-shaped horns. The ewe is of somewhat lighter build and does not have horns. They are very variable in pelage colour and several races have been recognized on this basis. The three most distinctive are the Uganda (*thomasi*), with an overall rich dark reddish-brown coat with relatively fewer distinct white markings on the face; in the white-eared (*leucotis*) the adult rams are dark brown to almost black, with contrasting white underparts, throat patch, facial markings and ears wholly white, while the ewes and young are similar to the Uganda; Buffon's (*kob*) is similar to the Uganda but smaller, and dark markings are usually present on the front faces of the legs.

DISTRIBUTION Buffon's has the most extensive distribution, extending over the moister savanna zone from Sudan to Senegal. The Uganda occurs in the west of Uganda and then extends marginally into the north-eastern DRC and extensively through southern Sudan. The white-eared is restricted to the swamp country in south-eastern Sudan, reaching into the adjacent area of Ethiopia.

STATUS Although populations have generally declined, all three races still occur in substantial numbers, probably more than 1,25 million individuals remain.

HABITAT Occupy floodplains and gentle hill country with good grass cover, but never found far from water.

BEHAVIOUR Live in herds of 15 to 40 animals and occasionally more, with gatherings of thousands being formed during certain seasons. The most dramatic of these gatherings involves the white-eared where densities of more than 1 000 animals per km^2 are usual at the grazing grounds. In general, however, nursery herd units are usually maintained and non-territorial rams form 'fluid', or loosely attached bachelor herds. In areas of high density adult rams defend a very small (about 50 m in diameter) circular territory, which may have as many as 15 abutting but non-overlapping territories within a prime core area and more surrounding it. These territorial groupings are also known as leks. Ewes move freely through the rams' territories. When a ewe is in breeding condition the ram tries to hold her briefly within his area in order to mate with her.

FOOD Purely grazers, with aquatic species included in the diet in some areas.

REPRODUCTION Although births are not tied to seasons in most areas, peaks have been recorded. After a gestation period of about 210 days, a single young weighing about 4 to 5 kg is dropped.

Uganda kob ram: Note the white throat patch. Inset: *Uganda kob ewe with suckling young*

PUKU
Kobus vardoni
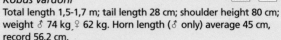

Total length 1,5-1,7 m; tail length 28 cm; shoulder height 80 cm; weight ♂ 74 kg ♀ 62 kg. Horn length (♂ only) average 45 cm, record 56,2 cm.
Identification pointers Similar to kob.
Similar species Kob (but ranges do not overlap), lechwe.

Front

67 mm

Back

Puku

DESCRIPTION Upperparts are a golden-yellow colour, with somewhat paler sides. Underparts are off-white, as are throat, sides of muzzle and the hair around the eyes. The legs are uniformly brown and the tail is golden-yellow. There are no markings, thus distinguishing it from the lechwe where ranges overlap. The ram carries relatively short but stout, lyre-shaped and deeply ringed horns. Lambs are very similar to the ewe in appearance. Some authorities consider the puku to be a subspecies of the kob.

DISTRIBUTION Widely fragmented across southern Central Africa; the principal limitation being restrictive habitat requirements.

STATUS Zambia probably has the largest populations, particularly those occurring in the north, in the Luangwa Valley. There are perhaps 40 000 animals in Tanzania. The Angolan and Congolese populations have been greatly depleted. The most southerly occurring population, in the Chobe National Park in extreme north-eastern Botswana, numbers only about 150 animals.

HABITAT Open flatland adjacent to rivers and marshes, but it rarely moves on to the exposed, open floodplains.

BEHAVIOUR Herds usually number between five and 30 individuals but these are rather unstable with individuals moving freely among groups. Nursery herds consisting of ewes and their young move over the territories of several rams. Established male territories are temporary, and may be held for a few days and up to several months in some cases. Rams attempt to keep nursery herds within their territories when ewes are in oestrus.

FOOD Predominantly grasses.

REPRODUCTION Young may be dropped at any time of year but, at least in parts of its range, births peak during the dry winter months. A single lamb, weighing some 5 kg, is born after a gestation period of approximately 240 days. The lamb hides for the early part of its life and on joining the herd usually moves as a group with other lambs.

■ *Kobus leche leche*
■ *Kobus leche kafuensis*
■ Area of overlap
■ *Kobus leche smithemani*

LECHWE *Kobus leche*

Total length 1,5-1,6 m; tail length 34 cm; shoulder height 96-100 cm; weight ♂ 100 kg ♀ 80 kg. Horn length (♂ only) average 70 cm, record 93,98 cm.
Identification pointers Medium size; rump higher than forequarters; ewes and young chestnut upperparts, white underparts, black markings on leading face of legs; rams of different races range from similar to ewes to very dark; rams have long, lyrate horns.
Similar species Puku (separated on body markings).

DESCRIPTION The rump is noticeably higher than the shoulders, and the ram carries long, strongly laterally ridged, lyre-shaped horns. Three distinctive and non-overlapping subspecies are recognized, within

which the ewes and young are very similar to each other but the adult rams are clearly separated by pelage coloration. All races and both sexes have black markings on the forward-facing surfaces of the legs,

Puku ewes

Puku ram

Red lechwe ram and ewes: Note the bright chestnut-brown colour. Inset (left): *The black lechwe ram is blackish-brown over much of the body.* Inset (right): *Kafue lechwe rams: This subspecies has dark shoulder patches.*

80 mm

Lechwe

and the underparts are white, with white facial patches that are most prominent in the black race. The red (*leche*) is overall bright chestnut-brown; the Kafue (*kafuensis*) ram has dark shoulder patches; the black (*smithemani*) ram is blackish-brown over much of the body.

DISTRIBUTION All races have very limited distributional ranges, with the bulk of the entire population occurring in Zambia. The red occurs in several separated populations in western Zambia, the Eastern Caprivi, Namibia, and well-watered areas of northern Botswana. The Kafue only occurs on the floodplains in south-central Zambia, and the black is centred on the Bangweulu Swamps in north-eastern Zambia.

STATUS Distribution is marginal in the DRC and Angola, and they may be extinct in those countries. The population in extreme north-eastern Namibia has been greatly reduced, by as much as perhaps 98%, in the last ten years.

HABITAT They occupy floodplains and seasonal swamps, and rarely wander more than two or three kilometres from permanent water.

BEHAVIOUR Next to the sitatunga, this is the most water-loving of all African antelope and it takes readily to water to feed or if threatened. They usually occur in herds of up to 30 individuals, but on occasion temporary herds of many thousands may form. Adult rams establish small territories within which they attempt to hold nursery herds for mating with receptive ewes, but these herds move freely over numerous ram territories. Rams hold their territories with elaborate displays. On the edges of the mating grounds groups of non-territorial rams gather.

FOOD Dominated by semi-aquatic grasses.

REPRODUCTION Although lambs may be seen at any time of the year, there appear to be seasonal peaks, e.g. from October to December in northern Botswana. A single lamb, weighing about 5 kg, is born after a gestation period of some 225 days. Lambs remain hidden for two to three weeks after birth.

NILE LECHWE
Kobus megaceros
Total length ♂ 2,15 m ♀ 1,8 m; tail length ♂ 50 cm ♀ 45 cm; shoulder height ♂ 1 m ♀ 80 cm; weight ♂ 90-120 kg ♀ 60-90 kg. Horn length (♂ only) average 76 cm, up to about 87 cm.
Identification pointers Rump higher than shoulders; ram very dark, white stripe along nape, white shoulder patch; long, ridged S-shaped horns; ewe uniform yellowish-brown.
Similar species None.

DESCRIPTION Medium-sized, with the rump standing higher than the forequarters. Dimorphism in coloration of ram and ewe is considerable. The coat of the ram is quite long and shaggy and the overall colour is dark chocolate-brown to almost black, with white underparts and a contrasting white stripe along the back of the neck which terminates in a large patch on the shoulders. The ears are pale to white, as is the area around the muzzle and circling the eyes. The horns are long, relatively thin, forming a very shallow 'S', with strong lateral ridging, and diverge widely towards the tips. Ewes are uniform yellowish-brown in colour. The hoofs are long and pointed.

DISTRIBUTION Restricted to two very limited areas of southern Sudan, with the main population centred on the Sudd Swamps.

STATUS About 95% of the 30 000 to 40 000 black lechwe are thought to be restricted to the Sudd, with fewer than 1 000 in the Machar.

Nile lechwe ram showing the extensive white shoulder/neck patch.

Nile lechwe ewes and juvenile ram.

HABITAT Swamps and flooded grasslands.

BEHAVIOUR Occur in herds of up to 50 individuals, reaching to several hundred in areas of most favoured habitat. Nursery herds may be accompanied by one or more adult rams, but rams also form bachelor groups. Rams accompanying ewe and juvenile herds expend considerable energy trying to monitor female condition and inseminating ewes in oestrus, as well as chasing and fighting off intrusions by other rams. Closely tied to aquatic environments, they readily take to water and spend considerable periods in neck-high water.

FOOD Aquatic and semi-aquatic grasses.

REPRODUCTION A single young is dropped, weighing between 4,5 and 5,5 kg.

BOHOR REEDBUCK
Redunca redunca

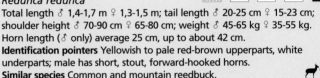

Total length ♂ 1,4-1,7 m ♀ 1,3-1,5 m; tail length ♂ 20-25 cm ♀ 15-23 cm; shoulder height ♂ 70-90 cm ♀ 65-80 cm; weight ♂ 45-65 kg ♀ 35-55 kg. Horn length (♂ only) average 25 cm, up to about 42 cm.
Identification pointers Yellowish to pale red-brown upperparts, white underparts; male has short, stout, forward-hooked horns.
Similar species Common and mountain reedbuck.

Front

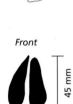

45 mm

Back

Bohor Reedbuck

DESCRIPTION Small and medium-sized, does not have any outstanding features. The overall body colour is yellowish to pale red-brown, and the underparts are white. The tail is short, bushy and brown above, with a white underside. There is a bare, grey patch below each ear. Only the ram carries the short, stout, ringed and forward-hooked horns. The Sudanese subspecies *cottoni* has long, thin horns, with a wide spread between the tips.

DISTRIBUTION Occurs across the West African savanna zone, extending widely through southern Sudan and Ethiopia. In East Africa it is widespread but of somewhat patchy distribution.

STATUS Within West Africa it has an extensive, although very fragmented, distribution and numbers are considerably higher in East Africa, with perhaps as many as 100 000 in that region.

HABITAT Closely tied to river floodplains, reed beds as well as seasonally flooded grasslands.

BEHAVIOUR Up to five ewes and their fawns may live within the breeding territory of a ram; larger groupings are occasionally seen, but these usually indicate a response to a particularly favourable food supply. The male territory varies in size according to region but in one study undertaken in Serengeti it was found to range between 25 and 60 ha, with each ewe utilizing a home range of some 15 to 40 ha. Rams defend access to ewes, rather than entire territories. Bachelor groups are generally tolerated by territory-holding rams but they are chased off when ewes are in the vicinity. In areas of prime habitat, densities may be very high, and 110 animals per km^2 have been recorded in north-east Uganda. Most activity takes place at night.

FOOD Grasses.

REPRODUCTION Through much of its range there is no distinct birth season, although peaks are probable at least in some areas. A single fawn is dropped after a gestation period of about 210 to 220 days.

Bohor reedbuck ram. Inset: *The Bohor reedbuck ewe lacks the short, stout horns of the ram.*

COMMON REEDBUCK *Redunca arundinum*

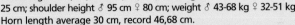

Total length ♂ 1,6-1,8 m ♀ 1,4-1,7 m; tail length
25 cm; shoulder height ♂ 95 cm ♀ 80 cm; weight ♂ 43-68 kg ♀ 32-51 kg.
Horn length average 30 cm, record 46,68 cm.
Identification pointers White, bushy underside of tail prominent when
fleeing; dark lines on front faces of forelegs; ram has forward-curved horns.
Similar species Bohor and mountain reedbuck (separated on habitat).

Front

65 mm

Back

Common Reedbuck

DESCRIPTION Medium-sized, with uniformly brown or greyish-fawn upperparts, the head and neck are usually slightly paler. Underparts and the underside of the tail are white, but the upper surface of the latter is similar in colour to the rest of the body. There is a vertical black stripe on the forward-facing surface of the front legs. The ears are broad, rounded and white on the inner surface. The ram has fairly long, forward-curved horns, which are transversely ridged from the base for about two thirds of their length; the bases of the horns are usually narrowly ringed with pale grey growth tissue.

DISTRIBUTION Across southern Central Africa, extending into Tanzania and then southward into the extreme northern and eastern reaches of Southern Africa.

STATUS Still widespread and locally abundant.

HABITAT Requires areas with tall grass and reed beds, and the close proximity of permanent water.

BEHAVIOUR Normally occur in pairs or family parties, but larger numbers may be observed feeding in close proximity. Territories are defended by the ram. In a study in KwaZulu-Natal, South Africa, ram home ranges averaged 0,73 km² and those for ewes 1,23 km², while territory sizes in the Kruger National Park are apparently influenced by the season. Common reedbuck emit frequent whistles when communicating.

FOOD Predominantly grasses, but also browse.

REPRODUCTION In the south there is a distinct summer birth peak which coincides with rains. A single fawn of about 4,5 kg is born after gestation of 220 days and remains hidden for up to two months in dense grass or other vegetation, with the ewe returning to suckle it once or twice per day. After each suckling session the fawn moves to a new lying-up location.

MOUNTAIN REEDBUCK

Redunca fulvorufula

Total length 1,3-1,5 m; tail length 20 cm; shoulder height 72 cm; weight
30 kg. Horn length (♂ only) average 14 cm, record southern Africa 25,4 cm,
East Africa up to 38 cm.
Identification pointers Grey-fawn upperparts, white underparts; bushy tail,
grey above, white under, latter showing when animal is running away; ram
short, forward-hooked horns.
Similar species Common reedbuck, grey rhebok (separated on size
and appearance), Bohor reedbuck.

DESCRIPTION The smallest of the reedbuck species, it has grey-fawn upperparts and white underparts, including lower surface of tail, which is prominent when fleeing. Hair on the neck and head is usually more yellow-fawn and the lower legs are often somewhat paler than the rest

of the upper body. The ears are long and narrow and lined with white hairs on the inner surface. Only the ram has horns, and these are short, stout, forward-curved and heavily ringed towards base. There is a black, glandular bare skin patch behind each ear.

Common, or southern, reedbuck ram

Common, or southern, reedbuck ewe

Mountain reedbuck ewe from South Africa

Chanler's mountain reedbuck ram (E. Africa)

Front

43 mm

Back

Mountain Reedbuck

DISTRIBUTION Three very widely separated populations. In the south they are restricted to South Africa for 90% of their range. The highly fragmented East African population (Chanler's) occurs at lower densities than in the south. The Cameroon population is totally isolated.

STATUS Still fairly abundant in the south. The Cameroon population is considered to be endangered.

HABITAT Restricted to mountainous and rocky slopes but showing a preference for broken hill country with scattered bush, trees or grassy slopes. Access to drinking water is said to be essential in some areas but not in others. They have been recorded as high as 5 000 m on Mount Kilimanjaro.

BEHAVIOUR Once established, a ram attempts to hold a territory on a year-round basis, but small groups of two to six ewes and their young are less stable and move from herd to herd, covering the territories of several rams, although they have been reported to remain for relatively long periods within the territory of one ram. Bachelor herds also form but these are unstable. Activity takes place both at night and during the day. Male territories range from 10 to 28 ha, and female home ranges, at least in one area, varied from 36 to 76 ha.

FOOD Grasses.

REPRODUCTION Breeding takes place throughout the year but ill-defined birth peaks are evident at the time of the rains. A single lamb, weighing about 3 kg, is born after a gestation period of about 242 days. The ewe gives birth away from the group, and the lamb remains hidden for two to three months.

GREY RHEBOK
Subfamily Peleinae (sometimes placed with Reduncini)

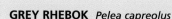

GREY RHEBOK *Pelea capreolus*
Total length 1,1-1,4 m; tail length 10 cm; shoulder height 75 cm; weight 20 kg. Horn length (♂ only) average 20 cm, record 30,16 cm. **Identification pointers** Small; woolly grey coat; long, narrow ears; large black nose; ram has straight, upright horns.
Similar species Mountain reedbuck (separated on coloration, hair form and horns).

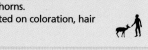

■ *High concentration area*
□ *Total distribution area*

Front

45 mm

Grey Rhebok

DESCRIPTION Gracefully built, with a thick, woolly grey coat. Underparts are white, as is the underside of the tail, which is conspicuous when the animal runs away. The long, narrow ears are mule-like, and the large black nose has a somewhat swollen, bulbous appearance. Ram has thin, vertical, almost straight to fractionally forward-facing horns.

DISTRIBUTION Restricted to suitable habitat in South Africa and Lesotho.

STATUS Not threatened; interestingly reaches its highest densities in the cultivated stretches of southern Western Cape, South Africa, and adjacent hill country.

HABITAT Shows a strong preference for hill and mountainous country but also occurs in the wheatlands of southern South Africa. It occurs in high rainfall montane areas and broken hill country in areas receiving less than 100 mm of precipitation per annum.

BEHAVIOUR The normal unit consists of a family party of ewes and their young and a single aggressively territorial ram. They appear to be almost entirely diurnal. When alarmed or disturbed they give vent to sharp snorting whistles and run off with a 'rocking horse' motion, showing white underside of the tail.

FOOD Selective feeders which predominantly browse but occasionally take grass.

REPRODUCTION A single lamb is dropped in November/ December in some areas after a gestation period of about 260 days.

Grey rhebok ram: Note the long straight horns and the bushy tail.

Grey rhebok ram and ewes, photographed in typical habitat in the Karoo National Park, South Africa.

HARTEBEEST, TSESSEBE/TOPI, BONTEBOK AND WILDEBEEST
Subfamily Alcelaphinae; Tribe Alcelaphini

HARTEBEEST
Alcelaphus buselaphus

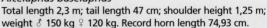

Total length 2,3 m; tail length 47 cm; shoulder height 1,25 m; weight ♂ 150 kg ♀ 120 kg. Record horn length 74,93 cm.
Identification pointers Shoulders much higher than rump; long, narrow face; horns in both sexes, races identified by their shape and structure; coloration varies with race.
Similar species Tsessebe, topi/korrigum/tiang.

- Alcelaphus buselaphus major
- Alcelaphus buselaphus lelwel
- Alcelaphus buselaphus tora
- Alcelaphus buselaphus swaynei
- Alcelaphus buselaphus cokei
- Alcelaphus buselaphus caama

Horn development

0 – 3 months

3 – 9 months

9 – 18 months

18 – 30 months

30 – 36 months

36⁺ months

(after O.B. Kok, 1975)

DESCRIPTION The hartebeest group is something of a taxonomist's nightmare but the simplest line is followed here with six distinct races which can be more or less separated on distribution, horn structure and coloration. All races have very similar body build, tails and habitat requirements. They are of medium size and high-shouldered and low-rumped, which gives them a rather awkward and clumsy appearance, but they are nimble and fast runners. The head is long and pointed, as are the narrow ears. Another common characteristic is the tail, very short-haired at the base and over much of the under-surface but with longish dark brown to black hairs on the outer surface. Both sexes carry horns, but those of the cows are more slender. Horns are set very close together at the base, curving forward to a greater or lesser degree, turning outwards and then pointing backwards; all are heavily ringed for more than two thirds of their length from the base. Horns of the red, western, Jackson's and Lelwel are similar, with the horns approximating a U- or V-shape. The horns of the Tora, Swayne's and Coke's are usually more slender, lighter at the base, less dramatically back-swept and with tips spread much further apart. Within each of the races there is some variation in coat colour. The red (*caama*) is generally fawn to golden-brown, but darker from the shoulders and down the centre of the back to the rump, and bulls are darker than cows; the rump and upper thighs are paler than rest of body, a black blaze runs down the front of the face and there are black markings on the

legs. Coloration is similar in Swayne's (*swaynei*) but horns are different and ranges do not overlap. The other races are more uniform in colour, from a reddish-brown to sandy-fawn, and in all cases the rump and underparts are paler. The calves are a uniform sandy-fawn in all races.

DISTRIBUTION Has a wide but fragmented distributional range, with a number of races being isolated. Western (*major*) extends through West Africa from Senegal to western Chad. The Lelwel (*lelwel*) extends from the limits of the last race over much of northern Central Africa and into western reaches of East Africa, where the rare Jackson's (*jacksoni*) occurs. The Tora (*tora*) only occurs in limited areas of adjoining Ethiopia and Sudan. Swayne's has an equally limited range in Ethiopia and in adjacent Somalia. Coke's (*cokei*), or the kongoni, is the principal East African race but restricted to adjacent areas of Kenya and Tanzania. The red is the only race occurring in southern Africa.

STATUS The red, Coke's, western and Lelwel still occur in substantial numbers but all have undergone declines. Swayne's and Tora are considered to be endangered races, with perhaps only 2 000 Swayne's and a lesser number of Tora still surviving.

HABITAT Occupy open savanna country and wooded grassland, extending into semi-arid country and into desert fringes after rain.

BEHAVIOUR Normally live in herds of about 20 individuals, but up to several hundred and even thousands may gather. These larger groupings

Red, or southern, hartebeest cow with calf of approximately nine months old.

Red hartebeest herd: Note the overall body colour and pale rump patch.

Hartebeest

100 mm

are normally associated with the onset of the rainy season and in arid areas they will travel great distances in search of fresh grass. Adult bulls are territorial and harem herds, made up of cows and their young, stay temporarily within such areas, which usually contain the best grazing. Bachelor herds occupy the areas around territories which often have grazing of poorer quality. Most activity takes place during the day but nocturnal feeding also takes place.

FOOD Mainly grazers but some browse included, usually from low shrubs and herbaceous plants.

REPRODUCTION A single calf is born away from herd, after a gestation period of 240 days, usually just before, or at the onset of rains. Remains hidden until it is strong enough to keep up with the herd.

LICHTENSTEIN'S HARTEBEEST
Alcelaphus lichtensteini

Total length 2,01-2,5 m; tail length 48 cm; shoulder height 1,25 m; weight ♂ 170 kg ♀ 165 kg. Horn length average 52 cm; record ♂ 61,92 cm.
Identification pointers Higher at shoulders than at rump; yellow-tawny body colouring, paler legs and rump; no distinctive markings; characteristic horn structure.
Similar species Tsessebe, topi (separated on coloration and horn structures).

DESCRIPTION There is some justification for including this as a subspecies of the common hartebeest (*buselaphus*), in part because of close similarity and the fact that it forms the distribution link between north and south. It has the typical hartebeest form, with the shoulders higher than the rump, the same tail appearance, a long, slender head and narrow, pointed ears. The overall body colour is yellow-fawn to pale reddish-fawn with a slightly darker 'saddle' stretching from the shoulders to the rump. The flanks, rump and lower legs are paler in colour. Both sexes have the horns flattened at the base, strongly ringed, except at the tips, and with a Z-shaped curvature similar to those of the red.

DISTRIBUTION A wide but fragmented distribution in southern Central Africa, extending into Tanzania, Mozambique and marginally south-eastern Zimbabwe.

STATUS The largest national population is located in Tanzania, with about 50 000 animals; elsewhere numbers are not known. Considered to be threatened in Zimbabwe and endangered in Malawi and the Congo. A small population has been established in the Kruger National Park from stock brought in from Malawi.

HABITAT Savanna woodland adjoining marshy areas and floodplains, with drinking water apparently essential.

BEHAVIOUR Small herds of up to 10 individuals form but on occasion larger, temporary herds occur. A territorial bull stays with a group of cows and their young within a fixed range, which usually incorporates the best grazing, with bachelor herds utilizing less favourable areas. In one study it was found that territories extended just over 2,5 km^2. A hierarchy exists amongst group females, which appears to be age-related. Although mainly active in the daytime, some nocturnal feeding takes place.

FOOD Almost exclusively grass but on rare occasions some browse is taken.

REPRODUCTION Seasonal breeders, with most births taking place in September in the south of their range. A single calf of about 15 kg is dropped after a gestation period of 240 days. Calf can follow mother soon after birth, but usually lies up between feeds, making no attempt to hide.

Jackson's race of the hartebeest is easily identified by its distinctive horns.

Coke's hartebeest, or Kongoni, female with young

Group of Lichtenstein's hartebeest: Note the Z-shape curvature of the horns.

HUNTER'S HARTEBEEST (HIROLA)
Damaliscus (Beatragus) hunteri

Total length 1,5-2,4 m; tail length 30-45 cm; shoulder height 98-125 cm; weight 75-160 kg (♂ consistently larger than ♀). Horn length average 60 cm, record 72,39 cm. **E**
Identification pointers Similar to other hartebeest; shoulders higher than rump; uniform tawny-yellow colour; white chevron between eyes; partly white tail; horns 'impala-like'.
Similar species None.

DESCRIPTION This species is medium-large, with a typical hartebeest-like build, although in general it is somewhat lighter and finer. Overall body colour is uniform tawny-yellow, but slightly darker on the legs, with paler underparts. The head is similar in colour to the body and is characterized by a distinct, narrow white chevron between the eyes. The long hairy tail is predominantly white. The lyrate, fairly heavy and ringed horns closely resemble those of the impala. It is sometimes placed as a subspecies of the 'common' hartebeest.

DISTRIBUTION Only found in a very small area of about 15 000 km² on the border of Kenya and Somalia and in Tsavo East.

STATUS Probably extinct in southern Somalia, with possibly fewer than 500 animals surviving in Kenya.

Almost 90% of the population has been lost over the past 20 years. A certain number were introduced to the Tsavo National Park outside their natural range but the status of this population is not known.

HABITAT Dry open grassland and scattered scrub country.

BEHAVIOUR No study has been undertaken on this rare species but they are known to live in herds of up to 25 animals. Most behavioural aspects probably approximate those of other hartebeest.

FOOD Grass.

REPRODUCTION A single calf weighing roughly 10 kg is dropped after a gestation period of about 240 days. Although not known with certainty, the birthing period probably coincides closely with the rains in its range.

TSESSEBE, TOPI, KORRIGUM AND TIANG
Damaliscus lunatus
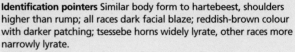
Total length 2,1 m; tail length 45 cm; shoulder height 1,2 m; weight ♂ 140 kg ♀ 126 kg. Horn length average 34 cm; record tsessebe 46,99 cm, in other races up to 72 cm.
Identification pointers Similar body form to hartebeest, shoulders higher than rump; all races dark facial blaze; reddish-brown colour with darker patching; tsessebe horns widely lyrate, other races more narrowly lyrate.
Similar species Hartebeest races (but separated on horn structure).

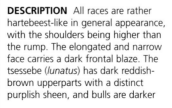

■ *Damaliscus lunatus korrigum*
■ *Damaliscus lunatus tiang*
■ *Damaliscus lunatus jimela*
■ *Damaliscus lunatus lunatus*

DESCRIPTION All races are rather hartebeest-like in general appearance, with the shoulders being higher than the rump. The elongated and narrow face carries a dark frontal blaze. The tsessebe (*lunatus*) has dark reddish-brown upperparts with a distinct purplish sheen, and bulls are darker

than cows. The head, lower shoulder and upper parts of legs are darker in colour than the rest of the body and the lower parts of the legs are brownish-yellow. All races have a black tassel on the tail. The horns of the tsessebe, present in both sexes, are widely lyrate and ringed except at

Hunter's hartebeest, or hirola

Tsessebe (subspecies lunatus) *bull*

Topi female with young. The topi (subspecies jimela) *occurs in scattered populations throughout East Africa.*

Front

90 mm

Tsessebe

Tsessebe form seasonal herds numbering in the thousands on the Bangweulu floodplains in north-east Zambia.

■ *Damaliscus pygargus phillipsi* (blesbok)
■ *Damaliscus pygargus dorcas* (bontebok)

the tip. The northern races are similar, with some variations in coloration and intensity of dark patches; mainly differentiated on the basis of horn structure, with these being thick, deeply ringed and closer together than those of the tsessebe.

DISTRIBUTION The korrigum (*korrigum*) is limited to a small area of West Africa but the tiang (*tiang*) is more widespread eastward from northern Cameroon and Chad to Ethiopia. The topi (*jimela*) of East Africa occurs in isolated populations scattered through the region, with the tsessebe occurring in the southern sector of the continent. The tsessebe is sometimes given full species status on the basis of, amongst others, horn structure and certain behavioural differences.

STATUS Topi, tiang and tsessebe still occur in substantial numbers, particularly the tiang with 700 000 animals. Of greatest concern is the West African korrigum, numbering in the very low thousands.

HABITAT Mainly occupy open savanna woodlands adjoining grassland plains.

BEHAVIOUR Tsessebe form herds of five or six individuals, each controlled by a territorial bull. This unit is quite stable, living permanently within defended territory. Larger herds of up to some 30 animals are sometimes seen but are usually of a temporary nature. Young bulls form bachelor

herds until they are able to contest their own territories or establish harems. The topi generally forms into larger herds, usually of 15 to 30 animals but larger groupings are not unusual. During rutting season adult bulls establish territories, across which nursery herds move freely, with bulls attempting to hold oestrus cows for mating. In some cases these territories are very small and may be tightly clustered, but are held purely as short-term mating grounds. Outside the rut bulls move freely without holding territories. In other cases bulls may hold territories of some 25 to 400 ha and cows remain within these areas for up to two or three years. Some populations are subject to nomadic movements in response to season, others are resident. Topi, tiang and korrigum frequently mix with other game animal species.

FOOD Grazers, with short to medium-long grasses being eaten but a preference being shown for new growth. Length of grasses selected seems to vary to some extent amongst different races.

REPRODUCTION A single young, weighing about 10 to 12 kg, is born after a gestation period of some 240 days, and it is able to keep up with the herd shortly after birth. In the south the tsessebe usually drop their calves from October to December. Elsewhere birth seasons are linked closely to the onset of rainy seasons.

BONTEBOK AND BLESBOK
Damaliscus (dorcas) pygargus

Total length 1,7-2 m; tail length 30-45 cm; shoulder height 90 cm; weight bontebok ♂ 62 kg blesbok ♂ 70 kg. Horn length both average 38 cm; record bontebok 43 cm, blesbok 52,39 cm.
Identification pointers Bontebok: rich dark-brown body colour, pure white buttocks, open white blaze from muzzle to between horns. Blesbok: reddish-brown colour, pale brown buttock patch, white blaze on muzzle broken by brown between eyes. **Similar species** None.

DESCRIPTION Bontebok and blesbok are separate, distinct subspecies. Both are higher at the shoulder than the rump, and have long pointed heads with both sexes carrying simple lyre-shaped horns, but with the

ewe's horns being the more slender. Bontebok has a rich, dark brown coat with a purple gloss, particularly rams, with the sides and upper limbs darker; the face has a white blaze, which is usually unbroken and

Bontebok ram. Inset (left): *Bontebok fawn.* Inset (right): *Bontebok ewe showing white rump and continuous facial blaze.*

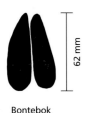

Bontebok

62 mm

Some populations of these two subspecies have hybridized and the purity of a relatively large number of animals/herds is now suspect. Hybrids may feature characteristics of either or both subspecies.

---

generally narrows between the eyes; the buttocks are white, as usually are the lower parts, and the horns are usually black on upper ringed surface. The blesbok has a reddish-brown colour, the white facial blaze is usually broken by a brown band between the eyes, the buttocks are usually pale, but rarely white, while the limbs are rarely as white as in the bontebok; the horns are usually straw-coloured on upper ringed surface.

DISTRIBUTION Bontebok were historically restricted to the Bredasdorp, Swellendam and Mossel Bay districts of the Western Cape, South Africa, are now restricted to a few reserves and private farms in a tiny area of the coastal belt within that same area; the largest single population is in the De Hoop Nature Reserve. Blesbok occur on the east-central plains of South Africa, centred on the Free State, and are well distributed on game farms and reserves in adjacent provinces.

STATUS At the end of the 19th, early 20th centuries, bontebok were brought to the brink of extinction but numbers have built up to about 2 000 animals. Some 50 000 blesbok occur, mainly on game farms.

HABITAT Bontebok are entirely restricted to the coastal plain in reserves with Cape heathland vegetation types, within which they require short grass, water and some cover. Blesbok occur on open grassland with access to drinking water.

BEHAVIOUR Both are diurnal, but are less active during the hotter midday hours. They characteristically stand head-down in groups facing the sun, frequently nodding the head, although this function is not understood. Territorial bontebok rams hold their areas throughout the year and nursery groups of ewes and lambs, numbering some six to 10 animals, wander at will through adjoining male territories. Nursery groups are herded during the January to March rut. Bachelor herds usually establish home ranges away from those held by territorial rams. Blesbok ewes move in harem herds numbering from two to 25, with each herd attended by a territorial ram. Unlike the bontebok, whose herd structure remains virtually unchanged throughout the year, blesbok do not occupy the same home range continuously and during the dry winter months come together in large mixed herds.

FOOD Predominantly grasses, but will browse occasionally.

REPRODUCTION Most bontebok lambs are born from September to October with a few as late as February. Most blesbok lambs are born from November to January with a distinct peak in December. The gestation period is approximately 240 days and the single lamb has a weight of 6 to 7 kg at birth. It is pale fawn to creamy in colour and can run with the mother within 20 to 30 minutes of birth.

Bontebok showing continuous facial blaze

Blesbok showing broken facial blaze

Blesbok ram with the unbroken blaze that occurs in a small percentage of these animals. **Inset:** *Blesbok ram with characteristic broken blaze. Apart from the similar bontebok, no other hartebeest-like antelope has white on its face.*

Blue Wildebeest

Horn development

3 months

7 months

10 months

16 months

24 months

36 months

(after J. Kingdon, 1982)

BLUE WILDEBEEST (BRINDLED GNU)
Connochaetes taurinus

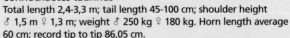

Total length 2,4-3,3 m; tail length 45-100 cm; shoulder height
♂ 1,5 m ♀ 1,3 m; weight ♂ 250 kg ♀ 180 kg. Horn length average
60 cm; record tip to tip 86,05 cm.
Identification pointers Forequarters higher, much heavier than
hindquarters; overall colour dark grey, some brown, slightly darker
vertical striping on neck and chest; long head, broad snout; horns
both sexes, superficially buffalo-like but much lighter.
Similar species Black wildebeest (but true ranges do not overlap).

DESCRIPTION Has lightly built hindquarters but is more robust at the shoulders and chest. Head is large and terminates in a broad snout. Both sexes have horns, although those of the cow are less robust, with horn bases forming a boss over the top of the head and the horns growing outward, turning sharply up and then turning inward. Tail is black and horse-like. Several subspecies have been recognized, of which the most distinctive are the blue (*taurinus*), with long black hairs down the length of the throat; the white-bearded (*mearnsi/albojubatus*) in which the throat fringe is white to dirty white; and Cookson's (*cooksoni*), which has a more brown tinge to overall pelage colour. Johnston's (*johnstoni*) has a white chevron between the eyes. In general all adult animals are dark grey tinged with brown, and in certain light conditions a silvery sheen is discernible. A number of vertical, darker stripes are present from the neck to just behind the rib cage, hence it is frequently referred to as the brindled (brown-streaked) gnu. A mane of long black hair runs down the back of neck. In the blue the front of the face is black, although an area of brown hair may be present at the horn base, particularly in younger animals. The calf is rufous-fawn, with a darker face and has a dark vertebral stripe.

DISTRIBUTION Three separate populations can be recognized, namely the black-bearded form of southern and south-western Central Africa, the totally isolated Cookson's which is concentrated along the Luangwa Valley of eastern Zambia, and the white-bearded race of East Africa found at its northernmost in southern Kenya.

STATUS The western race of the white-bearded is probably Africa's most abundant antelope, with an estimated 1,5 million animals, the vast majority of which are centred on the Serengeti/Maasai/Ngorongoro system. Elsewhere they have undergone considerable population declines, with the blue in Botswana having suffered greatly from the erection of many veterinary control fences; although accurate figures are lacking, that country has probably lost more than 80% of its once large herds in the past 30 years and today, all the principal herds are to a large extent confined to conservation areas.

HABITAT Shows a preference for open grassland savanna and savanna woodland; access to drinking water is essential.

BEHAVIOUR They occur in herds of usually up to 30 individuals, but much larger concentrations may be observed, numbering tens and even hundreds of thousands. One of the world's greatest land migrations involves the movement of more than one million wildebeest in a circuit between feeding and watering grounds within the Serengeti ecosystem of East Africa. Large migrations were also a feature of such countries as Botswana in the past. These movements are strictly governed by the seasons, and during them the integrity of the small herds is usually maintained. Territorial bulls defend a zone around their cows, even when on the move, indicating that it is not the ground which is defended but the right of access to receptive females. A territorial bull may control between two and 150 cows with their accompanying young, although cows may move through the territories of a number of bulls and mate with more than one.

Blue, or black bearded, wildebeest cow and calves, drinking in Mkuzi Game Reserve, South Africa.

Cookson's wildebeest bull, photographed in the Luangwa Valley, Zambia.

The white-bearded race of the blue wildebeest, East Africa.

Blue wildebeest, Kalahari

Front

90 mm

Black Wildebeest

Horn development

6 months

12 months

24 months

36 months

48 months

(after W. von Richter, 1971)

Outside the mating season the cow herds move freely and are not 'herded' by dominant bulls. Bachelor herds are usually located around the edge of the main concentration during the rut. Most activity takes place during the day, shade sought in hottest hours.

FOOD Grazers, showing a preference for short green grass when it is available.

REPRODUCTION Calves dropped at onset of rains in the south (mid-November to end December), with Serengeti/Ngorongoro animals being born in February and March. This varies in different areas; may be influenced by drought or early rains. A single calf of about 22 kg is born after gestation of approximately 250 days. Calf is able to run with the mother just a few minutes after birth.

BLACK WILDEBEEST (WHITE-TAILED GNU)
Connochaetes gnou

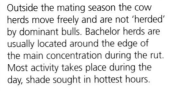

Shoulder height 1,2 m; weight 100-180 kg (♂ larger than ♀). Horn length average 52 cm; record tip to tip 74,62 cm.
Identification pointers Overall black appearance; long, white, horse-like tail; characteristic horn shape; extensive facial 'hair-brush'. **Similar species** Blue wildebeest (but natural ranges do not overlap).

DESCRIPTION More dark brown than black, but looks much darker from a distance. The long, white, horse-like tail contrasts strongly with the body colour and is diagnostic. It is somewhat grotesque in appearance, with shoulders standing higher than the rump, and has a large, broad-snouted head. The face is covered in a brush-like tuft of hairs which point outward, and there is long hair on the throat and chest between the front legs. An erect white-coloured, but black-tipped, mane runs from top of the neck on to shoulders. The horns with their stout boss (particularly bulls) bend steeply downward, forward and upward, with the cows' horns being thinner and generally less robust. Also known as the white-tailed gnu, the latter part of the name coming from the characteristic nasal call 'ge-nu'.

DISTRIBUTION Formerly distributed over a wide area of the interior plains of South Africa but it was brought to the brink of extinction towards the end of the last century. It occurs more or less throughout its former range but today it is restricted to reserves and game farms.

STATUS About 12 000 animals survive where once hundreds of thousands roamed.

HABITAT Low karoid scrub and open grassland.

BEHAVIOUR Bulls establish territories and during the rut they will attempt to 'herd' cows within their areas. The herds, consisting of cows and their young, normally wander freely over bull territories. Bulls mark their territories with urine, droppings and scent secretions, reinforcing the effect by performing elaborate displays. Bachelor herds consist of bulls of all ages. In the past this was a wide-ranging and migratory species, and its behaviour today may not in fact be typical of the species (a factor which always needs to be borne in mind with any animal no longer occurring on a free-range basis).

FOOD Principally grasses but they browse occasionally; access to drinking water is essential.

REPRODUCTION The majority of calves are dropped during the mid-summer months but the peak period varies in different areas. A single calf, weighing approximately 14 kg, is dropped after a gestation of about 250 days and it is able to keep up with the herd shortly after birth.

Black wildebeest: Note the overall black appearance.

Black wildebeest bull showing predominantly white mane and white tail.

IMPALA
Subfamily Aepycerotinae; Tribe Aepycerotini

IMPALA
Aepyceros melampus

Total length 1,6->1,72 m; tail length 28 cm; shoulder height 90 cm; weight ♂ 50 kg ♀ 40 kg. Horn length (♂ only) average 50 cm; record southern Africa 80,97 cm.

Identification pointers Black tuft of hair above hoof on rear surface of hind leg; thin black line down centre of white-haired tail, vertical black line on each buttock; ram has long, lyrate horns; **Similar species** None.

Front

47 mm

Impala

DESCRIPTION Medium-sized and lightly built, with the reddish-fawn upperparts becoming paler on the sides; the chest, belly, throat and chin are white. The tail is white with a central black line on the upper surface, and each buttock has a vertical black blaze. A diagnostic characteristic is the tuft of black hair on the lower rear-edge of the hindleg, as this is not shared with any other antelope. Ears are large, black-tipped and lined with white hair. Only the rams carry the long graceful lyrate horns that are deeply ringed for most of their length. Although six races have been recognized, they are only separated in the field with difficulty, with the possible exception of the black-faced (*petersi*), which has a distinctive black facial blaze and a somewhat bushier tail. The rams of some East African populations carry exceptionally long horns but otherwise resemble southern African populations.

DISTRIBUTION Has a wide distribution in the north-east of southern Africa, extending through Central Africa into East Africa, reaching its northern-most limits in central Kenya. An isolated western population, the black-faced, is located in north-western Namibia and marginally into south-western Angola.

STATUS Generally abundant, at least 500 000 animals occur in East Africa and probably an equivalent number elsewhere. The black-faced race probably numbers fewer than 3 000 but is secure for the present, being conserved in the Etosha National Park, Namibia.

HABITAT Open or light savanna woodland, avoiding open grassland unless scattered bush cover is available, with access to drinking water essential.

BEHAVIOUR Rams are very vocal during the rut, and give vent to a repertoire of growls, roars and snorts, and are only territorial at this time, with the rest of the year being spent in bachelor herds. The home range of a breeding herd, of ewes and their young, may overlap with the territories of several territorial rams. Rams separate out harem herds of 15 to 20 ewes, and their accompanying young, for mating. This disrupts the composition of the herds but they reunite at the conclusion of the rut. Bachelor herds tend to occupy those areas away from the breeding herds. Although they are mainly active during the cooler daylight hours, there is usually some nocturnal activity.

FOOD Mixed feeders, with considerable variation apparent in intake depending on the area and season.

REPRODUCTION A single lamb, weighing about 5 kg, is born at the beginning of the rainy season after a gestation period of 196 days.

Impala ewes. Insets: *Impala ram* (left), *black-faced impala ewe* (right).

GAZELLES AND DWARF ANTELOPE

Subfamily Antilopinae

This subfamily is broken down into two rather disparate and varied tribes, the **Antilopini** and the **Neotragini**.

The **Antilopini** includes 10 gazelle species, among them the springbok, as well as the gerenuk and the dibatag. The **Neotragini** consists of the dwarf antelope which include the royal antelope, pygmy antelope, suni, the dikdiks, klipspringer, steenbok, Cape and Sharpe's grysbok, oribi and the beira.

GAZELLES

Tribe Antilopini

GERENUK *Litocranius walleri*

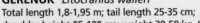

Total length 1,8-1,95 m; tail length 25-35 cm; shoulder height 95-100 cm; weight 30-50 kg. Horn length (♂ only) average 30 cm; record >44 cm.

Identification pointers Very long slender neck and legs; similar colour to impala; white eye ring, line extending towards snout; ram distinctive horns. **Similar species** Dibatag (separated on length of legs and neck).

Front

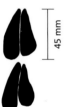

45 mm

Back

Gerenuk

DESCRIPTION One of the most easily identified medium-sized antelope, with very long legs and long thin neck, for which it has been given the alternative name of 'giraffe-necked' antelope. Upperparts are rufous-fawn in colour, with the sides paler, and a thin, dark line separates the white underparts. The head is short, with a somewhat 'pinched' appearance, the eyes are very large and ringed with white, and a line extends towards the snout. The ears are long and pointed. Only the ram carries the characteristic horns, which are relatively short, robust, heavily ringed, and approximate a tight lyre-shape.

DISTRIBUTION Restricted to the Horn of Africa and extending westward into Ethiopia, and southward through Kenya to north-eastern Tanzania to the east of the Great Rift Valley.

STATUS Up to 80 000 animals, with the most important protected populations centred on Kenya.

HABITAT Arid thorn scrub and thicket.

BEHAVIOUR Predominantly solitary, particularly the adult rams, but small mixed groups with a single ram are common, as are ewe and lamb groups, as well as single ewes with their lambs. Up to eight animals may be seen together but they are usually spaced several metres apart when feeding or lying up. When feeding they have a distinct advantage over many other browsers, which is increased by their ability to stand erect on the hind legs, a position that only the dibatag can also achieve. The home range of a single animal may vary from 2 to 6 km², largely dependent on local conditions, and rams are strictly territorial (2 to 4 km²), driving away any intruding males. Territorial rams tolerate subadult rams as long as they remain subservient, with non-territory holding animals forming into loose groupings. They are resident in specific areas and are not migratory.

FOOD Strict browsers, selecting new leaf growth, buds, fresh twig tips and the flowers of a wide variety of tree and bush species, particularly *Acacias*. They are independent of drinking water.

REPRODUCTION A single lamb, weighing about 3 kg, is born after a gestation period of up to 210 days, with births coinciding with the rainy seasons.

Gerenuk ewe. Inset: *Gerenuk ram feeding. The ability to stand erect on the hind legs when browsing is a distinct characteristic of both the gerenuk and the dibatag.*

DIBATAG
Ammodorcas clarkei

Total length 1,8-2 m; tail length 30-36 cm; shoulder height 80->88 cm; weight 22-35 kg. Horn length average 25 cm.
Identification pointers Long legs, neck; long tail, held erect when running; rams have short, forward-curved horns; pelage dark reddish-grey above, white below, including buttocks. **Similar species** Gerenuk.

DESCRIPTION Very similar in build to the gerenuk but neck slightly shorter and more slender. The horns are short, forward-pointing and ringed, like those of reedbuck, and carried only by the male. The tail is long, slender and black. Overall colour of upperparts is reddish-grey, with contrasting white underparts and buttocks. The lower legs are usually more brownish in colour. A distinct white ring circles the eye and extends in a line down the muzzle to the snout.

DISTRIBUTION Restricted to central Somalia and the Ogaden in Ethiopia.

STATUS The most viable populations occur in regions of Haradere-Awale Rugno and Hobyo, Somalia; stable in Ogaden.

HABITAT Semi-arid bush and open scrub land.

BEHAVIOUR Live in small groups, normally consisting of family or extended family, averaging three to six individuals, but up to nine have been recorded. Appear to be highly mobile, with a flexible home range size. As groups usually only include one adult ram it is probable that they are, at least in part, territorial.

FOOD Predominantly browsers, of mainly leaves and twig tips, but also take berries and will eat green grass growth.

REPRODUCTION A single lamb is dropped, probably in association with the rainy season.

GAZELLES
Genus *Gazella* Genus *Antidorcas*

A group of ten species of strikingly similar antelope, with only one species occurring in southern Africa and the rest restricted to northern and eastern Africa. Most species occur in arid and semi-arid areas and those occurring in the Sahel, Sahara and fringing areas are generally seriously threatened, with a few endangered.

DAMA GAZELLE
Gazella dama

Total length 1,65-2 m; tail length 25-35 cm; shoulder height 90-120 cm; weight 40-75 kg. Horn length (♂ only) average 33 cm; record 41,27 cm.
Identification pointers Largest true gazelle; slender build, longish neck, legs; white head, varying amounts of white on upperparts, fully on underparts, remainder rufous to chestnut brown; characteristic horns. **Similar species** None.

E

DESCRIPTION Three distinct races are recognized, the western *mhorr*, with the greatest extent of rufous on the upperparts; *permista*, which has more white on the sides and the white rump patch tapering to the back of the ribcage; and the most easterly *ruficollis*, only having rufous in the shoulder

region and on the neck. All three have a distinct white throat spot. Apart from its large size, the legs and neck are proportionately long. Both sexes carry horns, which are short, bent back strongly from the base and curved at the tip, and strongly ringed, with those of the female being less robust.

The western race of the dama gazelle: Note the distinctive white throat spot characteristic of all three races.

Of all three races, the western race of the dama gazelle, or mhorr, has the greatest extent of rufous on the upperparts.

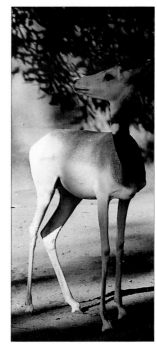

The eastern race of the dama gazelle, also known as the red-necked gazelle

DISTRIBUTION Previously occurred throughout the Sahel and extending into the Sahara Desert, through southern Morocco to the Sudan, but today they are reduced to a few tiny isolated populations in Mali, Niger and Chad. Some tiny populations may survive elsewhere.

STATUS Endangered and reduced to fewer than 500 animals, mainly through habitat modification and hunting.

HABITAT Desert and adjoining arid areas with sparse vegetation cover.

BEHAVIOUR Previously lived in large, temporary nomadic herds that moved to fresh feeding grounds, with the herds at other times of the year numbering up to 15 individuals, although often smaller, with solitary animals not unusual. The migrations followed a set pattern, with a southward movement during the driest month, turning northwards when the sparse desert rains fell. Their current behaviour is unknown, however, but their southern range has been greatly modified and affected by domestic stock and is now largely unsuitable for most of the wild ungulates found in dry areas. Given their nomadic movements, this species undoubtedly occupies very large home ranges. Herds consist of ewes, their young and a territorial ram, with non-territorial animals forming bachelor groups. This species frequently associates with the dorcas gazelle.

FOOD Predominantly browsers but will feed on a wide range of herbaceous plants and fresh grass growth.

REPRODUCTION Births take place at the onset of the rains, with a single lamb being dropped after a gestation period of approximately 198 days.

SOEMMERING'S GAZELLE
Gazella soemmeringi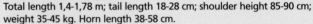
Total length 1,4-1,78 m; tail length 18-28 cm; shoulder height 85-90 cm; weight 35-45 kg. Horn length 38-58 cm.
Identification pointers Large; distinct black and white facial pattern; no dark flank stripe; white rump, underparts, inner legs; tail white with black tip; horns long.
Similar species Grant's gazelle (but separated on appearance).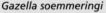

DESCRIPTION Relatively large, with no dark flank stripe but a distinctly white rump, and distinctive black and white facial markings. Underparts and inner surface of legs are white, with a white patch on the throat. The rest of the body and outer leg surfaces are pale rufous-fawn. Both sexes carry the rather long, ringed horns, with those of the ewe being more slender, similar to those of Grant's gazelle but shorter and usually more inward-pointing.

DISTRIBUTION Restricted to the Horn of Africa and extending about halfway up the Red Sea in Ethiopia and southern Sudan.

STATUS Still occur in reasonable numbers but populations have been much reduced throughout their range, with particularly drastic declines in Somalia.

HABITAT Semi-arid grassland and open scrub and hill country, usually dominated by Acacia trees and bushes.

BEHAVIOUR Live in small groups usually consisting of family parties, but larger herds form temporarily, and in some parts of their range they move in accordance with sporadic rainfall which encourages new vegetation growth. Larger herds include rams and ewes, but adult rams are frequently solitary. Herds often join in company with other antelope species. Little is known about their behaviour.

FOOD Mixed feeders, taking grass and browse.

REPRODUCTION A single lamb, weighing up to 4,5 kg, is dropped after a gestation period of about 198 days. Birthing takes place in April and May.

Soemmering's gazelle ewe: Note the white rump patch and upper tail surface.

Soemmering's gazelle ram showing the distinctive black and white facial markings.

SPEKE'S GAZELLE
Gazella spekei

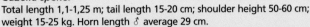

Total length 1,1-1,25 m; tail length 15-20 cm; shoulder height 50-60 cm; weight 15-25 kg. Horn length ♂ average 29 cm.

Identification pointers Overall similar to Thomson's; fawn upperparts, white underparts separated by dark brown flank band; dark vertical buttock stripe; expandable nose/snout; horns as in Thomson's.

Similar species Thomson's gazelle

DESCRIPTION Very similar to Thomson's gazelle and could be closely related. The main character separating the two is the ability to inflate the snout when excited or alarmed, hence the alternative name of flabby-nosed gazelle. Upperparts pale brownish-fawn, with a dark-coloured flank stripe separating the white underparts. Distinctive dark and white facial markings. The white buttocks are flanked by a vertical dark-coloured band. The horns of the ram are slightly divergent, curved backwards and with upward curved tips, and those of the ewes more slender and shorter.

DISTRIBUTION Restricted to the Horn of Africa.

STATUS Occur at very low densities.

HABITAT Open plains and plateaux at medium altitude.

BEHAVIOUR Occur normally in herds of five to 10 individuals, and occasionally more. Each herd is apparently controlled by a territorial ram.

FOOD Mixed feeders; take grasses and browse.

REPRODUCTION Nothing is known.

GRANT'S GAZELLE
Gazella granti

Total length ♂ 1,5-1,8 m ♀ 1,2-1,4 m; tail length ♂ 25-35 cm ♀ 25-30 cm; shoulder height ♂ 85-95 cm ♀ 80-85 cm; weight ♂ 55-80 kg ♀ 35-50 kg. Horn length ♂ 55-81 cm.

Identification pointers Large; uniform fawn upperparts; white underparts and white buttocks with black vertical streak at outer edge; lateral body line faint to very faint; long, well-ridged horns.

Similar species Thomson's and Soemmering's gazelles.

DESCRIPTION Large with uniformly fawn upperparts, white underparts, including inner leg surfaces. A distinct vertical black stripe runs down either side of the white buttocks. Lateral body stripe usually very faint. A circle of white hair surrounds the eye and extends as a white stripe to the snout. Tail is white towards base, with longer black hair towards tip. Its horns are arguably the most magnificent within the genus: those of the ram are long, robust, well ringed and slope slightly backwards, then outwards, the points finally inward; those of the ewes are considerably shorter and very slender. Several races have been recognized,

based on the form of the horns, which range from the widely diverging horns of *robertsi*, with their downward pointing tips, to the close-set horns of *raineyi* in northern Kenya and Somalia.

DISTRIBUTION Occur in East Africa, mainly in northern Tanzania and Kenya, but spilling over into Ethiopia and marginally in south-eastern Sudan, north-eastern Uganda and Somalia.

STATUS Probably more than 350 000 animals.

HABITAT Wide habitat tolerance, semi-desert scrub to open savanna woodland.

Front

51 mm

Back

Grant's Gazelle

Speke's gazelle group; the rams carry longer, heavier horns than the females.

Grant's gazelle ewe. Both sexes carry the long slender horns.

Grant's gazelle ram of the raineyi race

BEHAVIOUR Normally form small herds of up to 30 animals, with an adult ram controlling a group of ewes and their offspring. Adult territorial rams execute elaborate displays when confronting each other: they stand parallel facing in opposite directions, with chins up and heads turned away, and then rapidly whip the heads round to face each other; this may proceed to a head-on-head position, with the chin tucked into the neck and the horns held vertically, with the final stage before conflict involving head lowered to the ground and horns pointing at the opponent. Although the display may be sufficient to drive off a potential competitor, serious fighting does occasionally occur. Younger and non-territorial rams may form into bachelor groups that move around the edges of territorial ram ranges. In some areas they tend to be nomadic, with larger temporary herds forming at certain times of year, but in others they do not move out of fixed home ranges. This is largely a measure of the level of rainfall in a given area. Mingle freely with other ungulates.

FOOD Mixed feeders, taking browse and grass.

REPRODUCTION Young may be dropped at any time of year but in the driest areas birth peaks may coincide with rains. After a gestation period of about 198 days a single fawn weighing 5 to 7 kg is dropped.

SLENDER-HORNED (SAND) GAZELLE
Gazella leptoceros

Total length 1,15-1,3 m; tail length 15-20 cm; shoulder height 65-70 cm; weight 20-30 kg. Horn length ♂ 30-40 cm.

E

Identification pointers Palest gazelle; no dark markings; horns long, more slender in males than other gazelles; very limited distribution.
Similar species Dorcas and red-fronted gazelles.

DESCRIPTION Also known as the sand, rhim and Loder's gazelle, this is the palest of all African gazelles, being a dull greyish-fawn colour with white underparts and facial markings lacking clarity. The distal half of the tail is black. The horns are long, slender and well ringed, but shorter and more slender in the ewes. The hoofs are well developed and broad, an adaptation to the sandy habitats that it occupies.

DISTRIBUTION Recent definite records only exist from Niger and apparently the Quattar Depression region of Egypt, but it is certain that pockets still survive in the more remote sand areas of the Sahara. It is certainly extinct throughout virtually all of the northern and southern Saharan fringes.

STATUS Estimated to be about 5 000 animals but indications are that there could be considerably fewer. Given its adaptation to sandy desert regions it probably survives in the more isolated Saharan 'sand-seas' where it cannot be reached by poachers.

HABITAT Predominantly sandy desert but previously probably also occupied adjacent hill country.

BEHAVIOUR Strongly nomadic, moving widely through the desert, with their broad hoofs allowing access to deep and extensive areas of sand. In the past they were reported to live in small herds probably constituting family groups, with several family herds coming into loose and temporary association during migrations, particularly in search of feeding grounds. Each small group of females and associated young is accompanied by an adult ram.

FOOD Probably mixed feeders.

REPRODUCTION Birthing seasons variable, given wide range, but mostly tied to the fall of the meagre rains. Gestation period of the single fawn has been given as 156 to 169 days; its birth weight is about 2 kg.

Grant's gazelle ram of the robertsi *race*

Slender-horned, or sand, gazelle ewes. When in their natural habitat, these gazelles are strongly nomadic.

RED-FRONTED GAZELLE

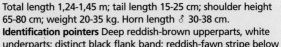

Gazella rufifrons
Total length 1,24-1,45 m; tail length 15-25 cm; shoulder height
65-80 cm; weight 20-35 kg. Horn length ♂ 30-38 cm.
Identification pointers Deep reddish-brown upperparts, white
underparts; distinct black flank band; reddish-fawn stripe below
black band. **Similar species** Dorcas and Soemmering's gazelles.

DESCRIPTION Upperparts are deep
reddish-brown in colour, with the white
underparts separated by a reddish
band and a narrow black flank stripe
(the only Sahelian gazelle with such
a stripe). The horns of the ram are
short, stout and distinctly ringed but
only slightly curved. The forehead and
muzzle are a rich reddish-brown colour.

DISTRIBUTION Restricted to the Sahel
zone, with an apparently small and
isolated population in northern Togo. A
widely separated population occurs to
the east of the Nile River, on the border
of Sudan and Ethiopia (the subspecies
tilonura, referred to as Heuglin's gazelle
and sometimes considered to be a
distinct species although differing only
slightly in horn structure).

STATUS Probably more than 10
000 animals survive, although some
populations are under severe hunting
pressure, and they also suffer from
competition with domestic stock.

HABITAT Semi-desert savanna but
avoiding areas of dense bush cover.

BEHAVIOUR Live alone, in pairs, or
small family parties of three to five
individuals, the latter usually led by an
adult ram. Larger groups of 10 to 15
are occasionally encountered. As with
most gazelles occurring in this region,
knowledge of their behaviour is virtually
non-existent and, given their increasing
scarcity, it is unlikely to improve.

FOOD Mixed feeders, taking grasses
and feeding from a wide range of
bushes, shrubs and small trees.

REPRODUCTION Birthing seasons
appear to be tied to the sparse rains,
with a single lamb weighing about
2,5 to 3 kg being dropped after an
estimated gestation period of 187 days.

CUVIER'S GAZELLE (EDMI)

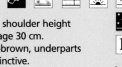

Gazella cuvieri
Total length 1,1-1,25 m; tail length 15-20 cm; shoulder height
60-80 cm; weight 35 kg. Horn length ♂ average 30 cm.
Identification pointers Upperparts dark grey-brown, underparts
white; dark lateral band; facial markings distinctive.
Similar species Dorcas gazelle.

E

DESCRIPTION Small to medium-
sized, with dark grey-brown
upperparts and clean white underparts
which are clearly separated by a dark
lateral band. In most of these animals
a paler shadow stripe runs above
the dark lateral stripe. The horns are
heavily ringed and of moderate length,
but are shorter and more slender
in the ewes. Some authorities feel
that the edmi is a subspecies of the
mountain gazelle (*Gazella gazella*) of
Arabia but recent thinking is that it
warrants full species status.

DISTRIBUTION Restricted to high
country in northern Algeria and
southern Morocco, with a marginal
population occurring in western
Tunisia.

STATUS Slightly more than 1 000
animals are thought to survive, having
suffered greatly from hunting and
competition with domestic stock
for food.

HABITAT Fairly wide habitat
tolerance, inhabiting open forest to
areas of low rainfall rocky desert.

Red-fronted gazelle ewe showing the distinct black band on the flanks.

Cuvier's gazelle, or edmi. The facial markings of this gazelle are distinctive.

This wide range is probably the main reason for its survival.

BEHAVIOUR No detailed study has been undertaken but they are known to live in small groups of three to five related individuals, and never form large herds. These groups, usually controlled by a territorial ram, may on occasion mix with dorcas in the south of its range. Home ranges are believed to be small but this probably varies from higher to low rainfall areas.

FOOD Mixed feeders; take browse and graze.

REPRODUCTION Nothing accurately known but births are probably seasonal, with a single lamb dropped.

DORCAS GAZELLE
Gazella dorcas

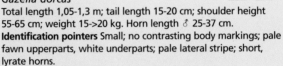

Total length 1,05-1,3 m; tail length 15-20 cm; shoulder height 55-65 cm; weight 15->20 kg. Horn length ♂ 25-37 cm.
Identification pointers Small; no contrasting body markings; pale fawn upperparts, white underparts; pale lateral stripe; short, lyrate horns.
Similar species Slender-horned and Cuvier's gazelles.

DESCRIPTION Small, with no distinct markings. Overall body colour is pale to sandy fawn, with white underparts. There is a flank band, or lateral body stripe but this is pale and indistinct, particularly from a distance. There are 'typical gazelle' facial stripes but these are less distinct than those of several other species. Horns are short to medium length, lyrate and strongly ringed. The female is almost identical to the male but the horns are more slender and lightly built.

DISTRIBUTION The widest distribution of any African gazelle, although populations are now highly fragmented and not present in much of the former range. Races also occur through the Middle East and as far as north-western India.

STATUS Once abundant throughout the Sahara and fringing areas, it now occurs in greatly reduced numbers although accurate estimates are not available. Based on recent observations there are probably at least 10 000 or more animals remaining.

HABITAT Semi-desert to desert plains, extending on to sandy areas.

BEHAVIOUR Live in small herds rarely containing more than 20 members, but larger groups may form during certain seasons when movement is stimulated towards fresh vegetation growth following the rains. The normal herd size would seem to be affected by the level of rainfall in an area and therefore food availability, as in true desert the incidence of pairs is apparently higher. Non-territorial rams usually form into bachelor groups but solitary rams are not unusual.

FOOD Mixed feeders, taking grass as well as browse and, unusually for antelope, they have been recorded as feeding on locusts and will therefore presumably take other insects as well.

REPRODUCTION Births are largely allied to the rainy seasons, with a single lamb, weighing some 1,3 to 1,7 kg, being dropped after a gestation period of approximately 169 to 180 days.

Dorcas gazelle ram. Although once abundant in the Sahara, this species occurs in greatly reduced numbers today.

- Gazella thomsoni thomsoni
- Gazella thomsoni albonotata

Front

48 mm

Back

Thomson's Gazelle

THOMSON'S GAZELLE
Gazella thomsoni

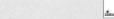

Total length 1-1,38 m; tail length 20-28 cm; shoulder height 55-65 cm; weight 15-25 kg (rarely more than 28 kg). Horn length ♂ 25-43 cm.
Identification pointers Small; broad black lateral stripe separating white underparts from yellowish-fawn upperparts; distinct white eye ring; short black-haired tail constantly flicking; ram horns well developed, almost parallel, well ringed. **Similar species** Grant's gazelle.

DESCRIPTION An abundant species, usually referred to as 'Tommy' (plural 'Tommies') within its range. Upperparts are usually pale yellowish-fawn to reddish-fawn, with a distinct, broad black lateral stripe, or band, clearly separating the clean white underparts. There is a distinct white ring around the eye, and the short, constantly flicking tail is covered with black hair. The horns grow fairly close together, are quite long, and are strongly ringed, but those of the ewes are shorter and very slender, and are frequently deformed. The Mongalla (*albonotata*) of southern Ethiopia and Sudan differs in having a white eye ring extending to the forehead, white forehead patch and horns turned slightly inward at the tips, but it is otherwise easily recognizable as Thomson's.

DISTRIBUTION Two population 'centres' are recognized, one straddling the Kenyan/ Tanzanian border, and extending slightly north and south; and Mongalla occurring in south-eastern Sudan and south-western Ethiopia.

STATUS Despite very limited distribution, this is by far Africa's (and the world's) most abundant gazelle. There are almost 1 million animals, of which approximately 300 000 make up the Mongalla population. In the Serengeti/Ngorongoro/Mara system they have benefitted greatly from the huge increase in the blue wildebeest population, giving access to finely cropped grass.

HABITAT Open savanna grassland.

BEHAVIOUR Form small herds consisting of up to 60 animals which are led by an old female, and accompanied by a single mature male. The herds are not stable and there is considerable emigration and immigration. During the peak mating periods territoriality in rams reaches its highest point but at other times large numbers of the smaller herds congregate on feeding grounds and may number tens of thousands. Non-territorial rams may gather in herds of several hundred individuals. During the mating season the territorial rams establish and defend small areas with a diameter of between 100 and 300 m, attempting to mate with any receptive ewe that enters his area. The rams will fight aggressively for territorial rights, with very little posturing involved. When threatened both sexes will 'pronk', executing stiff-legged jumps, or 'stotting', with the white rump hairs flared. Another significant identifying character is the constant flicking of the very short, black tail.

FOOD Predominantly grazers, and requiring regular access to drinking water.

REPRODUCTION Although lambs may be dropped at any time of the year there is a very distinct peak towards the end of the rainy season. A single lamb, weighing 2 to 3 kg, is born after a gestation period of approximately 188 days.

Thomson's gazelle ram. Inset: *Young Thomson's gazelle ewe. This species is by far the most abundant gazelle in Africa.*

SPRINGBOK

Antidorcas marsupialis
Total length 1,12-1,27 m; tail length 25 cm; shoulder height 75 cm;
weight 26-41 kg (♂ heavier and slightly larger than ♀).
Horn length ♂ average 35 cm; record 49,22 cm.
Identification pointers Only gazelle in southern Africa; dark brown
band separating upper- from underparts; white head, brown stripe
through eye to corner of mouth; short lyrate horns; broad white
rump patch when displaying.
Similar species Should not be confused with any other species
within range.

Front

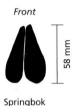

58 mm

Springbok

DESCRIPTION The only gazelle occurring in southern Africa. The hindquarters appear to be slightly higher than the forequarters. A dark red-brown stripe along each flank separates the fawn-brown upperparts from white underparts. The head is white with a thin brown stripe running through the eye to the corner of the upper lip. A large white patch on the rump is bordered by a brown stripe. A long-haired, white dorsal crest extends from the mid-point of the back to the rump; this is normally seen only when the crest is erected, for example when the animal 'pronks' (jumping with stiff legs accompanied by arching of the back). The tail is white with a terminal tuft of black hairs. Both sexes carry the heavily ridged, lyre-shaped horns but those of the ewe are much more slender. Some farmers in South Africa selectively breed springbok with white or black coats and these may be seen in separate herds, or mixed with normally coloured animals.

DISTRIBUTION Restricted to north-west and north-central southern Africa, extending marginally into south-western Angola. Eradicated from the arid interior plains of South Africa in the past but it has been widely reintroduced to farms and reserves within its former range and is now one of the most important sources of venison.

STATUS Well over 100 000 animals, although no accurate estimate is available. They were once involved in vast migrations involving hundreds of thousands, or even millions, of animals.

HABITAT Open, arid plains. Though independent of water, will drink when it is available.

BEHAVIOUR Normally live in small herds but when moving to new feeding grounds may form into herds of several thousands. Large herds are now largely restricted to the Kalahari Desert where they can move unimpeded by fences. Small herds may be mixed or contain only rams; solitary rams are also common. Rams are territorial and during the rut they herd ewe groups; however territories are only held temporarily and for the rest of the year they move freely. Although mainly diurnal, feeding during the cooler hours, night-time activity is common.

FOOD Mixed feeders, grazing and browsing, and they will also dig for roots and bulbs with the front hooves.

REPRODUCTION A single lamb, weighing about 3,8 kg is born after a gestation period of 168 days, with births falling during the summer months when food is abundant. Lambs join herd two days after birth when they are able to keep up.

Springbok ram

Springbok ewe

Both the 'black' and the 'white' springbok (inset) are selectively bred by farmers in South Africa.

DWARF ANTELOPES
Tribe Neotragini

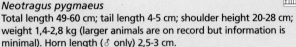

ROYAL ANTELOPE
Neotragus pygmaeus
Total length 49-60 cm; tail length 4-5 cm; shoulder height 20-28 cm; weight 1,4-2,8 kg (larger animals are on record but information is minimal). Horn length (♂ only) 2,5-3 cm.
Identification pointers Smallest horned ungulate; brown upperparts, white underparts, rufous throat collar.
Similar species Duikers within its range (separated on size).

DESCRIPTION The world's smallest horned ungulate, with its size and restricted distribution excluding any confusion with the duikers that share its range. The head and neck are dark brown, the back is somewhat lighter brown, becoming even lighter and bright reddish-brown on the flanks and legs. There is a rufous collar around the throat. Underparts are pure white, as are the underside and tip of the tail. Only the ram carries the tiny but sharp-pointed horns.

DISTRIBUTION Entirely restricted to the Guinean forest zone of West Africa.

STATUS No accurate information is available but it is believed to be abundant and not under any serious threat, although it does appear regularly in the 'bush meat' markets.

HABITAT Dense high forest, although there is some evidence that it can survive in disturbed secondary forest.

BEHAVIOUR Occurs singly and in pairs but because of the dense nature of its habitat, its small size and apparent nocturnal activity, virtually nothing is known about this species.

FOOD Probably approximates the diet of the pygmy antelope, which is a browser.

REPRODUCTION Nothing is known but young are probably born at any time of the year.

SUNI
Neotragus moschatus
Total length 68-75 cm; tail length 12 cm; shoulder height 35 cm; weight 5 kg. Horn length (♂ only) average 8 cm; record 13,34 cm.
Identification pointers Very small; constantly flicking white-tipped tail; ears pink-lined, translucent appearance; white flecked upperparts.
Similar species Sharpe's grysbok, blue duiker.

DESCRIPTION Tiny and elegant, with rich rufous-brown upperparts flecked with white hairs, and white underparts. There are two slightly curved pale to white bars on the throat and above each hoof is a narrow dark band. The fairly long tail is dark brown above and has a white tip, and is flicked regularly and rapidly (a useful identification character). The pink-lined ears give the appearance of being almost transparent. Only the ram carries the thick, prominently ridged horns, sloping backwards in line with the facial profile. The ram has a prominent, dark-coloured preorbital gland. Southern race *livingstonianus* is slightly larger than northern animals.

DISTRIBUTION Largely restricted to the coastal plain and adjacent country from far-eastern South Africa to southern Kenya. It penetrates deeply into the interior following the course of the Zambezi River and lives at up to 2 700 m on some East African mountains.

Front

23 mm

Back

Suni

Suni ewe. These animals frequent dry thickets and riverine woodland.

Only the suni ram carries the short, straight and heavily ringed horns.

STATUS Secure, although hunted in some areas. Densities appear to be at their lowest in the southernmost part of its range.

HABITAT Dry thickets and riverine woodland with dense underbrush.

BEHAVIOUR Usually occur in pairs or small groups of one adult ram and up to four ewes and associated young. Rams are territorial, marking territories with glandular deposits and dung heaps; in some areas these cover about 3 ha although this varies. Predominantly nocturnal but also active in the cooler morning and afternoon hours in areas of low disturbance. If disturbed they run off, following a zigzag resembling that followed by a startled hare. Normal movements follow regular pathways, making them vulnerable to snaring.

FOOD Principally browse but they also take a wide range of plants.

REPRODUCTION In south of range most births seem to coincide with the rains; further north young expected at any time of year, although in northern Tanzania there is a birth peak between November and February. A single fawn, born after about 180 days, spends first few weeks under cover, only emerging to suckle.

BATES'S PYGMY ANTELOPE
Neotragus batesi

Total length 54-62 cm; tail length 4,5-5 cm; shoulder height 25-32 cm; weight 2-3 kg. Horn length (♂ only) 2,2-3,8 cm.
Identification pointers Very small; similar colour to royal antelope but darker; tail uniformly dark; ranges do not overlap.
Similar species Duikers, particularly blue (separated on coloration and size).

DESCRIPTION Overall pelage colour of this, Africa's second smallest ungulate, is a rich reddish-brown with a distinct gloss, with white chevrons on the throat and black and white ear markings. Main identifying character is its small size.

DISTRIBUTION Fragmented, occurring in the north-east of the DRC and marginally in forests of western Uganda, with an apparent gap across the forest belt to the north of the Congo River, westward. However, given the unexplored nature of this area it is probably present, linking up with populations to the west. In the west there is a population in Gabon, Cameroon and the Congo, with an apparently isolated population in southeastern Nigeria.

STATUS Although hunted for meat, habitat destruction is minimal throughout much of its range and it is probably under no major threat.

HABITAT Various forest types with significant undergrowth, also disturbed habitats and 'rehabilitated' agricultural areas.

BEHAVIOUR The only study ever undertaken was in Gabon, where home ranges covered 2 to 4 ha, with all parts of a range being utilized on a rotational basis. They are predominantly solitary, with males probably being territorial and having ranges overlapping those of two or more females but not those of other males. There is some female range overlapping but distances are maintained between individuals. In the Gabon study area it was estimated that densities were as high as 75 individuals per km^2. They are active throughout the 24-hour period but show distinct peaks of resting and feeding behaviour.

FOOD Browsers, taking a wide range of plant species, although selectivity seems to be quite high. They readily enter cultivated patches to feed on certain crops.

REPRODUCTION Young are born throughout the year but there are two birth peaks. It is not known with certainty but the gestation period is about 180 days, after which a single fawn is dropped.

Suni ram: Note the fairly long, bushy tail. These animals are principally browsers and feed on a wide range of plants.

ORIBI
Ourebia ourebi

Total length 1,1 m; tail length 6-15 cm; shoulder height 60 cm; weight 14-20 kg (♂ smaller than ♀, weighing on average 2 kg lighter). Horn length (♂ only) average 10 cm; record southern Africa 19,05 cm.
Identification pointers Steenbok-like but larger; yellow-orange rufous above, white below; short, black-tipped tail in most races; long neck; ram has erect, partly ridged horns.
Similar species Steenbok (separated on size), grysbok (separated on habitat).

Front

40 mm

Back

Oribi

DESCRIPTION The largest of the 'small' antelope, with usually rufous yellow-orange upperparts and white underparts and inner thighs, which extends on to the front of the chest. It has a relatively long neck, medium-sized ears and short tail with distinguishing black tip (sometimes absent). There is a pale throat patch and off-white areas on either side of the nostrils and above eyes. Hair on the back and underparts may have a curly appearance, is more obvious in some populations than in others. Only the ram has horns and these are short, erect and partly ridged. Some races have been raised to species level based on size, horn shape and colour differences, but these are not likely to be valid and represent geographical races.

DISTRIBUTION Very wide but fragmented sub-Saharan distribution, particularly in southern and East Africa. It is absent from desert and the lowland tropical forest zone.

STATUS Abundant in some areas but seriously threatened in others, e.g. the Eastern Cape, South Africa. The greatest numbers, possibly as many as 100 000, are located in West Africa although even there it has lost ground to habitat destruction.

HABITAT Open short grassland with taller grass patches to provide cover.

BEHAVIOUR Occur in pairs or small parties consisting of one ram, which is vigorously territorial, and up to four ewes. Communal dung-heaps serve a territorial marking function, as do secretions from the preorbital glands and other glands, which are 'pasted' on to grass stalks. When disturbed they give a sharp whistle or sneeze and run off rapidly with occasional stiff-legged jumps displaying the black-tipped tail. They are inquisitive, however, and will turn to look back at the source of disturbance after running a short distance. Animals are very bound to their range and rarely leave it, even when under stress. They also lie down in long grass when disturbed, with the head erect, making them difficult to detect. In the most suitable habitats they can occur at quite high densities and closely grouped territories may range from 0,3 to about 1 km^2. Actual core areas within territories may be even smaller than this, although it has been suggested that they are much larger in other regions; as with most species, range size is to a large extent dependent on quality of food and other factors. They are independent of drinking water.

FOOD Principally grazers but browse is occasionally taken. They show a marked preference for short grass and will move if grass becomes too long.

REPRODUCTION Births occur throughout the year but there are marked peaks during the rains. At least in southern Africa births are seasonal but in the tropics peaks are less well defined. A single lamb is born after a gestation period of about 210 days. After birth the lamb remains hidden for up to three or four months before accompanying the group.

Group of oribi rams and ewe, photographed at Lake Mburo, Uganda. The young ram will be driven away by the territorial ram as it reaches maturity.

Oribi ewe showing the short, black tail and the fairly long dorsal hair.

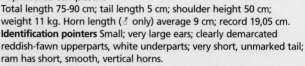

STEENBOK
Raphicerus campestris
Total length 75-90 cm; tail length 5 cm; shoulder height 50 cm;
weight 11 kg. Horn length (♂ only) average 9 cm; record 19,05 cm.
Identification pointers Small; very large ears; clearly demarcated
reddish-fawn upperparts, white underparts; very short, unmarked tail;
ram has short, smooth, vertical horns.
Similar species Oribi (but separated on size and black-tipped tail),
Sharpe's grysbok.

Front

Back

Steenbok

DESCRIPTION Small, elegant and large-eyed, with upperparts normally rufous-fawn but variable from pale fawn to deeper chestnut. Underparts including insides of legs are clean white, and there is a white patch on throat and above eyes. The very short tail is uniform rufous-fawn. Only the ram carries the short, sharp-pointed, smooth-surfaced and vertical horns.

DISTRIBUTION Two widely separated populations, the major one being in southern Africa and the other in Kenya and Tanzania.

STATUS Still abundant, although reduced in areas of high human densities.

HABITAT Open country but with some cover, and dry river-bed associations in arid areas. Independent of drinking water.

BEHAVIOUR Occur singly or in ram/ewe pairs, with the ram and ewe both strongly defensive of their own

overlapping territories. Territories in the Kruger National Park are about 0,03 km^2 in extent, but in the Namib Desert they average more than 0,5 km^2. Unlike other antelopes, they defecate and urinate in shallow scrapes dug with the front hoofs, and then cover these. They lie up in cover during the heat of the day, feeding during the cooler hours, but nocturnal feeding is also common, particularly in disturbed areas.

FOOD Mixed feeders, taking grasses, browse, seed pods and fruit, and also roots and bulbs which they dig out with their front hoofs.

REPRODUCTION A single lamb weighing approximately 900 g is born after gestation of 170 days. In the south births are closely linked to the rainy season but young can be expected throughout the year. They remain hidden for the first few weeks after birth.

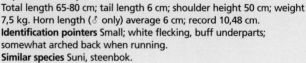

SHARPE'S GRYSBOK
Raphicerus sharpei
Total length 65-80 cm; tail length 6 cm; shoulder height 50 cm; weight
7,5 kg. Horn length (♂ only) average 6 cm; record 10,48 cm.
Identification pointers Small; white flecking, buff underparts;
somewhat arched back when running.
Similar species Suni, steenbok.

Front

Sharpe's Grysbok

DESCRIPTION Small and stoutly built, with reddish-brown upperparts which are liberally flecked with white hairs. The incidence of white hairs diminishes down the sides and the legs. Underparts are buff to buff-white but never pure white, and the area around the mouth and eyes is off-white. Only the ram has short, sharp, slightly

back-angled horns. 'False hoofs' are normally absent (see Cape grysbok). Some believe the two grysbok species should be given subspecies status.

DISTRIBUTION Restricted to north-eastern southern Africa, extending north to Tanzania and marginally westward into Angola.

Steenbok ram. Inset: *Steenbok ram testing ewe for readiness to mate.*

Sharpe's grysbok ram

Sharpe's grysbok ewe

STATUS Not uncommon through much of their range but they are secretive and not often seen.

HABITAT Good vegetation cover, with a preference for low thicket with adjacent open grassed patches. They are frequently associated with vegetated rocky hills and in scrub at their base.

BEHAVIOUR Almost entirely nocturnal but can be seen in early morning and late afternoon hours. Although usually seen singly it is possible that a pair may live in loose association within same home range. Rams are probably territorial, but this has not been established with certainty; little is known of its ecology.

FOOD Mostly browse but also grass and fruits, berries and pods.

REPRODUCTION Lambs may be dropped at any time of year but there may be a peak during rainy seasons. A single lamb is born after a gestation period of approximately 200 days.

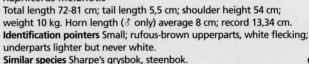

CAPE GRYSBOK
Raphicerus melanotis
Total length 72-81 cm; tail length 5,5 cm; shoulder height 54 cm; weight 10 kg. Horn length (♂ only) average 8 cm; record 13,34 cm.
Identification pointers Small; rufous-brown upperparts, white flecking; underparts lighter but never white.
Similar species Sharpe's grysbok, steenbok.

Front

34 mm

Back

Cape Grysbok

DESCRIPTION Small and squat, with rufous-brown upperparts abundantly flecked with white hairs. Flanks and neck have fewer white hairs and underparts are lighter brown than upperparts. The tail is very short, and the grey-brown ears are proportionately large with white hairs on the inside. Only the ram has short, smooth, slightly back-angled horns. There is a pair of 'false hoofs' above the fetlock.

DISTRIBUTION Restricted to a narrow belt along the south-western and southern Cape coastal belt and the adjacent interior, South Africa.

STATUS Still fairly abundant but its secretive nature often causes it to be overlooked.

HABITAT Relatively thick scrub-bush, and almost entirely restricted to the fynbos, or heathland, vegetation of the Cape, South Africa, including scrub-covered sand dunes and wooded gorges on mountain slopes. In the extreme southern Karoo, they are found along rivers and on scrub-covered hillsides. They are frequently found along the fringes of agricultural land where belts of natural vegetation remain, and will also lie up in commercial orchards and stands of cash crops such as alfalfa.

BEHAVIOUR Mainly nocturnal but active in the early morning and late afternoon if not disturbed, or on overcast and cool days. They are usually solitary except when mating or when the ewes are tending lambs. Rams are territorial, with non-overlapping ranges measuring in size from 0,01 to 0,09 km², depending on the habitat occupied. The territories of females overlap. At least in captivity a hierarchy plays a role, but this is as yet poorly understood. Large dung heaps are used and rams mark twigs and grass stalks with secretions from the preorbital glands.

FOOD Predominantly browsers but grass is taken, particularly fresh growth. In the vineyards of the Western Cape it is considered to be a nuisance as it feeds on young grapes and terminal buds.

REPRODUCTION There are birth peaks in spring and summer (September to December), but lambs are dropped throughout the year. A single lamb is born after a gestation period of approximately 180 days.

Cape grysbok ram. Inset: Cape grysbok ewe: Note the large ears and white flecked coat.

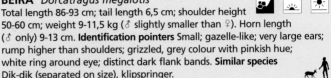

BEIRA *Dorcatragus megalotis*

Total length 86-93 cm; tail length 6,5 cm; shoulder height 50-60 cm; weight 9-11,5 kg (♂ slightly smaller than ♀). Horn length (♂ only) 9-13 cm. **Identification pointers** Small; gazelle-like; very large ears; rump higher than shoulders; grizzled, grey colour with pinkish hue; white ring around eye; distinct dark flank bands. **Similar species** Dik-dik (separated on size), klipspringer.

DESCRIPTION Very similar to the steenbok in overall build, including having very large ears, similar horns and large eyes. The rump stands higher than the shoulders, the coat is thick and coarse, generally a grizzled grey colour with a slight pinkish hue, and a darker-coloured band runs from the lower shoulder to the flank. Underparts are paler with white where the legs join the body, and the short, bushy tail is white below. The head is usually more chestnut in colour, with a whitish ring around the eyes. The horns, carried only by the ram, are short and straight, and widely separated.

DISTRIBUTION Restricted to northern Somalia close to the Red Sea and the Gulf of Aden, and possibly also Djibouti and the adjacent areas of Ethiopia.

STATUS Rare and threatened by competition with domestic stock for food and hunting. Densities are apparently low.

HABITAT Stony hills and mountain ranges in arid areas but, unlike klipspringers, they do not utilize very steep slopes.

BEHAVIOUR Very little is known but they live in pairs, or in groups of up to seven individuals including one or two rams. They live in fixed home ranges, and their rather pointed hoofs, with their rubbery pads, are an adaptation for life in broken, rocky hill country. They are independent of drinking water.

FOOD Mixed feeders, taking browse and grass; *Acacia* is an important food source.

REPRODUCTION Nothing is known.

KLIPSPRINGER *Oreotragus oreotragus*

Total length 80-100 cm; tail length 8 cm; shoulder height 60 cm; weight ♂ 10 kg ♀ 13 kg (slightly larger in some subspecies). Horn length (♂ only) average 8 cm; record South Africa 15,9 cm (some populations have horned females). **Identification pointers** Stocky; short muzzle; walks on hoof tips; rocky habitats. **Similar species** Beira (but separated on appearance).

DESCRIPTION Small and stocky, with coarse, spiny hair, which may have a cushioning function when the animal falls but more likely serves as a heat regulator. General colour is yellow-brown to grey-yellow, with an overall grizzled appearance. Coloration is variable in some regions; e.g. the *somalicus* race is pale creamy yellow. Underparts, chin and lips are white to off-white. Ears are rounded, broad and usually bordered with black. The heavily built appearance is caused by hair standing on end instead of

lying flat as in other antelope. It characteristically walks on the tips of the hoofs. In most races only the ram has horns; these are short, widely separated at the base, vertically placed and ringed only near the base. In some East African races, such as the *schillingsi* race, the ewes also often have horns but this is not completely consistent.

DISTRIBUTION An extensive, but habitat-bound, distribution in southern and eastern Africa and north to the

Klipspringer

20 mm

Klipspringer ram

Klipspringer ewe

Klipspringer ewe. In most races the ewes do not carry horns.

The Klipspringer is sometimes placed in a separate tribe, the Oreotragini, within which it is the sole species.

Red Sea. There are two widely spaced and separated populations, one in the Central African Republic and the other on the Jos Plateau in eastern Nigeria.

STATUS Still common throughout much of its range, although certain isolated populations may be under threat.

HABITAT Rugged, rocky habitat, but may move short distances on to plateaux to feed, and in altitude from coastal hills to 4 500 m on the summit of Mount Meru in northern Tanzania.

BEHAVIOUR Occur in pairs or small family parties, with the ram being territorial. They are extremely agile in moving across rocky terrain and up steep, rock-covered slopes. They frequently stop to look back when running from a disturbance and both sexes give loud nasal alarm whistles. Communal dung-heaps, or middens,

are scattered, generally on flat sites, through a group's home range and probably act as markers. Both sexes mark twigs with a secretion from the preorbital glands. They are active in the morning and cooler afternoon hours but throughout the day when overcast or cool. The size of the home range is strongly linked to rainfall and consequent abundance of food, and sizes of 8 to 49 ha have been recorded.

FOOD Predominantly browsers but grass is taken on occasion.

REPRODUCTION Give birth at any time of the year, although there is some evidence of seasonal peaks, at least in some regions. The single lamb, weighing about 1 kg, is dropped after a gestation period of 210 days, and remains hidden for two to three months after birth.

DIK-DIKS
Genus Madoqua

This group of four (or arguably five) species of tiny, delicate-looking antelope are easily recognized by the elongated and somewhat swollen appearance of the nose, the distinctive crest of erectile hairs on the forehead and the very large eyes. Only the rams have the short, spiky horns, that may be hidden by the head crest. All species occur in the drier areas of north-eastern Africa.

The Damara Dik-dik is now separated from Kirk's Dik-dik, which is restricted to East Africa. They were previously considered to be one species within widely separated populations.

HABITAT Live in relatively dry and arid bush country, particularly favouring areas with *Acacia* trees provided there is dense undergrowth to provide food and cover. They also occupy bush-covered hill slopes and fringing scrub cover at their bases.

BEHAVIOUR Usually live singly, in pairs or small family parties; some evidence that pairs live within a defended territory and that mating is for life. Pairs establish communal dung middens within the home range and twigs are marked with secretions from the preorbital glands. Both diurnal and nocturnal. In certain interactions, particularly between rams, and also when animals are suddenly alarmed, the crest on the forehead is raised, giving the head a much bigger outline. In the Serengeti, they were estimated to occupy territories covering from 5 to 30 ha, but smaller territories have been recorded elsewhere. Within

territories the same pathways are used between resting and feeding sites; these frequently radiate from the dung middens.

FOOD Predominantly browsers but some green grass is eaten, and they also feed on leaves, pods and flowers knocked down by larger species such as greater kudu, elephant and baboons. There are, at least in some areas, seasonal feeding preferences. They scratch out roots with the front hoofs.

REPRODUCTION Gestation period for all species probably around 170 days; a single fawn of 600 to 760 g is dropped. Kirk's dik-dik drop most fawns during summer; in some areas in East Africa there appear to be two birth peaks. Unusual for antelope, both ram and ewe have regular contact with fawn, the ram also licking and grooming offspring.

All dik-diks have very large eyes.

Kirk's dik-dik: Note the short, spiky horns of the ram.

Dik-dik ewe. The crest of erectile hairs on the forehead and the somewhat swollen appearance of the nose are characteristic.

SALT'S DIK-DIK
Madoqua saltiana

Total length 55-70 cm; tail length 4 cm; shoulder height 37 cm; weight 2,7-4 kg. Horn length 3,6-8,8 cm.
Identification pointers Back grey-grizzled; flanks grey to reddish-brown; legs, forehead, nose bright red-brown; white ring around eye.
Similar species Other dik-diks.

DESCRIPTION The coat is thick, with the back grey and speckled, and the flanks are variable from grey to reddish-brown. The legs, forehead and nose are bright red-brown in colour. There is a white ring around the eye.

DISTRIBUTION Widely distributed in the Horn of Africa, extending in a relatively broad belt up along the Red Sea coast to south-eastern Sudan.

STATUS Still common and widespread.

KIRK'S DIK-DIK *Madoqua kirki*
DAMARA DIK-DIK *Madoqua damarensis*

Total length 64-76 cm; tail length 5 cm; shoulder height 38 cm; weight 5 kg. Horn length average 8 cm; record 11,43 cm.
Identification pointers Elongated nose (less than Guenther's); white eye-ring; yellowish-grey grizzled, greyer towards rump.
Similar species Guenther's and Salt's in East Africa, none elsewhere.

Front   *Back*

21 mm

Kirk's Dik-dik

DESCRIPTION The elongated, very mobile nose is not as well developed as in Guenther's. Upperparts are yellowish-grey and grizzled, but the neck is paler than the shoulders and flanks, and underparts are white to creamish in colour. A white ring of short hairs circles the eye.

DISTRIBUTION The most widespread dik-dik in East Africa, with a separate population located in northern Namibia and south-western Angola.

STATUS Common to abundant over much of its range.

PIACENTINI'S DIK-DIK
Madoqua piacentinii

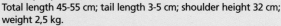

Total length 45-55 cm; tail length 3-5 cm; shoulder height 32 cm; weight 2,5 kg.
Identification pointers Body silver-grey, legs fawn-yellow; chestnut-red blaze on snout.
Similar species Other dik-diks.

DESCRIPTION Piacentini's dik-dik is also known as the silver dik-dik. The lower legs are fawn, with similar colouring on the cheeks, ears and forehead crest. There is a chestnut-red blaze on the front of the face. The hairs inside the ear are white, as is the upper throat. There is no white ring around the eye.

DISTRIBUTION Restricted to a narrow strip of coastal plain in eastern Somalia.

STATUS Common.

Kirk's, or Damara, dik-dik ewe from East Africa. This species is common to abundant over most of its range.

Kirk's dik-dik ram: Note the white ring of short hairs around the eyes.

GUENTHER'S DIK-DIK

Madoqua guentheri
Total length 62-70 cm; tail length 3-5 cm; shoulder height 34-38 cm; weight 3,7-5,5 kg. Horn length 5-10,8 cm.
Identification pointers Nose conspicuously elongated; overall greyish-fawn, grizzled; whitish underparts; forehead, nose rufous.
Similar species Other dik-diks.

DESCRIPTION Guenther's dik-dik has the most elongated and proboscis-like snout of all dik-dik species, but it usually lacks the clearly demarcated white eye-ring. Overall body colour is greyish-fawn and it is distinctly grizzled, while the underparts are white.

DISTRIBUTION Extends from the Horn of Africa into northern Kenya, westward through southern Ethiopia, and across to northern Uganda.

STATUS It is the most abundant dik-dik in eastern Africa.

DUIKERS

Subfamily Cephalophinae; Tribe Cephalophini
The duiker are placed in two genera, with perhaps as many as 18 species in the *Cephalophus* group, and only one in the genus *Sylvicapra*. Whereas the latter is discussed in the same way as are other species in this guide, the cephalophine, known as the forest duikers, are treated as a group. Aspects such as behaviour, food and reproduction are given on a communal basis (at the beginning of the section). The reason for this is that very little research has been undertaken on these secretive antelope, but the little that is known seems to indicate that there are many similarities between them. Although several of the forest duikers are taxonomically fairly clear-cut, others are very complex and numerous questions remain unanswered. Where this may be relevant to field identification, it is mentioned.

COMMON (GREY) DUIKER

Sylvicapra grimmia
Total length 90-135 cm; tail length 10-22 (average 12) cm; shoulder height 50 cm; weight ♂ 18 kg ♀ 21 kg (some records indicate weights as low as 10 kg but whether this refers to a distinct race or isolated individuals is not known). Horn length (♂ only) average 11 cm; record South Africa 18,1 cm.
Identification pointers Crest of long hair on top of head; often black facial blaze; narrowed snout where preorbital glands are located.
Similar species Oribi (separated on habitat).

Front

38 mm

Common Duiker

DESCRIPTION The general body coloration varies according to region from light grey to reddish-brown, with underparts being slightly paler to white. Some 18 subspecies have been described, based almost entirely on pelage coloration but the validity of most is very doubtful. In high altitude areas, particularly in East Africa, a quite long, shaggy coat is often developed. There is usually a crest of longish hair on the top of the head and a black blaze down the centre of the face. The preorbital glands emphasize the narrowness of the muzzle, giving the black snout a slightly bulbous appearance. The front surfaces of the legs are usually darker than the rest of the pelage but this may be absent in some regions. Rams carry well-ringed, sharp-pointed horns but on occasion ewes also

Guenther's dik-dik has a very large, proboscis-like snout.

Common, or grey, duiker ram

Common duiker ewe

grow stunted, or deformed, horns. Unlike other duiker species, the back is held straight and the legs are proportionately quite long. The common duiker is also known as Grimm's, crowned, grey and bush duiker in the different parts of its range.

DISTRIBUTION The most widespread of all duiker species, with an almost complete sub-Saharan range, although it is absent from the lowland equatorial forests and true desert.

STATUS Abundant and widespread, and even though it is hunted widely, it is often found in close association with human habitation.

HABITAT Very wide habitat tolerance, showing a clear preference for savanna woodland, thickets and open bush country, and found up to relatively high altitudes where there is adequate cover. Open country is avoided completely.

BEHAVIOUR Usually solitary but not uncommonly encountered in pairs, and in areas of high density several individuals may be seen feeding in close proximity to each other. Rams are intolerant of each other and establish, mark and hold territories. They usually associate with the one female that remains within their range, and she readily drives off other females entering it. Home ranges in parts of their southern range have been measured between 12 to 27 ha. In areas of high food availability, they occur at very high densities, with individuals occupying ranges of 4 ha or less. Small heaps of droppings are deposited in close proximity to each other at several locations within the territory and both sexes mark twigs with secretions from the preorbital glands. They are active mainly at night but frequently feed in the cooler morning hours and may emerge an hour or more before sunset. When feeding they may maintain close proximity to other species, including savanna baboons, larger antelope and domestic stock, especially cattle and goats. They are independent of drinking water but will drink on occasion when it is available.

FOOD Feed on a wide variety of browse, including flowers, shoots, leaves, fruits, seeds, pods and fungi, and also a wide range of cultivated crops, for which they are considered a nuisance in some areas. Animal foods are also taken, such as termites, other insects, small vertebrates and carrion, and if the opportunity presents itself they will attempt to catch birds up to the size of the domestic hen. Prey captured is well chewed. They also use the front hoofs to excavate for bulbs, tubers and roots. This very wide dietary tolerance perhaps helps explain their success and wide distribution.

REPRODUCTION A single lamb, averaging 1,6 kg at birth, may be born at any time of year after a gestation period of about 190 days, although at least in some regions there may be a birthing peak coinciding with the rainy season. Young are active soon after birth but for the first part of life they lie up under cover, frequently moving their location. The parents are very protective and if a young is threatened they react to its alarm bleating.

Common, or grey, duiker ewe. Body coloration in this species varies according to region.

Common duiker ram: Note the narrow snout.

Common duiker ewe: Note the forehead crest.

THE FOREST DUIKERS

Genus *Cephalophus*

Several characteristics are common to all forest duikers including: a squat, stocky appearance; the hunched posture of the back and the head held close to the ground; short, thin legs and a well-developed crest, coming to a point at the top of the head and frequently covering the horns. Males always have horns but in some species the females may also have horns, which tend to be shorter than those of the male. The horns are very short (shorter than the head), partly ridged and then smooth, sharply pointed and angled back in line with the plane of the face. The ears are quite short and rounded. In front of each eye is a long, black, naked line, which is the outer surface of the scent-producing glands, giving the muzzle a somewhat pinched appearance. The snout is black, relatively large and somewhat cow-like. In all cases forest duiker pelage is sleek, usually with a distinct sheen. There is considerable confusion within certain groupings, e.g. the 'red duiker' complex, that incorporates Weyns', Peters', Natal and Harvey's duikers. Also the blue and Maxwell's duikers may constitute one superspecies with several recognizable races. Complicating the issue further is the possibility that as yet undescribed races and possibly even full species may come to light from some of Africa's more remote forests and montane areas. In cases where descriptions are not clear-cut, the distribution maps and habitat descriptions should be consulted for clues on identity.

BEHAVIOUR The name duiker is a Dutch word meaning 'diver', based on the animal's habit of plunging into dense cover on being disturbed. All the forest duikers share most aspects of behaviour, being largely solitary animals, although pairs frequently live in close association. Indications are that a few, probably all, are strongly and aggressively territorial, but because of the high productivity of their chosen habitats, their territories and home ranges are small. For example, in one area home ranges of the blue duiker cover between 2 and 4 ha. However, in some other areas the densities can be astonishingly high, the blue reaching 70 animals per km^2 of forest in one area of Gabon. In some species a pair may defend a mutually held territory against intruders of the same species. All species have well-developed preorbital scent glands, which secrete a substance used for marking twigs and other objects. This almost certainly has a territorial function. At least the blue duiker, and probably others, appear to be monogamous and pair for life; however, a pair spend little time together and feeding and resting frequently take place at different times. Times of activity seem to be variable in different species and even within the same species in different regions, and depend on the levels of disturbance. The blue duiker seems to be mainly diurnal in parts of its southern range but in other areas may be mainly nocturnal. The bay is believed to be nocturnal whereas the yellow-backed may be expected to be active at any time of day or night. The black-fronted duiker feeds primarily during the daylight hours but Abbott's duiker is nocturnal.

FOOD Duikers are unique in the antelope world, not only feeding on plant parts but also including animal food in their diet; further, they are also known to hunt actively. The bulk of the diet of most species is made up of a wide range of wild fruits, including those of many tree species. These animals are able to open their mouths considerably wider than most antelope can, thus enabling them to chew even relatively large fruit pips, or seeds, are usually not swallowed but are spat out. They also eat leaves, twig tips, bark, flowers, pods, fungi and resin. There are numerous records of different duikers eating a great variety of insects, other invertebrates, small mammals, frogs, reptiles, fish (scavenged) and carrion. They have been observed hunting for birds up to the size of domestic hens. Unlike other

Yellow-backed duiker

Blue duiker

Red-flanked duiker

Red duiker

antelope, their digestive systems cope very efficiently with this animal food.

REPRODUCTION This aspect is very poorly known but all have single lambs, although there are also reports of twins for species such as the yellow-backed duiker. Lambs may be dropped at any time of the year, but birthing peaks are known, or suspected, in some species; e.g. the young of the red-flanked duiker are born mainly during the dry season and in the south the red duiker has a distinct summer peak, as does the blue duiker in the same region. On average, in the smaller species at least, lambs weigh about 10% of the ewes' weight; in the case of the blue duiker, they average 400 g. Gestation periods are poorly known but most are

probably in the vicinity of 160 or more days; for Maxwell's and the blue duikers it is said to be 167 days.

GENERAL Duiker meat is a very important source of animal protein for millions of rural Africans and although several species have been greatly reduced by hunting, others such as the blue seem to be able to sustain a heavy offtake. The immensity of this harvest is indicated by the fact that of 46 tons of 'bush meat' entering the Bukavu (the DRC) over a six-week period, well over 30% was made up of duikers of several species, while in the markets of Kisangani 70% of 'bush meat' consisted of the blue. They are also important prey components of leopard, golden cat and the crowned eagle.

ABBOTT'S DUIKER *Cephalophus spadix*
Total length 1,1-1,3 m; tail length 8-12 cm; shoulder height 50-65 cm; weight up to 60 kg. Horn length 10-12 cm.
Identification pointers Large; dark chestnut-brown to black; no distinguishing markings; restricted distribution.
Similar species Yellow-backed duiker (separated on rump patch).

DESCRIPTION Third largest forest duiker, with a dark chestnut-brown to black coat without any markings.

DISTRIBUTION Restricted to the Uluguru/Uzungwe, Rungwe and Usambara mountains, and Mount Kilimanjaro in Tanzania. It is also suspected to be present on Mount Meru.

STATUS Not believed to be threatened, despite the fact that they live in isolated montane pockets, but at certain locations hunting and habitat loss are possibly having adverse impacts.

HABITAT Dense mountain forest.

OGILBY'S DUIKER *Cephalophus ogilbyi*
Total length 97-130 cm; tail length 12-15 cm; shoulder height 55 cm; weight 14-20 kg. Horn length 4-12,1 cm.
Identification pointers Overall reddish-orange, narrow black dorsal stripe shoulder to tail; some populations apparently white 'stockings', others darker legs. **Similar species** None.

DESCRIPTION There is some confusion as to the taxonomic status of Ogilby's, with the belief that it may only be a race of the bay duiker. It is reddish-orange overall with a narrow dark brown to black dorsal stripe extending from the shoulders to the base of the tail. Some populations have white leg 'stockings', others have darker coloured legs. Horns are noticeably conical and broad at the base.

DISTRIBUTION Fragmented in West Africa with one isolated population to the east of the Niger River and on the island of Bioko in the Gulf of Guinea.

STATUS Populations have become increasingly fragmented and are now rare almost everywhere in West Africa.

HABITAT Tropical lowland forests.

Ogilby's duiker: Note the narrow black dorsal stripe.

Ogilby's duiker: The horns are conical and broad at the base.

WHITE-BELLIED DUIKER *Cephalophus leucogaster*
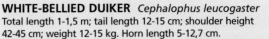

Total length 1-1,5 m; tail length 12-15 cm; shoulder height 42-45 cm; weight 12-15 kg. Horn length 5-12,7 cm.
Identification pointers Medium-sized; relatively pale fawn to reddish-brown, darker vertebral band; palest forest duiker in area; dark facial blaze; buttocks, belly white. **Similar species** Bay and Peters' duikers.

DESCRIPTION Medium-sized and paler than other forest duikers within range; buttocks and belly white, underparts generally pale. Overall body colour is light fawnish-brown to darker reddish-brown, usually more pronounced in rump region. A dark vertebral band and a dark facial blaze contrast with orange-red crest.

DISTRIBUTION See map.

STATUS Uncommon but probably secure.

HABITAT Lowland, secondary and gallery forests, and adjacent dense thicket areas.

YELLOW-BACKED DUIKER
Cephalophus silvicultor
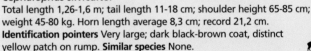

Total length 1,26-1,6 m; tail length 11-18 cm; shoulder height 65-85 cm; weight 45-80 kg. Horn length average 8,3 cm; record 21,2 cm.
Identification pointers Very large; dark black-brown coat, distinct yellow patch on rump. **Similar species** None.

DESCRIPTION This is the largest of all duikers and is easily identified by its overall dark brown to blackish coat and the distinctive yellow rump patch, which is broadest above the tail and tapers along the spine to terminate in a point behind the shoulders; this is raised when alarmed but presumably has some behavioural function. The hair around the muzzle may be silvery-white, and the head crest may be dark or dull chestnut in colour.

DISTRIBUTION The most extensive distribution of any of the large forest duikers.

STATUS Threatened in most of West Africa but given its relatively wide habitat tolerance, is probably secure elsewhere.

HABITAT Occurs in virtually all forest associations within the tropics, as well as savanna woodland and miombo.

ZEBRA (BANDED) DUIKER
Cephalophus zebra

Total length 90-105 cm; tail length 15 cm; shoulder height 40-50 cm; weight 9-20 kg. Horn length 2-4,8 cm.
Identification pointers Reddish-brown overall; 12 to 15 distinct vertical black body stripes. **Similar species** None.

DESCRIPTION Overall body colour is reddish-brown, and darker on the rump, shoulders and neck, with distinct vertical black body stripes from the shoulders to the rump. Black markings on legs; snout is dark in colour and tail is predominantly white.

DISTRIBUTION Very limited range, much of which falls within Liberia.

STATUS Considered to be endangered.

HABITAT Dense forests in lowlands and hills.

Yellow-backed duiker ram: Note the dark coloration and the pale rump patch.

The zebra duiker with its distinctive coat patterning cannot be mistaken for any other species.

RED-FLANKED DUIKER
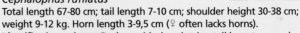
Cephalophus rufilatus
Total length 67-80 cm; tail length 7-10 cm; shoulder height 30-38 cm; weight 9-12 kg. Horn length 3-9,5 cm (♀ often lacks horns).
Identification pointers Dark greyish dorsal stripe tail base to nose; body reddish to reddish-yellow; legs partly greyish. **Similar species** None.

DESCRIPTION Overall reddish-brown to reddish-yellow body colour, which contrasts strongly with the broad grey dorsal stripe extending from the base of the tail to the nose, with the blaze being usually darker than the back stripe, and the stripe being darker in the eastern part of its range. The legs are bluish-grey and there are black and white markings on the ears.

DISTRIBUTION Extends right across West Africa in a broad belt from Senegal to Uganda.

STATUS Still found to be abundant through much of its range.

HABITAT Least tied to lowland high forest of all duikers; readily occupies forest fringes, secondary forest and woodlands, even those edging on savanna.

JENTINK'S DUIKER

Cephalophus jentinki
Total length 1,5 m; tail length 15 cm; shoulder height 80 cm; weight up to 70 kg. Horn length 15,5-17,5 cm.
Identification pointers Very large; black head and neck, white shoulder band; silver-grey rump; restricted distribution. **Similar species** None.

DESCRIPTION Second only in size to the yellow-backed, and easy to distinguish because of pelage patterning. The head and neck are black and a narrow white band extends across the shoulders on to the top of the front legs. The rest of the body is overall grizzled silvery-grey, but underparts are somewhat paler.

DISTRIBUTION Very limited range, found only in fragmented populations within Sierra Leone, Liberia and Ivory Coast.

STATUS Endangered as a result of hunting and habitat loss (2 000 to 10 000 remain).

HABITAT Lowland rainforest.

MAXWELL'S DUIKER *Cephalophus maxwellii*

Total length 62-98 cm; tail length 8-10 cm; shoulder height 32-40 cm; weight 8-9 kg. Horn length 2,2-9,8 cm.
Identification pointers Small (variable); overall colour grey-brown to blue-grey. **Similar species** Black duiker (separated on size and coloration).

DESCRIPTION Many taxonomists believe that this and the blue are the same, representing a superspecies. Both are variable in size and pelage coloration. Apart from small size and overall bluish-grey to grey-brown coloration, including legs, there are no distinguishing features.

DISTRIBUTION Widespread from the west of the Niger River to Senegal.

STATUS Abundant in most areas but heavily hunted as 'bush meat'.

HABITAT Lowland rainforests and gallery forests.

Jentink's duiker showing the distinctive white shoulder 'collar'.

Red-flanked duiker

Maxwell's duiker is widespread from the Niger River to Senegal.

PETERS' AND WEYNS' DUIKERS
Cephalophus callipygus/C. weynsi

Total length 90-130 cm; tail length 10-16 cm; shoulder height 45-60 cm; weight 15-24 kg. Horn length 5,5-13,8 cm.

Identification pointers Brownish-fawn merging to bright rufous on rump, some populations darker than others; legs darker than body; forehead/crest reddish-brown; dark (black) vertebral stripe always present in western populations (Peters'), absent in east (Weyns').

Similar species Other red duikers, bay duiker.

DESCRIPTION The similarities between members of the 'red duiker group', which includes Peters', Weyns', Harvey's red and the Natal, make the separation of these species very difficult in the field. Peters' and Weyns' occupy the Congolean tropical forest belt, with the other two to the east of the Great Rift Valley and south-east to South Africa. Some authorities believe that these should be lumped together and only separated on the subspecies level; others believe that some subspecies currently recognized should be raised to full species.

Peters' is in general brownish-fawn in colour on the forequarters, grading into bright rufous towards the rump, with animals in the west of the range tending to be lighter in colour than elsewhere. The forehead and crest are reddish-brown, the muzzle dark, with white on lips, chin and throat. A dark to black band runs along the spine, widening towards the rump. Legs are darker than rest of body. Weyns' is said to have somewhat coarser, longer hair but usually no vertebral stripe.

DISTRIBUTION Apparently occurs only within a few degrees of the equator, westward from the eastern DRC to the Atlantic, with Weyns' duiker said to occur from the DRC, extending into southern Uganda and marginally into Kenya, and southward along the eastern shore of Lake Tanganyika.

STATUS Probably abundant in the lowland tropical forests but numbers are low in the most eastern parts of the range.

HABITAT Lowland forest, as well as several associated forest types. Weyns' may also extend into montane forests in the eastern parts of the range.

BLACK DUIKER
Cephalophus niger

Total length 90-100 cm; tail length 12-14 cm; shoulder height 45-50 cm; weight 18-24 kg. Horn length 2,5-17,5 cm.

Identification pointers Very dark brown to black overall; chestnut hair on forehead.

Similar species Maxwell's duiker.

DESCRIPTION Uniformly very dark brown to black over the entire body, and has a relatively thick coat. The head and sides of the neck are usually very slightly paler in colour, as are the neck and throat. The only markedly different coloration is the bright reddish-brown crest and forehead.

DISTRIBUTION West of the Niger River to Guinea.

STATUS Considered to be endangered within the eastern parts of its range, particularly in Nigeria, but elsewhere, despite heavy hunting pressure, fairly secure.

HABITAT Lowland rainforests and their fringes.

The black duiker is endangered in some parts of its range.

The black duiker usually has a relatively thick coat and a bright reddish-brown forehead and crest.

Black duiker

BLACK-FRONTED DUIKER
Cephalophus nigrifrons

Total length 95-120 cm; tail length 10-15 cm; shoulder height 45-55 cm; weight 13-16 kg. Horn length 4-12 cm.
Identification pointers Reddish to dark brown overall; distinct very dark to black facial blaze, crest. **Similar species** Bay and Peters' duikers.

DESCRIPTION Overall body colour a uniform reddish, deep chestnut, or dark red-brown, with lower leg colouring darker to black. The main distinguishing character is the broad black blaze running from nose to forehead, usually incorporating the crest and often extending a short distance down the back of neck. The tail is black with a white tip. One subspecies, the Ruwenzori (*rubidus*), is sometimes recognized as a full species on the basis of the belly being white, the hair being thicker and minor colour differences.

DISTRIBUTION Main distribution centres are a few degrees north and south of the equator within Central Africa, with isolated outlying populations found on Mounts Kenya, Elgon and Kabobo, while the *rubidus* form occurs in the Ruwenzori Mountains.

STATUS Generally not threatened but subject to habitat destruction and hunting.

HABITAT Montane forests in the east, and elsewhere lowland and gallery forests.

ADER'S DUIKER
Cephalophus adersi

Total length about 75 cm; tail length 9-12 cm; shoulder height 30-32 cm; weight 6-12 kg. Horn length 3-6 cm.
Identification pointers White band across buttocks; white spotting on legs. **Similar species** Red duiker (separated by lack of buttock band).

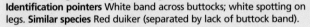

DESCRIPTION Overall tawny red colour becoming greyer on the neck, but easily identified by the white band around the buttocks. There is some white spotting, or freckling, on the legs. Some believe it to be a subspecies of the red (*natalensis/harveyi*) but others feel that it justifies its own identity.

DISTRIBUTION Most limited distribution of all duikers; restricted to island of Unguja, Zanzibar, and forest pockets along Kenyan coast.

STATUS Threatened by habitat loss and hunting. May be extinct on mainland.

HABITAT Coastal forest, woodland and thickets.

RED DUIKERS
Cephalophus natalensis/C. harveyi

Total length 80-110 cm; tail length 9-15 cm; shoulder height 45 cm; weight 10-16 kg. Horn length average 6 cm; record 10,48 cm.
Identification pointers Rich reddish-brown to deep chestnut overall; black and white tipped tail; many variations.
Similar species Peters' and Weyns'.

DESCRIPTION Overall body colour is rich reddish-brown to deep chestnut, but in the case of *harveyi* there is a black facial blaze, the centre of the

crest is black, which may extend on to the upper neck, and the legs may be somewhat darker. The tail is tipped in black and white.

Natal red duiker: The large preorbital gland secretes a sticky, tar-like substance used for marking territories.

Ader's duiker is easily identified by the while band around the buttocks.

Red Duiker

Front

Back

Blue Duiker

DISTRIBUTION Not known with certainty where the two species/ subspecies occur, but to a large extent they are restricted to the coastal plain and adjacent interior from eastern South Africa to Kenya and Somalia, and in a few locations extending inland, usually in conjunction with riverine forest. There is an apparently isolated population in the south of the Ethiopian Highlands but its exact identity has not been established.

STATUS In general secure, despite there being a number of isolated populations.

HABITAT Most forest types and associated thickets within its range.

BLUE DUIKER
Cephalophus monticola

Total length 62-84 cm; tail 7-12 cm; shoulder height 35 cm; weight 3-6 kg.
Horn length average 3 cm; record 7,3 cm.
Identification pointers Tiny (bigger than Bates's pygmy antelope); overall body colour light slate-grey to dark brown, most shades between; leg colour usually slightly different to body. **Similar species** None.

DESCRIPTION The smallest duiker, and very delicate in appearance. Overall body colour is very variable, from pale slate-grey to dark brown, and although largely tied to regional differences, there is also some variation within specific populations. Unlike Maxwell's duiker, the legs are usually some shade of brown, or brown-grey, contrasting with the rest of the body. The throat and chest may be somewhat paler, and the hair around the eyes may be lighter. Many different subspecies have been described.

DISTRIBUTION Very widely distributed in Central Africa, with substantial population centres in East Africa, mainly in Uganda and southern and eastern Tanzania. In the south, populations are limited to the coastal plain and to a narrow strip of the adjacent interior.

STATUS Probably the most abundant of all duikers, despite very heavy hunting pressure for their meat, particularly in Central Africa.

HABITAT Occupies probably the widest range of forest and wooded habitats of any other duiker, which in part explains its success, utilizing rainforests to coastal sand-dune forest, riverine and montane forest, even certain plantations.

BAY DUIKER *Cephalophus dorsalis*

Total length 78-110 cm; tail length 8-15 cm; shoulder height 40-55 cm; weight 19-25 kg. Horn length 5,5-10,5 cm.
Identification pointers Brown-yellow to brown-red; distinct dark dorsal stripe nose to tail base; dark on legs; medium-sized.
Similar species Peters' duiker.

DESCRIPTION Bright brownish-yellow to brownish-red with a distinct dark dorsal stripe extending from nose to base of tail. Dark markings on legs; some animals have almost wholly darkened legs extending on to shoulders and rump. A dark stripe, of varying intensity and length, may run down centre of ventral surface. Forehead crest is very poorly developed and may be almost absent.

DISTRIBUTION Occurs virtually throughout the tropical lowland forest belt to the eastern DRC.

STATUS Probably secure but precarious in west.

HABITAT Lowland and dense secondary forest.

The blue duiker is the smallest of the duikers. Inset: *Blue duiker showing the large preorbital gland.*

Blue duiker from the northern DRC.

Bay duiker.

GOAT ANTELOPES (GOATS AND SHEEP)
Subfamily Caprinae

Front

85 mm

Nubian Ibex

NUBIAN IBEX
Capra ibex nubiana

WALIE IBEX
Capra ibex walie

Total length 1,55-1,9 m; tail length 15-25 cm; shoulder height
65-100 cm; weight ♂ 60-80 (one record up to 125) kg ♀ 50-70 kg
(♂ consistently larger and heavier than ♀). Horn length ♂ up to 1,14 m.
Identification pointers Only African wild goat; variable brown above,
white to paler below; ram longish beard, massive swept-back horns.
Similar species Barbary sheep (Ibex are separated on size and
appearance from domestic goats).

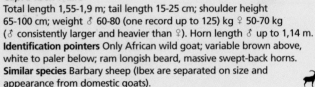

DESCRIPTION Large and easily
identified by robust build, and in
the ram a longish beard under the
chin and massive, semi-circular horns
with transverse knobs along their
entire length, except for the tips. The
ewe lacks a beard and carries short,
slightly curved horns. Overall body
coloration is dark brown to yellowish-
brown but in the walie the colour is
generally richer and tending towards
dark chestnut. Darker lines, or
bands, usually separate upper- from
underparts, the latter being white
to creamy-fawn. Black and white
markings are located on the forward-
facing surfaces of the front legs. The
tail is short and tufted, and is dark
brown to black. There is some doubt
as to whether the two races should
be given full species status, and it is
assumed here that they are forms of
the more widespread Palaearctic ibex.

DISTRIBUTION The walie ibex is
found only in and around the Simien
National Park in northern Ethiopia,
although recent reports indicate
that it may no longer occur in that
park. The Nubian ibex occurs in the
narrow belt of arid and rugged Red
Sea hills, through Eritrea and Sudan
and possibly into southern Egypt.
It is also present in the hills of the
Egyptian Sinai.

STATUS Both races occur in greatly
reduced numbers, with well below
400 walie and several hundred of the
slightly more secure Nubian.

HABITAT Nubian are restricted to
arid, rugged hill country, whilst the
walie occur at altitudes above 2 800
m in mountainous plateau country
with subalpine heathland and
grassland vegetation.

BEHAVIOUR Live in small herds
of fewer than 10 individuals, with
ewe/lamb groups being relatively
stable and periodically joined by adult
rams. Dominant rams circulate range,
checking on breeding condition of
ewes, but move on if there are no
oestrus females. Males of the walie
occupy home ranges from about
0,5 to >10 km^2. No work has been
undertaken on the Nubian in Africa.

FOOD Mixed feeders, browsing
and grazing.

REPRODUCTION Nubian are said to
be mainly seasonal breeders, with kids
being born in March to April, while
the walie may breed throughout
the year with a peak in rutting from
March to May. A single young is
usual but twins and even triplets have
been recorded. Kid birth weight is
approximately 2 kg, after a gestation
period of 150 to 165 days.

Nubian ibex ram and ewe. The Nubian and walie ibex are Africa's only wild goats.

Walie ibex ram

Nubian ibex ram: Note the massive swept-back horns.

BARBARY SHEEP *Ammotragus lervia*

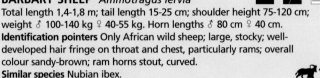

Total length 1,4-1,8 m; tail length 15-25 cm; shoulder height 75-120 cm; weight ♂ 100-140 kg ♀ 40-55 kg. Horn lengths ♂ 80 cm ♀ 40 cm.
Identification pointers Only African wild sheep; large, stocky; well-developed hair fringe on throat and chest, particularly rams; overall colour sandy-brown; ram horns stout, curved.
Similar species Nubian ibex.

DESCRIPTION Large and stockily built, with the ram markedly larger than the ewe. A well-developed fringe of long hairs, particularly extensive in the ram, extends down the throat, on to the chest and front legs. Tail is fairly long and well haired and the ears are rather short. The horns of the ram are stout and very broad at the base, and are curved back, down and forward in mature animals; the horns of the ewes are thinner and shorter. (Also known as the aoudad).

DISTRIBUTION Once occurred in virtually all suitable habitats throughout the Sahara and fringing areas but now reduced to only a few locations.

STATUS Numbers are greatly reduced and they have completely disappeared from some areas. Total population is considerably lower than 50 000 animals, with some of the largest localized populations, perhaps up to 3 600 animals, located in the Aïr Mountains and Termit Massif. Extensive hunting and competition with livestock are the major factors influencing declines.

HABITAT Arid hill and mountain country.

BEHAVIOUR Live in small groups of between three and six animals but up to 20 individuals occur occasionally, particularly during the dry season. Each group consists of an adult ram, a number of ewes and their accompanying offspring. Older rams are usually solitary. They make their way easily over the rugged terrain in which they live and during the hottest daylight hours they seek shade amongst the boulders or under rock overhangs. Harem rams will vigorously defend their ewes against intrusions by other rams, particularly during oestrus.

FOOD Graze and browse.

REPRODUCTION Mating peaks in October/November, with lambs being dropped after a gestation period of 150 to 165 days. One to three lambs are born but a single lamb is most usual, weighing 1,5 to 3 kg.

HIMALAYAN TAHR *Hemitragus jemlahicus (introduced)*

Total length ♂ 1,65-1,9 m ♀ 1,55-1,7 m; tail length 15-20 cm; shoulder height ♂ 90-100 cm ♀ 80-90 cm; weight ♂ 80-90 kg ♀ 60-70 kg. Horn length ♂ up to 42 cm, ♀ shorter.
Identification pointers Goat-like; was found on Table Mountain, Cape Town. **Similar species** None.

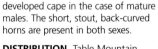

DESCRIPTION Goat-like, having a long shaggy coat, with a well-developed cape in the case of mature males. The short, stout, back-curved horns are present in both sexes.

DISTRIBUTION Table Mountain, Cape Town.

STATUS Plans to exterminate them have been largely successful, and few, if any, remain.

HABITAT Mountain heath (fynbos).

BEHAVIOUR Males move in bachelor groups or singly; join nursery herds during rut.

FOOD Browse and graze.

REPRODUCTION One kid is born after 180 days.

Barbary sheep ram: Although it resembles the Nubian ibex, it is in fact not a wild goat but the only African wild sheep.
Inset: The Himalayan tahr is native to the Himalayas and was introduced to Table Mountain, South Africa.

ELEPHANTS Order Proboscidea

AFRICAN ELEPHANT
Family Elephantidae; *Loxodonta africana*

FOREST ELEPHANT
Loxodonta africana cyclotis

SAVANNA ELEPHANT *Loxodonta africana africana*
Forest Elephant Shoulder height ♂ 2,35 m ♀ 2,1 m;
weight ♂ 2 800-3 200 kg ♀ 1 800-2 500 kg.
Savanna Elephant Total length ♂ 7-9 m ♀ 6,5-8,5 m;
shoulder height ♂ 3,2-4 m ♀ 2,5-3,4 m;
weight ♂ 5 000-6 300 kg ♀ 2 800-3 500 kg.
Identification pointers Unmistakable.
Long trunk; usually tusks; large ears.
Similar species None.

Front

500 mm

Back

Elephant

Recently some
authorities have
recognized the two
subspecies as full
species based on DNA
sequencing.

DESCRIPTION Several subspecies have been described, but today only the larger savanna and the forest races are recognized. Apart from differing in size and habitat preferences, the forest has proportionately smaller and more rounded ears and the tusks are usually more slender, straighter and downward pointing. Although there are distinct populations of both subspecies, there is considerable interbreeding between the two races in areas of habitat overlap. The African elephant is the largest living land mammal, easily identified by its long, highly mobile and sensitive trunk, very large ears and two tusks extending from the upper jaw. Some individuals, and in some cases localized populations, lack tusks. The largest tusks on record were removed from an elephant in Kenya, weighing 102,3 and 97 kg respectively. Although tusks grow throughout an animal's life, they never reach maximum potential length as a result of wear and breakages. The large ears serve as display and signalling devices, as well as being used to cool the blood as it circulates through the numerous vessels on the inner surface. This cooling is sometimes aided by squirting water behind the ears with the trunk. The grey-brown skin is virtually hairless, except at the tip of the tail, and usually takes on the coloration of local soils as a result of frequent dust-and mud-bathing.

DISTRIBUTION Occupied virtually all habitats in sub-Saharan Africa within historical times, and up to some 1 500 years ago still occurred along the Mediterranean seaboard of North Africa. Populations are becoming increasingly fragmented, with principal concentrations located in Central, East and the northern parts of southern Africa and only isolated and small numbers surviving in West Africa. Free-ranging herds are increasingly rare, with most populations being restricted to conservation areas.

STATUS Massive declines in both numbers and range over the past three decades, from an estimated 5 to 10 million in 1930 to some 600 000 by 1992, primarily as a result of illegal hunting for the ivory tusks, although this is now largely under control. The principal threat is loss of range and habitat as a result of rapidly increasing human populations.

HABITAT Extremely wide habitat tolerance, including coastal, montane, forest, different savanna associations, semi-desert and swamp, with the only requirements being access to adequate food, water and usually shade.

Savanna elephant bull. Elephants have a wide habitat tolerance, their only requirements being access to food and water.

BEHAVIOUR Nearly all behavioural studies have been undertaken on the savanna race. Home range size varies considerably and usually relates to the abundance of food and access to water, with matriarchal, or family, groups ranging over 15 to >50 km^2; those of bulls may be up to 1 500 km^2, but are frequently smaller, although up to 3 120 km^2 was recorded in the semi-arid Tsavo East National Park, Kenya. Ranges of the forest race are generally much smaller, primarily because of greater abundance of food. They are highly social, living in small family herds consisting of an older (matriarch) cow and her offspring, with larger groups including other related cows and their calves of different ages. At certain times, usually at waterpoints or at abundant and localized food sources, several of these matriarchal groups may gather to form temporary 'herds', sometimes up to several hundred, but each family unit retains its integrity. Adult males move freely amongst the matriarchal herds seeking out receptive cows. On reaching maturity the young cows remain with their birth group but as the unit grows, subgroups of young adult cows separate to form their own family units. Young bulls, on reaching puberty, leave the birth group but reluctant males will be driven off by the matriarch. As younger bulls are unable to compete with larger and more experienced males they seldom mate before their twentieth year. They have complex and intricate means of communication, including visual signals, touch, and sound both audible and inaudible to humans; these can carry for several kilometres but the exact limits have not been determined. Adults have no enemies except for man, but young are on occasion killed by spotted hyaenas and lions. Up to 50% of animals die before reaching 15 years, but some attain up to 60 years of age.

FOOD Very wide variety of plants and plant parts. In wet seasons the savanna race eats increased quantities of grass, while more woody and herbaceous food is taken during the dry seasons. Tusks are used to strip tree bark and dig for roots, and the front feet are sometimes used to kick loose grass clumps and shrubs. Flowers and fruits of certain trees such as the marula (Sclerocarya birrea) are favoured and may attract animals from considerable distances. Because of the large quantities of seeds consumed they are very important dispersers, particularly of certain tree species. Average daily food intake of adults is from 150 to 300 kg, and daily water consumption is between 100 and 220 litres.

REPRODUCTION A single calf, weighing about 120 kg (smaller in forest race), is born after a 22-month gestation period. Although birth peaks are evident in some areas during the rainy season, calves are dropped throughout the year, depending largely on abundance and quality of food. The forest race has less defined birth seasons. Mature cows give birth every three to four years, with intervals largely depending on conditions and increasing in times of drought.

Forest elephant

Savanna elephant

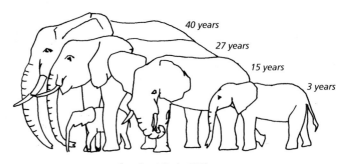

40 years

27 years

15 years

3 years

(based on J. Hanks, 1979)

Elephant herd at water. A single elephant consumes between 100 and 220 litres of water per day.

Elephant cow feeding in a shallow swamp, Amboseli, Kenya.

CARNIVORES Order Carnivora

FOXES, JACKALS AND WILD DOG Family Canidae

Twelve members of the canid, or dog, family occur in Africa, ranging in size from the diminutive fennec to the wild dog. The presence of **Blanford's fox** (*Vulpes cana*) on the African continent was recently confirmed when a specimen was collected at Wadi Qiseib on the western shore of the Red Sea in Egypt.

Front

50 mm

Red Fox

The Arabian race of the wolf (*Canis lupus*) occurs in the Sinai Peninsula of Egypt and recent records indicate it may occur in parts of North Africa.

RED FOX *Vulpes vulpes*

Total length 85-95 cm; tail length 35-40 cm; shoulder height about 30 cm; weight 4-8 kg (♂ heavier than ♀; North African races average smaller than foxes from Europe). **Identification pointers** 'Typical' fox, largest within range; long, bushy tail, usually white-tipped; large ears, black outside, white inside; overall colour yellowish-red to grey-russet. **Similar species** Rüppell's and pale foxes, golden jackal (separated on size and coloration).

DESCRIPTION Large, with a long, bushy, white-tipped tail. Ears large, dark on outer surface and white on inner. Overall pelage colour greyish-russet to yellowish-grey, with a deeper coloured dorsal band running from tail base to head. Underparts variable, from greyish to occasionally darker, or dirty white, with the lower legs being dark and the lips, chin and throat pale to white.

DISTRIBUTION Restricted to a narrow belt in the north-west through Morocco, Algeria, Tunisia, and in north-east Libya, widely in Egypt, southward into northern Sudan.

STATUS Common.

HABITAT Coastal plains, mountains – especially foothills – scrub and woodland, true desert (except extensive sand areas).

BEHAVIOUR Usually territorial, with a monogamous pair sharing a range, sometimes with their non-breeding family members. Measured home ranges vary from 1 to 10 km^2 but in Africa these are not known, although in arid regions they are almost certainly near the larger size, given the lower food densities. Most activity takes place at night or during crepuscular hours, although diurnal movement is not unusual in areas where they are not disturbed.

FOOD Extremely varied, including invertebrates, small vertebrates, carrion, wild fruits and berries.

REPRODUCTION From 3 to 12 pups dropped after a gestation period of about 51 days. Weight in range of 50 to 150 g, depending on litter size; weaned at 6 to 8 weeks.

CAPE FOX *Vulpes chama*

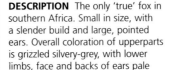

Total length 86-97 cm; tail length 23-34 cm; shoulder height 30-36 cm; weight 2,5-4 kg. **Identification pointers** Fox-like; bushy dark-tipped tail; upperparts grizzled silvery-grey; head, ears, lower legs pale tawny-brown. **Similar species** Bat-eared fox.

DESCRIPTION The only 'true' fox in southern Africa. Small in size, with a slender build and large, pointed ears. Overall coloration of upperparts is grizzled silvery-grey, with lower limbs, face and backs of ears pale tawny-brown to reddish-brown. The bushy tail is dark-tipped and pencilled with dark brown to black, and looks darker than rest of coat. Ears are reddish-brown to yellowish-fawn on the back surface and white on inside.

The red fox is often found in close association with man. **Left inset:** *Arabian Wolf.* **Right inset:** *Blanford's fox probably occurs throughout the hills of the Red Sea coast. It is a small species that occupies arid, rugged terrain, often with steep cliffs.*

Adult Cape fox, photographed in the central Namib Desert, Namibia.

The Cape fox is restricted to southern Africa, and is the only true fox in the region. Many are killed as presumed killers of domestic livestock.

Front

38 mm

Back

Cape Fox

Underparts off-white to very pale fawn. White to off-white patches on cheeks may be distinct, or almost absent.

DISTRIBUTION Endemic to southern Africa.

STATUS Locally abundant.

HABITAT Open areas, such as grassland and arid scrub, agricultural areas, and in south-west of its range heathland (fynbos).

BEHAVIOUR Form pairs but male and female forage and hunt alone. Parties are rarely formed, but several individuals have been recorded to share a den site in the Kalahari. Dens are located in burrows excavated by other species, amongst dense vegetation and in crevices and rock scree. Most activity takes place at night; in areas of low disturbance they are also crepuscular. Home range sizes have been measured from 1 to 4,6 km^2 in one area. Pups begin to forage on their own at about 16 weeks, remaining with the mother until fifth month.

FOOD Wide range: small rodents, young hares, insects and other invertebrates, reptiles, birds and some plant food. Will also scavenge and take very young lambs and goat kids on occasion.

REPRODUCTION In some areas breeding is non-seasonal but in others there are distinct peaks, usually spring, early summer months. Litter size 1 to 5 (usually 3) pups, dropped after gestation of 50 to 52 days.

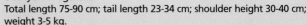

BAT-EARED FOX
Otocyon megalotis
Total length 75-90 cm; tail length 23-34 cm; shoulder height 30-40 cm; weight 3-5 kg.
Identification pointers Jackal/fox-like; very large ears; bushy, silver-grey coat, black legs; bushy tail black above and at tip; facial markings black and silvery-white; arched back when on the move.
Similar species Cape fox.

Front

35 mm

Back

Bat-eared Fox

DESCRIPTION Small and jackal-like, with slender legs and a sharp-pointed, fairly long muzzle. Ears are very large (14 cm), dark to black on the back surface, particularly towards the tip, white on the inside and pale grey around the edges. The body is covered in fairly long, silvery-grey hair with a distinctly grizzled appearance and the legs are black. The bushy tail is black above and at the tip. The front of the face is generally black, with a light, or white, band running across the forehead to the base of ears.

DISTRIBUTION Two separate populations, one in southern Africa, marginally extending into Angola, Zambia and Mozambique, and the other in East Africa, from Tanzania into Ethiopia and Somalia. The southern part of the range has expanded considerably in recent decades. Distribution is linked with that of the harvester termite – its most important item of prey.

STATUS Not threatened, with range expansion probably having resulted from changes in agricultural practices.

HABITAT Open country, such as short scrub, grassland and lightly wooded areas, and farm land.

BEHAVIOUR Both nocturnal and diurnal, largely dependent on disturbance levels and, in some areas at least, the time of year. Activity usually ceases during the hot midday hours. They are active diggers and although they dig their own burrows, will frequently modify those of other species. They normally occur in groups of two to six individuals, consisting of a pair, which mate for life, and their offspring. Occasionally more may be seen together but such groupings are temporary. Records of more than two adults at a den may

Bat-eared fox: Note the contrasting black and white facial markings and the very large ears.
Inset: *Bat-eared fox pair*

indicate that more than one female is present. Home range size varies from 0,25 to about 3 km^2, with varying levels of overlap. The density of individuals ranges from one to 28 per km^2. When foraging they appear to wander aimlessly, stopping periodically with the ears turned to the ground; when food is located, shallow holes are dug with the front paws.

FOOD Mostly insects, particularly harvester termites (Hodotermes).

Occasionally eat small vertebrates and wild berries.

REPRODUCTION Most births in southern Africa take place from September to November, and there and elsewhere largely coincide with the rains when insect densities are at their highest. A litter of 1 to 6 pups is dropped after gestation of 60 to 75 days. If more than two females share a den, the pups are cared for and suckled by all lactating animals.

RÜPPELL'S FOX
Vulpes rüppelli
Total length 65-90 cm; tail length 25-39 cm; shoulder height 30 cm; weight 1,2-3,6 kg.
Identification pointers Overall pale sandy coat; black facial patches; bushy white-tipped tail; slender build.
Similar species Pale fox, red fox, fennec.

DESCRIPTION Small and lightly built. Overall pelage colour is pale fawn, to almost white in some cases, and the bushy tail has a distinctly 'bright' white tip. Coloration along the back may be more brownish, as with the backs of the large ears.

DISTRIBUTION Occurs in broad belt through northern and central Sahara from the Atlantic to the Red Sea. Occurs widely in Arabian Peninsula and western Afghanistan.

STATUS Secure.

HABITAT Stony and sandy desert.

BEHAVIOUR Groups of three to 15 animals are on record. However, the little evidence available indicates that territorial pairs form the typical grouping. In Oman they occupy ranges estimated at about 50 km^2. Nocturnal and crepuscular.

FOOD Omnivorous, with a large invertebrate intake, and wild fruits and berries.

REPRODUCTION Litter size of 2 to 3 pups.

PALE FOX
Vulpes pallida
Total length 61-74 cm; tail length 23-29 cm; shoulder height 25 cm; weight 2-3,6 kg.
Identification pointers Small; proportionately long legs and ears; overall pale fawn, tail reddish, black-tipped; underparts off-white; desert habitat.
Similar species Red fox, Rüppell's fox, fennec (separated on ear size).

DESCRIPTION Similar to the red but smaller, with proportionately longer limbs and ears, the latter rounded at the tips. Overall pelage colour is pale fawn but legs and sometimes the back are more reddish-brown. Underparts, face and

inside of ears are paler, towards off-white. The bushy tail has a distinct black tip.

DISTRIBUTION Across the Sahel belt from the Atlantic to the Red Sea.

STATUS Probably secure.

The hair of the Rüppell's fox is soft and fine.

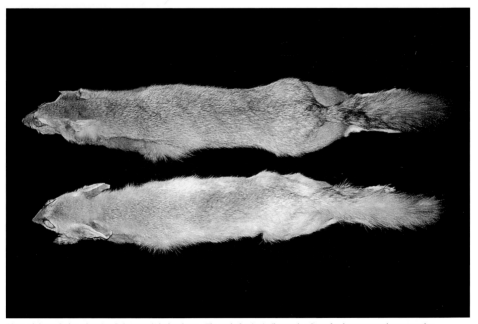

Skins of the pale fox, showing lighter and darker forms. The pale fox is similar to the Cape fox but ranges do not overlap.

HABITAT Sandy and stony dry savanna, extending into true desert.

BEHAVIOUR Apparently occur in family parties, made up of adult male and female and their young. Excavate their own dens, descending 2 to 3 m and extending up to 15 m. Nocturnal and crepuscular.

FOOD The bulk of the diet is made up of fruits and berries but on occasion small vertebrates are taken. Almost certainly also take invertebrate prey.

REPRODUCTION Litter size numbers 3 to 4 pups.

FENNEC
Fennecus zerda

Total length 42-72 cm; tail length 18-31 cm; shoulder height 19-21 cm; weight 1-1,5 kg.
Identification pointers Tiny; very large ears; cream-coloured pelage, black-tipped tail; sandy desert habitat.
Similar species Pale and Rüppell's foxes.

DESCRIPTION The world's smallest fox, easily recognized by its extremely large ears (15 cm) and overall cream-coloured fur, with some dark pencilling. Some animals may be lightly tinged with fawn. The tail tip is black.

DISTRIBUTION Throughout Sahara Desert, extending to Nubian Desert on the Red Sea.

STATUS Unknown but hunted by desert tribes.

HABITAT Sandy desert.

BEHAVIOUR Nocturnal; have been observed in groups of up to 10 animals. Males mark and hold territories but it is not known whether continuously or seasonally. Females actively defend the den when pups are present. Pups leave the den permanently when three months old.

FOOD Wide range of animal and plant food.

REPRODUCTION Mating recorded January and February; 1 to 5 pups dropped after gestation of 50 to 52 days. Pups weigh about 45 g.

ETHIOPIAN WOLF
Canis simensis

Total length 1,33 m; tail length 33 cm; shoulder height 60 cm; weight ♂ 14-19 kg ♀ 11-16 kg (very few measurements available). **E**
Identification pointers Relatively large; bright reddish coat, white throat patch, inner ears and underparts; darker tail.
Similar species Golden (common) jackal.

DESCRIPTION Very handsome, with long legs and long, quite narrow muzzle. Overall colour tawny-rufous to reddish-brown with contrasting white underparts, including throat and chest patches. Much of the face, muzzle and backs of ears are more reddish than the rest of the body. The bushy tail is mostly white below towards the base, but black and darkly pencilled towards tip.

DISTRIBUTION Isolated locations in the Ethiopian Highlands above 3 000 m; majority in the Bale Mountains National Park.

STATUS Due to habitat loss, hybridization and disease, probably only as few as 450 survive.

HABITAT Afro-alpine moorlands at 3 000 m to more than 4 000 m, with areas of short grass and herbaceous plants favoured.

The fennec is characterized by its small size and huge ears.

The Ethiopian wolf is considered the most endangered canid in Africa, even more so than the wild dog.

Ethiopian wolves with cubs. This species is threatened by hybridization with domestic and feral dogs.

BEHAVIOUR Although social, they are predominantly solitary hunters. Before dispersing to forage, between two and 12 animals congregate in the morning, midday and evening with considerable vocalizations. Average observed group size is seven, and more than one adult male may be present. Each pack defends a territory against intruders but up to 70% of matings observed in one area involved pack females being covered by males from packs in adjacent territories. When pups are present in a den, both parents as well as subadults feed them by regurgitation. Group home ranges vary in size from 2,4 to 12 km².

FOOD Rodents make up 90% of the diet; they also take hares and calves of mountain nyala and reedbuck, and scavenge too.

REPRODUCTION Two to 6 pups are dropped after 60 to 62 days, and weaned at 6 to 8 weeks. Mating is seasonal and takes place between August and December.

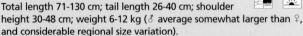

BLACK-BACKED JACKAL *Canis mesomelas*
Total length 71-130 cm; tail length 26-40 cm; shoulder height 30-48 cm; weight 6-12 kg (♂ average somewhat larger than ♀, and considerable regional size variation).
Identification pointers Dog-like; dark, white-flecked 'saddle' on back; most of tail black; fairly large, pointed reddish-backed ears; distinctive call. **Similar species** Golden (common) and side-striped jackals.

Front

54 mm

Back

Black-backed Jackal

DESCRIPTION Medium-sized and dog-like, with a characteristic black 'saddle', broad at the neck and shoulders, narrowing towards the base of the tail, and liberally sprinkled with white hair. The face, flanks and legs are reddish-brown, ranging from very pale to much richer in colour. The lips, throat and chest are white and underparts vary from almost white to the colour of the flanks. Ears are fairly large and pointed, reddish on the back surface with the interior lined with white hair. The tail is overall blackish but paler towards the base.

DISTRIBUTION Two separate populations, the one restricted to southern Africa, the other in East Africa (Tanzania to Ethiopia).

STATUS Common, but local extinctions have occurred, mainly in South Africa, as a result of hunting pressure.

HABITAT Extremely wide tolerance, from desert (relatively dry areas preferred) to areas with rainfall exceeding 2 000 mm. Absent from forests.

BEHAVIOUR Mainly nocturnal in farming areas and locations where they come into conflict with man but in undisturbed regions they forage during the cooler daylight hours. Normally solitary or occur in pairs, but family parties are not unusual. Pairs form a long-term bond, with both sexes marking and defending a territory which can vary considerably in size, depending on factors such as the availability of food and competition with other jackals. Recorded pair ranges cover 2 to 33 km². The call is characteristic and has been described as a screaming-yell, finishing off with three or four short yaps. Calling, at least in southern Africa, is more frequent during the winter months when mating takes place.

FOOD Very wide range of food items, including young antelope, rodents, hares, birds, reptiles, invertebrates, as well as wild fruits and berries. Carrion readily taken. Some individuals, but not all, prey heavily on domestic stock, particularly the young of sheep and goats.

REPRODUCTION Seasonal breeders; 1 to 8 (usually 3 or 4) pups born July to October in southern Africa. Gestation about 60 days. Male, female and subadult 'helpers' from previous litter bring food to young.

The black-backed jackal is easily identified by its dark 'saddle' flecked with white hair.

The colour of the face ranges from pale to rich reddish-brown, while the lips, throat and chest are white.

The black-backed jackal commonly buries its surplus food in shallow holes for later use.

SIDE-STRIPED JACKAL
Canis adustus
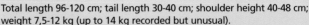
Total length 96-120 cm; tail length 30-40 cm; shoulder height 40-48 cm; weight 7,5-12 kg (up to 14 kg recorded but unusual).
Identification pointers Overall grey; light and dark stripe along each side; no 'saddle' on back; tail nearly always white-tipped; ears smaller than black-backed; more moist habitats favoured.
Similar species Black-backed and golden (common) jackals.

Front

52 mm

Back

Side-striped Jackal

DESCRIPTION Appears more or less uniform grey from a distance, but there are some regional differences with more brown evident. At close quarters a light-coloured stripe, or band, liberally fringed with black, is seen along each flank (hence its name). Underparts and throat generally paler but seldom white. Tail is quite bushy, mostly black but usually with a distinct white tip.

DISTRIBUTION Central Africa, with distributional extensions into eastern southern Africa, Ethiopia and also westward to north-eastern Benin, but apparently absent from the northern Congolean forests.

STATUS Generally rare but not threatened.

HABITAT Well-watered, wooded areas are preferred, but not forest, and very open grassland is avoided. Recorded from sea level to altitudes of about 2 700 m.

BEHAVIOUR Predominantly nocturnal but there may also be some crepuscular activity. Most sightings are of solitary animals, although pairs and family parties are not infrequently observed. The limited information available indicates that a home range/territory is occupied by a mated pair. The call has been likened to an owl-like hoot or a series of short yaps, quite unlike that of the black-backed jackal.

FOOD Omnivorous, taking a wide range of food items, including small mammals, birds, reptiles, invertebrates, carrion, as well as wild fruits and berries.

REPRODUCTION Three to 6 pups per litter are dropped between August and January in southern Africa. Mating recorded in June/ July and September/October in East Africa, and June to November in southern Africa. Gestation of 57 to 70 days.

GOLDEN (COMMON) JACKAL   *Canis aureus*
Total length 80-130 cm; tail length 20-30 cm; shoulder height 38-50 cm; weight 7-15 kg.
Identification pointers Usually pale golden-brown, black/grey hair on back; tail black-tipped. **Similar species** Black-backed and side-striped jackals (separated on appearance), red fox (separated on size and coloration).

DESCRIPTION Coat coloration is variable but usually pale golden-brown with liberal sprinkling of black and grey hair on back. The head, ears, flanks and lower legs may be reddish and underparts paler, or dirty white. The tail is variably black, brown or grey, but always black-tipped.

DISTRIBUTION Occurs throughout the North and Horn of Africa, extending southward to north-

western Tanzania, and from sea level to altitudes of 3 800 m. Probably best observed in Africa in the Serengeti.

STATUS Widespread and abundant.

HABITAT Wide habitat tolerance, with preference for open country, with scattering of trees and bushes.

BEHAVIOUR Normally a mating pair occupies and defends a territory of 0,5 to 2,5 km², but this may be larger

Side-striped jackal from central Kenya. Inset: *Side-striped jackal from northern Botswana: Note the different colour forms.*

Golden, or common, jackal drinking. In some areas this animal is closely associated with human settlements. Inset: *Skins of Africa's three jackal species* (top to bottom): *Golden jackal, black-backed jackal and side-striped jackal.*

in the more arid parts of its range. A pair tolerates subadults from previous litter as they help in the care and feeding of current litter. Generally diurnal but in areas of disturbance may switch to mainly nocturnal activity. In areas of high food abundance the normal social structure may be disrupted and as many as 20 individuals may associate in a group, and home ranges may be very small. Co-operative hunting by mating pairs greatly increases prey capture success.

FOOD Omnivorous, taking fruits, small mammals, including young antelope, birds, reptiles and invertebrates. Carrion is also readily taken. In the Serengeti the time of birthing in January and February coincides with the dropping of Thomson's gazelle fawns, which are an important food source at that time.

REPRODUCTION In Tanzania mating takes place during October/November, and occasionally June/July, with most births taking place in January/February. Birthing times poorly known elsewhere on continent. Litter of 1 to 9 (usually 5 or 6) pups dropped after gestation of about 63 days; weaned at about 8 to 10 weeks.

WILD DOG *Lycaon pictus*

Total length 1,05-1,5 m; tail length 30-40 cm; shoulder height 65-80 cm; weight 17-36 kg (animals from East Africa on average smaller than those from southern Africa; genetic differences also known). **E**

Identification pointers Heavily blotched black, white, yellow-brown; slender body, long legs; tail usually white-tipped; large, dark, rounded ears; black muzzle, black stripe from eyes over top of head; largest African canid; always in packs. **Similar species** None.

DESCRIPTION Similar in size to domestic German shepherd, unlikely to be mistaken for any other African canid. Ears are large, rounded and dark, legs are long and bushy tail usually white-tipped. Body is irregularly blotched with black, white, brown and yellowish-brown. No two dogs have exactly the same markings and coloration. Muzzle is black, with black continuing as a line from muzzle to between ears. Forehead on either side of black line pale fawn to white.

DISTRIBUTION Once found virtually throughout sub-Saharan Africa, with the exception of the forests, but has been greatly reduced; distribution very fragmented.

STATUS Viable populations probably only survive in six countries, namely Botswana, Kenya, Tanzania, South Africa (Kruger National Park only), Zambia and Zimbabwe. Total population is somewhere between 2 000 and 3 000.

HABITAT Desert plains to relatively high rainfall regions, open and lightly wooded savanna, moderately bushed country, such as miombo woodland and, rarely, forest margins.

BEHAVIOUR Highly social, living in packs that are very variable in size, but average 10 to 15 adults and subadults. Each pack includes several related adult males, and one or more related adult females originating from a different pack. Usually only the dominant female in a pack will successfully raise a litter of pups. There is intensive rivalry among adult females for the top breeding position and they may fight savagely. She, and her young at the den, are fed with regurgitated meat by other members of the troop. Hunting is done by the pack, with the dogs moving slowly towards the intended prey, gradually increasing the tempo as the targeted animal starts to move away; once the target animal is selected the pack rarely deviates and will maintain the chase for several kilometres if necessary. Hunting success rates are influenced by such factors as season and the type of prey hunted, and they have the highest

Front

76 mm

Back

Wild Dog

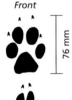

The wild dog, or hunting dog, is Africa's largest canid.

Once found virtually throughout sub-Saharan Africa, the wild dog has in recent decades become extinct as a viable breeding species in 19 sub-Saharan countries. Most populations are now restricted to conservation areas.

overall hunting success rate (about 70%) of all the large carnivores. Packs only kill for their immediate needs and are not, as generally believed, wanton killers. One of the few truly nomadic carnivores; pack home ranges vary from about 450 to probably >1 500 km², with considerable overlap (up to 80% has been recorded); pack ranges contract considerably when there are small pups at the den requiring regular feeding. They do not establish, or defend, territories. Primarily diurnal, with most hunting taking place during the cooler morning and late afternoon hours. They are very vocal, with a wide range of calls.

FOOD Wide range of mammals, ranging in size from steenbok to buffalo, although medium-sized ungulates form the most important prey component. Impala are the most important prey in the Kruger National Park (South Africa), springbok in the Kalahari (Botswana), and Thomson's gazelles and blue wildebeest in Serengeti/Mara ecosystem (East Africa). Also recorded in their diet are rodents, hares and birds, including ostrich.

REPRODUCTION Young are dropped during the dry winter months (March to July in the south) when grass is short and hunting conditions at their best. In the Serengeti three quarters of all litters are dropped between January and June. Two to 19 (average 7 to 10) pups are born after gestation of 69 to 73 days. Young are born in abandoned burrows of other species; remain in close proximity to den for first three months. Pups begin to follow pack at about three months, only joining hunt at 12 to 14 months.

OTTERS, WEASELS, POLECATS AND BADGER
Family Mustelidae

CAPE CLAWLESS OTTER *Aonyx capensis*

CONGO CLAWLESS OTTER *Aonyx congica*
(There is some uncertainty about the status of these, but they are probably the same species.)
Total length 1,1-1,6 m; tail length 50 cm; shoulder height 35 cm; weight 10-18 (maximum 25) kg.
Identification pointers Quite large, elongated; dark-brown coat, appearing black when wet; lips, upper chest white; arched back walking on land; unclawed, finger-like digits. **Similar species** Spotted-necked otter, water mongoose (separated on size).

■ *Aonyx capensis*
■ *Aonyx congica*
■ Area of overlap

Front

100 mm

Back

Cape Clawless Otter

DESCRIPTION Largest of Africa's otters. Overall coloration is dark brown but with white fur extending from lips to upper chest (extent varies). Legs are short and stout, and the long tail is heavy at the base and tapers towards the tip. On land, it walks with the back arched. Toes are finger-like and lack claws. In water, or when wet, it is almost black in colour and somewhat seal-like. When swimming, only the head is usually visible.

DISTRIBUTION Occurs widely in sub-Saharan Africa, except Horn and arid southern Africa.

STATUS Secure, but occurs in low densities.

HABITAT Most wetland types, including dry stream beds with permanent pools. Coastal habitats also utilized. Unlike the two other otter species, they may wander several kilometres from water.

BEHAVIOUR Mainly crepuscular but activity is recorded at all times of day or night. Occur singly, in pairs, or small family parties, and lie up in dense vegetation, or in self-excavated dens (holts) in sandy soils of water-bodies during non-active periods. Latrine areas

All of the otters, in this case the Cape clawless, appear much darker when wet.

Cape clawless otter. Inset: *Note the finger-like digits of the Cape clawless otter.*

with numerous droppings made up largely of crab-shell fragments are a useful indication of their presence. Although the clawless hunt by sight in water, much of their food is located by feeling with the fingers and they are thus not adversely affected by dirty water with poor visibility. They hunt regularly in vegetation fringing water-bodies.

FOOD Crabs, fish, frogs, as well as small mammals, birds, insects and molluscs.

REPRODUCTION Two to 3 cubs are dropped after a gestation period of 60 to 65 days.

SPOTTED-NECKED OTTER *Lutra maculicollis*

Total length <1 m; tail length 30-50 cm; shoulder height <30 cm; weight 3-5 kg.
Identification pointers Overall coloration brown to dark brown; pale blotching on throat, upper chest; rarely far from water.
Similar species Clawless otter, water mongoose.

DESCRIPTION Smallest of sub-Saharan otters, with a long, slender body and somewhat flattened tail. Feet fully webbed and toes clawed. Overall colour dark brown to reddish-brown but appears black when wet; throat and upper chest variably mottled/blotched with creamy-white.

DISTRIBUTION Primarily in tropics, with isolated populations in eastern South Africa.

STATUS Generally common except in south.

HABITAT Rivers, lakes, swamps and dams; rarely moves away from water.

BEHAVIOUR Diurnal, usually associating in groups of two to six animals, although larger groups occur on occasion. Quite vocal, group members retaining contact with whistling calls. Droppings deposited at latrine sites close to water's edge. Most prey is caught in water and usually carried to the bank for eating. Unlike the clawless otters, they hunt mainly by sight; clear water is therefore essential.

FOOD Mostly fish but also crabs, insects, frogs and birds.

REPRODUCTION Two to 3 cubs born after about 60 days.

EURASIAN OTTER *Lutra lutra*

Total length 1 m; tail length 40 cm; shoulder height 30 cm; weight 6-10 kg (African specimens generally smaller than elsewhere).
Identification pointers Typical otter; dark brown above, paler lips, throat, upper chest; only otter in North African range.
Similar species None.

DESCRIPTION Body coloration dark brown, with lips, cheeks, throat and upper chest being white to fawnish-white, but appearing much darker when wet. The feet are well webbed and each toe has a claw.

DISTRIBUTION Restricted to a narrow belt in Morocco, Algeria and Tunisia.

STATUS Threatened by habitat loss and hunting in African range.

HABITAT Rivers and permanent water bodies.

BEHAVIOUR Adult males patrol a territory within which one or more females, and their dependent young, are resident. They communicate with whistling sounds.

FOOD Mainly fish, also insects, birds, rodents.

REPRODUCTION One to 5 (usually 2 or 3) cubs of 220 g each, dropped after 59 to 63 days.

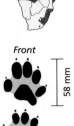
Front

58 mm

Back

Spot-necked Otter

Unlike the clawless otter, the spotted-necked otter has well-developed claws. Also note the well-webbed feet and the white neck spotting characteristic of this animal.

The Eurasian otter is restricted to a narrow belt in north Africa, but is very widespread in Europe and Asia.

■ *Ictonyx striatus*
■ *Poecilictis libyca*
■ *Mustela putorius*

Front

22 mm

Back

Striped Polecat

STRIPED POLECAT (ZORILLA) *Ictonyx striatus*
Total length 57-67 cm; tail length 26 cm; shoulder height 10-15 cm; weight 600-1 400 g.

LIBYAN STRIPED WEASEL *Poecilictis (Ictonyx) libyca*
Total length 34-50 cm; tail length 12-20 cm; shoulder height 6-8 cm; weight 500-750 g.
Identification pointers Both species have longish black and white coats; white hair longer, more dominant in weasel; legs have shorter black hair; head black, white blaze between eyes.
Similar species Each other, polecat, striped (white-naped) weasel.

DESCRIPTION Both with conspicuous black and white markings, from top of head to rump striping, particularly in polecat. There is a white blaze on the forehead between the eyes and a larger white patch at the base of the ears. The tail is predominantly white. Hair on legs is shorter and black.

DISTRIBUTION Polecat with wide sub-Saharan range, excluding lowland forest and adjoining high rainfall savanna. Weasel throughout North Africa, including the Sahara.

STATUS Common.

HABITAT Polecat very tolerant but absent from lowland forest. Weasel in arid and semi-arid habitats.

BEHAVIOUR Both species similar. They are strictly nocturnal and usually solitary but pairs and family parties may be seen. They shelter in burrows excavated by other species, amongst rocky outcrops, dense vegetation and not infrequently in association

with human habitation, but will also excavate their own burrows. If threatened they turn their rump towards the aggressor, with the back arched and tail erect, and as a last resort spray foul-smelling fluid from anal glands. Nothing is known about home range, or territoriality.

FOOD Mostly insects and rodents as well as other small animals.

REPRODUCTION A litter of 1 to 3 (up to 5) pups is dropped after 36-day gestation period. In southern Africa at least, polecat gives birth during the summer months.

Another species, the **Polecat** (*Mustela putorius*), is restricted to a very tiny area in northern Morocco and adjacent Algeria, but is also found in Europe. Overall coloration is dark brown with glossy white on the muzzle and the throat, and with a fairly short, bushy tail. Total length is about 50 cm and weight 600 to 1 500 g. They are nocturnal, crepuscular and solitary.

■ *Poecilogale albinucha*
■ *Mustela nivalis*

STRIPED (WHITE-NAPED) WEASEL *Poecilogale albinucha*
Total length 40-50 cm; tail length 12-16 cm; shoulder height 5 cm; weight 220-350 g.
Identification pointers Long, thin body; bushy white tail; very short legs; black colour, with white cap, four white or yellowish stripes.
Similar species Striped polecat (zorilla) (separated on size and hair length).

DESCRIPTION Long, slender and short-legged, with an overall black coat and four off-white to yellowish stripes running from the nape to the tail base, converging into a white cap

on top of the head. The body hair is coarse but short, and the tail is bushy and predominantly white in colour. When walking or running, the back is arched.

Striped polecat. Inset: *Skins of the Libyan striped weasel* (Poecilictis libyca) *from North Africa.*

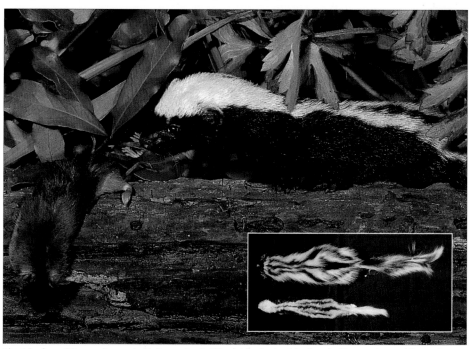

The striped, or white-naped, weasel with its prey. Inset: *Skin of striped polecat* (top) *and white-naped weasel* (bottom).

Front

21 mm

Back

Striped Weasel

Front

54 mm

Back

Honey Badger

DISTRIBUTION Has a limited range in southern and Central Africa.

STATUS Uncommon.

HABITAT Mainly savanna associations but recorded from lowland rainforest in the DRC. Most records from grassland.

BEHAVIOUR Mainly nocturnal and solitary, but pairs and family parties have been recorded. Although efficient diggers, they readily use burrows excavated by small rodents.

FOOD Principally rodents, many of which are caught in their burrows. Their surplus prey is hoarded.

REPRODUCTION In southern Africa most births are from November to March, with 1 to 3 young, weighing about 4 g, dropped after a 32-day gestation period.

The Weasel (*Mustela nivalis*) is restricted to extreme north-western and north-eastern Africa and should not be confused with any other species. Total length is only 16 to 23 cm, with a 5-cm tail and a weight of 45 to 200 g. Upperparts are reddish-brown with white to yellowish underparts. They are solitary animals, both nocturnally and diurnally active, territorial, and feed mainly on small rodents.

HONEY BADGER (RATEL)
Mellivora capensis
Total length 90-100 cm; tail length 18-25 cm; shoulder height 30 cm; weight 8-14 kg.
Identification pointers Stocky, short legs; upperparts silvery-grey, underparts, legs black; short, bushy tail, often held erect when walking.
Similar species None.

DESCRIPTION Thickset and stocky, with short legs and a short, bushy tail. Upperparts are silver-grey and underparts and legs are black (diagnostic). Ears are very small.

DISTRIBUTION Very wide but absent from true desert. Also found throughout the Middle East and as far as India and south Russia.

STATUS Occurs at low densities.

HABITAT Virtually all, with the exception of true desert.

BEHAVIOUR Tough and aggressive, and recorded to attack large mammals such as elephant, buffalo and man when threatened. They are usually seen singly, but pairs and family parties may be observed. They are mainly nocturnal and to a lesser extent crepuscular and diurnal. No information available on territoriality or home range size.

FOOD Very wide range, including invertebrates and rodents, and to a lesser extent reptiles, birds, carrion and wild fruits. The name is derived from the tendency to break into beehives to eat the honey and larvae. They also frequently scavenge around rubbish dumps and in camps in savanna parks and reserves.

REPRODUCTION Apparently a non-seasonal breeder, with 1 to 4 young being dropped after a gestation period of about 180 days. Usually only 1 to 2 young, rarely more than 1 reared.

The honey badger is extremely tough and can be very aggressive. Parties of up to six males have been recorded.

Honey badgers are mainly nocturnal and to a lesser extent crepuscular. They will readily climb trees.

CIVETS AND GENETS Family Viverridae

AFRICAN CIVET *Civettictis civetta*

Total length 1,2-1,4 m; tail length 40-50 cm; shoulder height 40 cm; weight 9-15 kg.
Identification pointers Large; distinctive black and white facial and neck markings; walks with arched back, head held low.
Similar species Genets.

DESCRIPTION Long-bodied and - legged and heavily built, about the size of a medium-sized dog. The hair is long and coarse, with a light grey forehead, white muzzle and a broad black band running horizontally between the forehead and muzzle, continuing round the head to the throat. A distinct light band extends from the ear base towards the chest. Overall colouring greyish to grey-brown with many black spots, blotches and bands. Spotting is absent, or less distinct, on shoulders and neck. The legs are black and the bushy tail is banded white and black below, with the upperside and tip black. A ridge of dark, erectile hair runs along the spine to the tail.

DISTRIBUTION Widespread in the tropics.

STATUS Common.

HABITAT Wide tolerance, with preference for more densely wooded and forested areas, and nearly always near water.

BEHAVIOUR Mainly nocturnal but also crepuscular. Although generally solitary, pairs are also observed. Regular latrine sites, or 'civetries', are used throughout range, which is also marked with anal gland secretion. They are purely terrestrial.

FOOD Invertebrates, particularly insects, small rodents, hares, birds, reptiles, carrion and wild fruits, such as wild dates.

REPRODUCTION Two to 4 pups are dropped after a gestation period of 60 to 65 days.

Front

45 mm

Back

African Civet

GENETS *Genetta spp.*

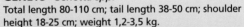

Total length 80-110 cm; tail length 38-50 cm; shoulder height 18-25 cm; weight 1,2-3,5 kg.
Identification pointers Long, slender bodies, long tails, short legs; fairly long snouts, longish, thin, rounded ears; black and white rings on tail; body darker spots, blotches, stripes, or combination of all. **Similar species** African civet (separated on size), African linsang (*Poiana richardsoni* – restricted to the Congolean rainforest and a limited area of forest in Liberia/Guinea and Ivory Coast), aquatic genet (*Genetta piscivora* – limited lowland forest distribution in north-eastern Congo).

■ *Genetta tigrina*
■ *Genetta servalina*
■ *Genetta abyssinica*
■ *Genetta maculata*

Some 17 genet species are recognized, but there is much uncertainty as to whether all are valid and the average observer would have great difficulty identifying them to species level. However, all are easily recognized as genets. Some species are very restricted in distribution, such as the **giant genet** (*Genetta victoriae*) of northern DRC, the **crested genet** (*G. cristata*) in the southern Nigeria/Cameroon border region, **Johnston's genet** (*G. johnstoni*) from a tiny area on the borders of Guinea, Liberia and Ivory Coast, and the **Abyssinian genet** (*G. abyssinica*) known from a handful of locations in Ethiopia, Eritrea and north-west Somalia. Two other species have wide distributions in the tropical forests, namely the **servaline genet** (*G. servalina*) of the Congolean region, and the common **rusty-spotted genet** (*G. maculata*) of the Guinean forests and marginally into the western Congolean forests, now considered to have

The African civet is strictly terrestrial, whereas the African Palm civet (inset) rarely comes to the ground.

- ■ *Genetta angolensis*
- ■ Area of overlap (*Genetta maculata* and *Genetta cristata*)
- ▨ *Genetta johnstoni*
- ■ Area of overlap

- ■ *Poiana richardsoni*
- ■ *Genetta piscivora*
- ■ Area of overlap

Front   *Back*

20 mm

Genets

- ■ *Genetta genetta* and *G. felina*
- ■ *Genetta thierryi*
- ■ Area of overlap
- ■ *Genetta victoriae*

a much wider range. The so-called **Angolan genet** (*G. angolensis*) occurs in a broad belt in Central Africa from the Atlantic to Indian Oceans, and the **Haussa genet** (*G. thierryi*) is restricted to the moister woodland savannas of West Africa. There are only two widely distributed species: The **Common Small-spotted genet** (*G. genetta, G. felina*, the **South African Small-spotted genet**), which occurs virtually throughout southern and East Africa, through the Sahel, with an apparently isolated population in north-west Africa, elsewhere extending into southern Europe and the Middle East; and the **Large-spotted genet** (*G. tigrina*) which is restricted to coastal South Africa. (The following accounts are generalized as the genets have many similarities and few overall differences.)

DESCRIPTION All are recognizable by long, elegant bodies and tails, with short legs, long, pointed snouts, and large, rounded, membranous ears. The tails of all are thickly haired, with black and white rings, and although the extent of ringing has been used as an identifying character, this is very variable even within one species. Some have short, soft fur, such as the large-spotted, but others, such as the small-spotted, have coarser coats with an erectile crest of longer hair down the back. Overall pelage colour varies from grey-white to reddish-fawn, with a liberal scattering of darker spots, blotches and in the case of the Abyssinian, stripes. Underparts are generally paler and all have black and white facial markings to a greater or lesser extent. When moving the tail is carried straight out behind and parallel to the ground. In southern and East Africa the most likely species to be encountered are the large- and small-spotted: the former has fairly large spots that are usually rusty-brown in colour, a dark brown or black-tipped tail and it has no crest of longer hair down the back; the latter usually has an overall greyish colour, with numerous black spots and bars, a white-tipped tail and an erectile crest of longer hair down the back.

DISTRIBUTION See introduction and maps.

STATUS Small- and large-spotted are common and widely distributed but the status of others is poorly known; those with very limited ranges probably at risk.

HABITAT Most are associated with forest or woodland, but the small-spotted also occurs in more arid country, where it may shelter on rocky hillsides or in burrows dug by other species. Eight species are entirely restricted to tropical lowland forests.

BEHAVIOUR Nocturnal, only occasionally crepuscular, lying up under dense cover during the day. Excellent climbers but at least some species forage mainly on ground. Normally solitary but pairs may also be sighted. Virtually no studies have been undertaken on the African genets but indications are that at least in some species females hold and defend territories but males do not. Within each home range/territory there is usually a single latrine site where droppings are deposited. They mark their territories with pungent secretions from the anal glands, with urine and tree scratching possibly also playing a marking role.

FOOD Invertebrates, particularly insects, are important, as well as small rodents. Reptiles, amphibians, birds and other small mammals (up to the size of hares) are taken. Wild fruits are also eaten but this may be more prevalent in some species than others. May kill more than they need when the situation presents itself, for example, in a poultry run.

REPRODUCTION In southern Africa the small- and large-spotted are summer breeders and seasonality is indicated in other regions and with other species. In the tropics they may be aseasonal and up to two litters per year have been recorded. Females den down amongst dense vegetation, in holes or rock crevices. Between 2 and 5 young per litter. The gestation period averages 70 days, with birth weights between 50 and 80 g.

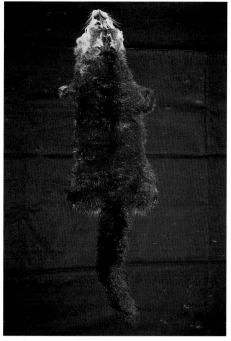

The South African large-spotted genet has fairly large spots, usually rusty-brown in colour, and a dark brown or black-tipped tail.

As far as we are aware, the attractive aquatic genet has never been photographed in the living state.

Skins of 'typical' large-spotted (left) and small-spotted genets (right), South Africa.

The small-spotted genet usually has an overall greyish colour, numerous spots and bars, and a white-tipped tail.

AFRICAN PALM CIVET Family Nandiniidae

AFRICAN PALM CIVET *Nandinia binotata*
Total length 87-97 cm; tail length 45-50 cm;
shoulder height 22 cm; weight 1,5-3 kg.
Identification pointers Long tail, fairly slender body; greyish-brown
to dark brown, darker spotting; whitish spot above each shoulder
blade; forest habitat. **Similar species** Genets.

DESCRIPTION Long and sleek body and tail, but less so than in the genets. Overall coat colour is greyish-brown to dark brown with small, irregularly shaped, dark brown to black spots over upperparts. The tail is dark-ringed, and usually there is a dark stripe down the back of the neck and a distinct white spot on top of each shoulder.

DISTRIBUTION Restricted to equatorial region, extending southward to eastern Zimbabwe.

STATUS Common.

HABITAT Forests, generally receiving more than 1 000 mm of rain per annum.

BEHAVIOUR Nocturnal, solitary and largely arboreal. Most foraging takes place at higher levels but they may move through the understory. More vocal than genets.

FOOD Mainly wild fruits, also insects, birds, rodents, fruit-bats, occasionally carrion.

REPRODUCTION Probably an aseasonal breeder; usually 2, up to 4, young per litter, born in tree holes after a 64-day gestation period.

MONGOOSES Family Herpestidae

At least 23 species of mongoose live in Africa, with all but one living south of the Sahara. The endangered **Liberian mongoose** (*Liberiictis kuhni*) is only known from a limited area of lowland forest on the joint borders of Guinea, Liberia and Ivory Coast, and has been observed once in the wild; it has a very long, narrow snout, long claws on the front feet, and two light-coloured neck stripes. **Pousargues' mongoose** (*Dologale dybowskii*) is a small species (total length 38 to 50 cm), known from only 30 museum specimens, no specimen having been collected, or observed, in the past 10 years; they resemble a slightly larger and darker version of the dwarf mongoose and occur in a narrow belt of moist woodland savanna from Uganda, through far north-eastern DRC and marginally into Central African Republic. The **long-nosed mongoose** (*Herpestes naso*), known from about 100 specimens and a handful of sightings, inhabits the forests from the Cross River, Nigeria, eastward across the DRC to the Ugandan border; it is large, stocky and shaggily haired, and could be confused with the water (marsh) mongoose but has a longer snout and longer legs.

SURICATE *Suricata suricatta*
Total length 45-55 cm; tail length 20-24 cm; shoulder
height 15 cm; weight 620-960 g. **Identification pointers** Small size; pale
coat, several irregular transverse bands on back; thinly haired, dark-
tipped tail; tail held rigidly vertical when running; lives in groups.
Similar species Banded mongoose (separated on habitat preference).

DESCRIPTION Overall body colour ranges from fawn to silvery-grey, with a number of darker, irregular transverse bands running from behind the shoulders to the base of the tail.

The tail is thin, tapered, short-haired and usually dark-tipped. The head is broad at the back, the muzzle sharply pointed and the ears small.

■ *Suricata suricatta*
■ *Herpestes naso*
▨ *Dologale dybowskii*
■ *Liberiictis kuhni*

Skin of the servaline genet, which has a wide distribution in tropical forests.

The Liberian mongoose is an endangered species and has been observed only once in the wild by a scientist.

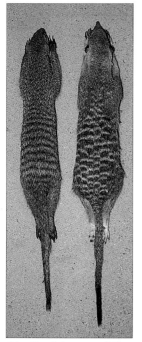

Skins of banded mongoose (left) and suricate (right)

The suricate is the common social mongoose of the arid interior of southern Africa. It frequently stands on its hind legs, using the tail as a 'fifth leg'.

Front

25 mm

Back

Suricate

DISTRIBUTION Restricted to the drier areas of southern Africa, extend marginally into Angola.

STATUS Common.

HABITAT Occupy open, dry and lightly vegetated country.

BEHAVIOUR Diurnal and terrestrial, and highly social, living in troops of 5 to 40 individuals. They excavate their own burrows but also use those dug by ground squirrels and yellow mongoose. They are quite vocal when foraging. Frequently stand on their hind legs.

FOOD Mainly insects and other invertebrates, also eat vertebrates opportunistically.

REPRODUCTION Two to 5 young are born in the summer months, after an average gestation period of 73 days.

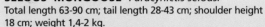

SELOUS' MONGOOSE *Paracynictis selousi*
Total length 63-90 cm; tail length 28-43 cm; shoulder height 18 cm; weight 1,4-2 kg.
Identification pointers Overall pale speckled grey to tawny-grey; tail light coloured, white towards tip; nocturnal, solitary.
Similar species White-tailed and yellow mongooses.

DESCRIPTION Probably closely related to the yellow mongoose. Overall coloration is pale speckled grey to tawny-grey, with brown to black legs and light-coloured, well-haired tail, white towards the tip.

DISTRIBUTION Restricted to northern parts of southern Africa, and southern Central Africa.

STATUS Uncommon.

HABITAT Savanna grass- and woodland.

BEHAVIOUR Terrestrial and solitary, but pairs and females accompanied by young occasionally sighted. Dig their own burrows.

FOOD Invertebrates and to a lesser extent small vertebrates.

REPRODUCTION Two to 4 young born August to March.

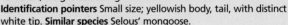

YELLOW MONGOOSE *Cynictis penicillata*
Total length 40-60 cm; tail length 18-25 cm; shoulder height 15-18 cm; weight 450-900 g.
Identification pointers Small size; yellowish body, tail, with distinct white tip. **Similar species** Selous' mongoose.

DESCRIPTION Coloration is reddish-yellow to tawny-yellow with a white tail tip over much of its range; in the north (Botswana) it is more grey and lacks white tail tip. Tail is quite bushy and held horizontal to the ground, or at 45°, when running. The chin, throat and upper chest are paler to off-white. Eyes orange-brown.

DISTRIBUTION A near southern African endemic, from mainly the central and western areas.

STATUS Common.

HABITAT Open grassland and semi-desert scrub, as well as agricultural land.

BEHAVIOUR Diurnal and terrestrial, and live in small colonies of five to 10 animals. Although colonial, individuals disperse to forage alone. Share burrow systems with ground squirrels and suricates.

FOOD Insects, other invertebrates, small vertebrates and carrion.

REPRODUCTION Two to 5 young, mainly in summer.

Front   *Back*

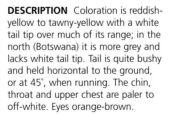

26 mm

Yellow Mongoose

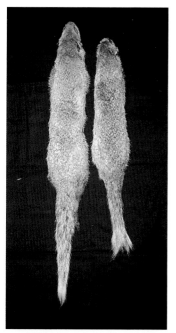
Skins of Selous' mongoose

Selous' mongoose

Yellow mongoose: Note the white-tipped tail. Inset: *The grey form of the yellow mongoose is found in the northern parts of southern Africa.*

- ■ *Bdeogale crassicauda*
- ■ *Bdeogale nigripes*
- ■ *Bdeogale jacksoni*

The population of the Small Grey mongoose in northern Namibia and adjacent south-west Angola is held to be a different species, the Kaokoland Slender Mongoose (*Galerella flavescens*)

- ■ *Galerella flavenscens*
- ■ *Galerella pulverulenta*

Front

28 mm

Back

Small Grey Mongoose

BUSHY-TAILED MONGOOSE *Bdeogale crassicauda*

Total length 65-92 cm; tail length 23-35 cm; shoulder height >20 cm; weight 1,5-2,9 kg.
Identification pointers Overall dark appearance, medium size.
Similar species Jackson's, black-footed and water mongooses.

DESCRIPTION Appears black at a distance but at close quarters more grizzled, although legs and long-haired bushy tail are jet black.

DISTRIBUTION Eastern Africa between the equator and the southern tropic.

STATUS Uncommon.

HABITAT Open woodland with rocky outcrops.

BEHAVIOUR Solitary and mainly nocturnal.

FOOD Invertebrates, small rodents, reptiles and amphibians.

REPRODUCTION Nothing is known.

Two other members of this genus are recognized: **Jackson's mongoose** (*B. jacksoni*), from a limited area of central Kenya and marginally into Uganda, is grey to grey-brown overall with black legs, a mainly white tail, and a yellowish neck and throat. The **black-footed mongoose** (*B. nigripes*) is restricted to the lowland rainforests in the Congolean belt, north of the Congo River, and is very similar to Jackson's but lacks differential throat colouring. These should be compared with the white-tailed but that species is longer in the leg and has shaggier hair, and is largely separated by favoured habitats. All three members of the genus are stoutly built, with fairly large heads and muzzles.

SMALL GREY MONGOOSE

Galerella pulverulenta
Total length 55-69 cm; tail length 20-34 cm; shoulder height 10-12 cm; weight 500-1 000 g. **Identification pointers** Small; uniform grizzled-grey; feet dark to black; bushy, grizzled-grey tail, held horizontal to ground when running. **Similar species** Slender mongoose.

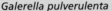
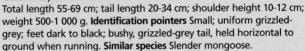

DESCRIPTION Small, with an overall light to dark grizzled-grey coat and long, bushy tail. In the north-west of the region, individuals may appear almost black. The legs are darker than the rest of body.

DISTRIBUTION Restricted to the south and north-west of southern Africa.

STATUS Common.

HABITAT Very wide habitat tolerance, from semi-desert to high rainfall coastal forest. They require some cover and avoid very open terrain.

BEHAVIOUR Diurnal and terrestrial, and mainly solitary although pairs and family parties are sighted. They make

use of regular pathways within the home range. Home ranges overlap considerably and although glandular secretions are used for marking, it is not known whether it is territorial. Female territoriality is a possibility. Home ranges covering <10 to 63 ha have been recorded.

FOOD Small rodents and invertebrates are most important, with birds, reptiles, amphibians, carrion and wild fruits being occasionally eaten.

REPRODUCTION Between 1 and 3 young are dropped in holes, amongst rocks or in dense vegetation, mainly between the months of August to December in the south of their range.

Skins of the bushy-tailed mongoose: Note the dark, glossy fur and short black tail.

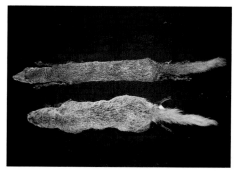

Skins of the black-footed mongoose (top) and Jackson's mongoose (bottom). Both are related to the bushy-tailed mongoose but have a more limited distribution. All three are stoutly built, with fairly large heads and muzzles.

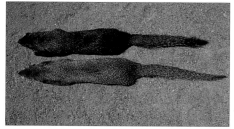

Skins showing colour variants of the small grey mongoose; the dark form (top) from the north-west of its range and the more typical grey form (bottom).

The small grey mongoose is the common solitary mongoose of the southern parts of South Africa.

Front

26 mm

Back

Slender Mongoose

Front

42 mm

Back

Large Grey Mongoose

SLENDER MONGOOSE

Galerella sanguinea
Total length 50-65 cm; tail length 23-30 cm; shoulder height 10 cm; weight 370-800 g.
Identification pointers Long, slender, short-legged; variable colour; fairly bushy, black-tipped tail, raised vertically or curved over body when running; nearly always solitary. There is great taxonomic confusion.
Similar species Small grey mongoose.

DESCRIPTION Small, very slender and long-tailed, which in most races is black-tipped. Colour ranges from almost black, through to grey, brown and a deep chestnut-red.

DISTRIBUTION Throughout the sub-Saharan savanna and semi-arid areas of Africa.

STATUS Common.

HABITAT Areas of high and low rainfall, but is absent from most dense forests and true desert.

BEHAVIOUR Terrestrial but climbs well; is usually solitary. It is one of Africa's most commonly seen carnivores but no detailed study has been undertaken.

FOOD A very wide range of invertebrates, small vertebrates and some wild fruits and berries.

REPRODUCTION The litter consists of 1 to 2, rarely 3, young, and these are dropped after a gestation period of approximately 45 days. The birth season varies from region to region.

LARGE GREY MONGOOSE

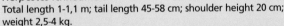

Herpestes ichneumon
Total length 1-1,1 m; tail length 45-58 cm; shoulder height 20 cm; weight 2,5-4 kg.
Identification pointers Large; long grey-grizzled coat; long, black-tipped tail, black lower legs.
Similar species None. (In South Africa, see the small grey mongoose.)

DESCRIPTION Large and grey, as its name implies. The tail is prominently black-tipped and the lower parts of the legs are black. The body and much of the tail-hair is long and uniformly grey-grizzled in colour. The hair is particularly long around the hindquarters and the basal half of the tail. Ears are short.

DISTRIBUTION Very widespread, including North Africa. Occurs elsewhere in parts of the Middle East and southern Europe.

STATUS Uncommon.

HABITAT Riverine vegetation and lives in close association with other water-bodies, although it may wander several kilometres away from its preferred habitat when foraging.

BEHAVIOUR Both nocturnal and diurnal, although mainly the latter. They may be solitary, in pairs or in family parties. When several animals are together they walk nose to anus, giving the group a snake-like appearance. They frequently stand on the hind legs to view the surrounding area. Droppings are deposited at regular latrine sites, and points within the home range are marked with anal gland secretions.

FOOD A very wide range of small vertebrates, particularly rodents, as well as invertebrates are eaten, and on occasion they will eat wild fruits.

REPRODUCTION Litter size has been recorded as 2 to 4 young, born after a gestation period of about 75 days.

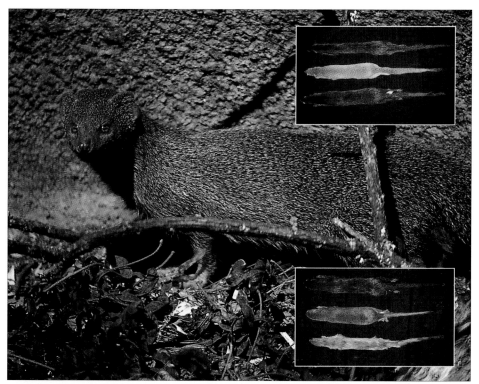

The dark grey form of the slender mongoose. Insets: *Principal colour variations of the slender mongoose; locations* (top to bottom): *Kenya, Sudan, Sierra Leone, Ruwenzori Mountains, Cameroon and Somalia.*

Large grey mongoose: Note the grizzled grey coat and the relatively long hair.

Front

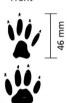

46 mm

Back

Water Mongoose

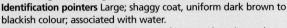

WATER (MARSH) MONGOOSE *Atilax paludinosus*

Total length 80-100 cm; tail length 30-40 cm; shoulder height 22 cm; weight 2,5-5,5 kg.

Identification pointers Large; shaggy coat, uniform dark brown to blackish colour; associated with water.

Similar species Long-nosed mongoose (separated on size and appearance), otters.

DESCRIPTION Large, usually uniformly dark brown, and shaggy-haired, but has short hair on face and feet. Some individuals may be almost black, or reddish-brown. The tail is relatively short, bushy at the base and tapers towards the tip.

DISTRIBUTION Very widespread in sub-Saharan Africa.

STATUS Common.

HABITAT Most well-watered habitats; will penetrate arid areas along water-courses as long as permanent pools are present, although occasionally it may wander several kilometres from water. It frequents the littoral zone and estuaries.

BEHAVIOUR Predominantly nocturnal but also crepuscular. They are probably territorial and sightings are mostly of solitary animals, although pairs and females with young are also seen. Home ranges tend to be linear, following rivers and streams or perimeters of other water bodies. When foraging they follow regular pathways. They swim readily. Droppings are deposited at regularly used latrine sites, close to water, and these are usually more concentrated than those of the otters.

FOOD Mainly crabs and amphibians but also a very wide range of other invertebrates and small vertebrates. Wild fruits are taken occasionally.

REPRODUCTION In southern Africa most births are between August and December but elsewhere they appear to be aseasonal although there are possible peaks. From 1 to 3 young, weighing on average 120 g at birth, are dropped in dense vegetation cover, in rock crevices or in burrows of other species.

MELLER'S MONGOOSE *Rhynchogale melleri*

Total length 60-90 cm; tail length 30-38 cm; shoulder height 18 cm; weight 1,7-3 kg.

Identification pointers Shaggy, light to dark brown coat; tail usually dark brown or black, also white, usually brown at base; crest-like parting on neck.

Similar species White-tailed mongoose (separated on size).

DESCRIPTION Has a shaggy appearance with light to dark brown pelage colour. The tail is usually dark brown to black but individuals with white tails are not uncommon. The legs are dark in colour. The head is quite short but the muzzle somewhat swollen, and a distinct crest-like parting on either side of the neck is diagnostic.

DISTRIBUTION Patchily distributed, mainly in the east between equator and southern tropic.

STATUS Rare.

HABITAT Open woodlands adjacent to savanna, but always near dense cover and water.

BEHAVIOUR Nocturnal and solitary.

FOOD Mainly termites, and other invertebrates and smaller vertebrates.

REPRODUCTION Two to 3 young are apparently born during the summer months.

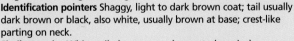

Water mongoose. Inset: *Note the dark, shaggy coat and the naked toes.*

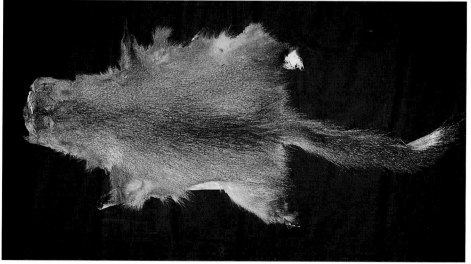

Skin of Meller's mongoose

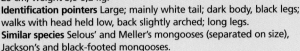

WHITE-TAILED MONGOOSE *Ichneumia albicauda*
Total length 90-150 cm; tail length 35-48 cm; shoulder height 25 cm; weight 3,5-5,2 kg.
Identification pointers Large; mainly white tail; dark body, black legs; walks with head held low, back slightly arched; long legs.
Similar species Selous' and Meller's mongooses (separated on size), Jackson's and black-footed mongooses.

Front   *Back*

45 mm

White-tailed Mongoose

DESCRIPTION A very large mongoose, which when walking holds the rump higher than the shoulders, and the head low. The coarse, shaggy hair is brown-grey to almost black on the legs and the bushy white tail is distinctive.

DISTRIBUTION Very widespread in savanna areas.

STATUS Common.

HABITAT Found in woodland savanna and forest margins, but absent from equatorial forest and desert.

BEHAVIOUR Nocturnal and mainly solitary but pairs and family parties may be seen. Home ranges of 8 km^2 have been recorded.

FOOD A wide range of invertebrates, small vertebrates (up to the size of hares and canerats) and wild fruits.

REPRODUCTION Between 1 and 4 young per litter, and a summer birth peak.

- Mungos mungo
- Mungos gambianus
- Area of overlap

BANDED MONGOOSE
Mungos mungo

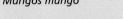

GAMBIAN MONGOOSE
Mungos gambianus
Total length 50-65 cm; tail length 18-25 cm; shoulder height 18-20 cm; weight 600-1800 g.
Identification pointers Pelage brownish-grey to dark brown; banded with 10-12 dark brown to black transverse stripes; the Gambian has distinct black stripe on side of neck, fawn-white throat; lives in troops; savanna woodland.
Similar species Suricate, cusimanse (separated on appearance).

Front

26 mm

Back

Banded Mongoose

DESCRIPTION Both have overall brownish-grey to dark brown coats but the underparts of the Gambian are rusty brown. The banded has 10 to 12 (occasionally more) dark brown to black transverse bands on the back, from behind the shoulders to the base of the tail. The Gambian lacks these stripes but has a distinct black stripe on each side of the neck, strongly contrasting with the buff-white throat (a pattern which is unique to this species). The tails are well haired but not bushy.

DISTRIBUTION The Gambian is restricted to the moister savannas of West Africa. The banded occurs virtually throughout the African savanna regions, penetrating into the arid Horn.

STATUS Banded is abundant, but little is known of the Gambian.

HABITAT Found in savanna and some woodland associations.

BEHAVIOUR Both live in troops but most information available is for the banded, which is highly gregarious and social, with troops numbering five to 30, and on occasion more. When foraging, troop members remain in contact with constant soft chittering and 'murmuring' calls. Recorded size of home ranges

The white-tailed mongoose is a large species, with a distinctive white tail.

Gambian mongoose

Banded mongoose

is from 80 ha to >4 km^2 but this is largely dictated by troop size and food availability. A troop's home range includes several shelters, usually in termitaria. Frequent marking with anal gland secretions is done by all troop members within the range, mainly on rocks and logs. Although territories appear not to be established, contact with different troops can result in conflict. They are diurnal and terrestrial.

FOOD Insects, other invertebrates, reptiles, amphibians, birds (including eggs), small rodents and carrion.

REPRODUCTION Non-seasonal breeders in some areas but seasonal peaks are discernible elsewhere, with breeding usually synchronized within any troop. Two to 6 young, averaging 20 g in weight, are born after a gestation period of approximately 60 days. Young may suckle from any lactating troop female. Nothing is known for the Gambian.

THE CUSIMANSE GROUP Crossarchus species

Four species are recognized, the **cusimanse** (*Crossarchus obscurus*), **flat-headed cusimanse** (*C. platycephalus*), **Alexander's cusimanse** (*C. alexandri*) and **Ansorge's cusimanse** (*C. ansorgei*). Very little is known about these and information is pooled.

■ *Crossarchus ansorgei*
■ *Crossarchus alexandri*
▨ *Crossarchus obscurus*
▨ *Crossarchus platycephalus*

CUSIMANSE GROUP

Total length 45-76 cm; tail length 15-32 cm; shoulder height 18-20 cm; weight 450-1 500 g.
Identification pointers Medium to small size; proportionately short tails; elongated snouts; longish, shaggy, dark-coloured coats; forest habitat; live in groups. **Similar species** Long-nosed mongoose (separated on size and behaviour).

DESCRIPTION Fairly small mongooses, with short legs, proportionately short and tapered tails and elongated snouts. The body is covered with longish, coarse hair, and coloration is variable in different species, from almost black to brown and greyish-yellow. Head coloration is usually marginally paler than the rest of the body but otherwise there are no characteristic markings.

DISTRIBUTION The cusimanse occurs in the tropical rainforests of West Africa. The flat-headed has the most restricted range, in south-eastern Nigeria and adjacent areas of Cameroon. Alexander's is present north of the Congo River, extending marginally into the Central African Republic and Uganda, while Ansorge's is found only south of the Congo River, although recent evidence indicates that the ranges of the two last mentioned species do in fact overlap.

STATUS No reliable information is available as yet but the species in West Africa are probably under threat from increasing habitat loss.

HABITAT Restricted to lowland rainforest.

BEHAVIOUR Live in troops of 10 to more than 20 individuals and in many ways are the forest equivalent of the savanna-dwelling banded and Gambian mongooses (Mungos). Troops are believed to be made up of one to three family groups, each a mated pair accompanied by offspring of two to three litters. Nothing is known about home range sizes but they are apparently very mobile and have no fixed den to which they return. Diurnal and nocturnal movement has been recorded

FOOD Diet includes many insects, crabs, snails, reptiles and eggs, as well as fruits and berries.

REPRODUCTION Probably aseasonal and more than one litter may be dropped annually. Average litter size is thought to be 4 young; gestation period some 70 days.

Cusimanse: Note the elongated snout and rounded ears.

Left to right: *Ansorge's cusimanse, cusimanse (unusually pale) and two Alexander's cusimanse.*

The cusimanse (Crossarchus obscurus) *is highly social, living in troops of 10 to more than 20 individuals.*

- Helogale parvula
- Helogale hirtula

Front

16 mm

Back

Dwarf Mongoose

DWARF MONGOOSE
Helogale parvula

DESERT DWARF MONGOOSE
Helogale hirtula
Total length 35-40 cm; tail length 14-20 cm; shoulder height 7 cm; weight 220-350 (rarely up to 600) g.
Identification pointers Very small; uniform dark to greyish-brown, with gloss; always in troops.
Similar species Other mongooses (separated on size).

DESCRIPTION One of Africa's smallest carnivores, with a fairly short but sleek and glossy coat, ranging from dark to grey-brown and some with a reddish-brown tinge. Overall the appearance is somewhat grizzled at close quarters. The tail is the same colour as the body, and well haired but not bushy. No markings or contrasting colours.

DISTRIBUTION Widespread in suitable habitat from equator southward, with desert dwarf being restricted to the southern Horn region. The distribution of the two is continuous. Some doubt has been expressed as to the validity of the separate species status accorded to the desert dwarf mongoose but as no study has been undertaken on this form, we prefer to retain it here.

STATUS A generally common species in suitable habitat, with troops reaching fairly high densities in some areas.

HABITAT Open woodland and sparse woodland savanna, as well as rocky areas found within this habitat.

BEHAVIOUR Strictly diurnal and terrestrial, with troops of usually about 10 (up to 40 recorded) in number, each occupying a fixed home range of 2 to 30 ha. Within the home range a troop has up to 20 dens, often within termitaria. Each troop has a dominant female and male, with the rest of the colony falling into a 'pecking order'

with the younger animals ranking highest – an unusual departure from the rest of the mammal world – and females always dominant over males. Usually only the dominant female breeds but all troop members care for the young. When foraging they retain contact with one another by uttering soft 'twittering' calls.

The dwarf mongoose, along with the troop-living banded mongoose, is one of the most frequently sighted mongoose species. During the early morning they usually sun-bask on termitaria, rocks or logs, with much time being spent grooming, both individually and communally. Regularly used dens are characterized by middens of their small droppings that contain large quantities of fine insect fragments. As with most other mongoose species, they mark objects (rocks, branches, etc.) with secretions from anal and cheek glands, with troop members marking the same locations.

FOOD Insects, other invertebrates and to a lesser extent small reptiles, birds and their eggs. Fruit has also been recorded.

REPRODUCTION Births mainly coincide with the rainy season, with litter sizes ranging from 1 to 7 (average 2 to 4) young, which are dropped after a gestation period of 50 to 54 days. In some regions two litters annually are probable.

Dwarf mongoose

Left to right: *Two colour forms of the dwarf mongoose, and the desert dwarf mongoose.*

A troop of dwarf mongooses at their den. Termite mounds such as this, are often used as den sites by these animals.

HYAENAS AND AARDWOLF

Families Hyaenidae and Protelidae

There are three species of 'true' hyaena and one aardwolf, but a number of authorities consider the latter to belong to the Hyaenidae.

SPOTTED HYAENA

Crocuta crocuta

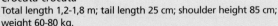

Total length 1,2-1,8 m; tail length 25 cm; shoulder height 85 cm; weight 60-80 kg.

Identification pointers Large; shoulders higher than rump; short, fawn-yellow, dark-spotted coat; rounded ears; usually in packs; distinctive call.

Similar species Other hyaenas.

Front

96 mm

Back

Spotted Hyaena

DESCRIPTION Best known of the hyaenas, with heavily built forequarters standing higher than the rump. The head is large with prominent rounded ears and a black muzzle. The overall colour is from fawn-yellow to grey-fawn, with scattering of dark brown spots and blotches. The head, throat and chest are not spotted. The tail is short with coarse hair, and a short, erect mane extends along the neck and shoulders. The call consists of whoops, groans, grunts, whines, yells and giggles, and once heard is never forgotten.

DISTRIBUTION Wide sub-Saharan range, but has been eliminated in much of southern Africa and is absent from the tropical lowland forest areas.

STATUS Still common in a number of savanna areas but greatly reduced, even locally extinct, in others.

HABITAT Open and lightly wooded savanna, denser woodland types, rugged, broken country; also penetrates drier areas along vegetated water-courses.

BEHAVIOUR Although solitary animals may be encountered, they usually live in family groups, or 'clans', led by an adult female. Clan size ranges from three to 15 or more individuals, with each clan defending a territory, which is marked with urine, anal gland secretions and the distinctive bright white droppings, usually deposited in latrine sites. They are both nocturnal and crepuscular, with more limited daytime activity. They frequently sunbask in the vicinity of their daytime shelters. Contrary to popular opinion, they are not skulking scavengers but skilled and aggressive hunters, although they are not above driving other predators such as lions from their kills.

FOOD Ungulates, including antelope, buffalo and plains zebra, form the bulk of prey and are actively hunted. They also scavenge, and in game parks they frequent camp dumps.

REPRODUCTION One to 2 cubs per litter is usual but up to 3 have been recorded, although more than one female may den down in the same location, giving the impression of larger litters. Young may be born at any time of the year, but slight seasonal peaks may be discernible in some areas. The gestation period is about 110 days and cubs are uniformly dark brown with lighter heads; the spots only appear in the fourth month. Cubs weigh on average 1,5 kg at birth.

The spotted hyaena is the best-known of Africa's three hyaena species. This species has an extensive range south of the Sahara.

A young spotted hyaena. Usually between one and two cubs are born per litter, and spots develop only in the fourth month.

STRIPED HYAENA *Hyaena hyaena*

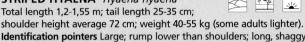

Total length 1,2-1,55 m; tail length 25-35 cm;
shoulder height average 72 cm; weight 40-55 kg (some adults lighter).
Identification pointers Large; rump lower than shoulders; long, shaggy
coat; distinct stripes on body, legs; head large; long, pointed ears;
solitary. **Similar species** Spotted hyaena, aardwolf.

DESCRIPTION Has the distinctive hyaena form, with the back sloping down to the rump and a large head, with a mainly naked muzzle. The ears are large and pointed (in contrast to the shorter, rounded ears of its spotted cousin). The coat is buff to grey in colour, shaggy in texture and extensively marked with transverse black stripes. The legs are also well striped and ringed. The muzzle and the throat are mainly black. A well-developed erectile mane extends from the neck base to the rump. The tail is fairly long and bushy.

DISTRIBUTION Occurs widely in North Africa, including the Sahara and Sahel, extending south to northern Tanzania. Also occurs throughout Arabia, the Middle East and into northern India.

STATUS Occurs at low densities but there is no known threat.

HABITAT Dry areas, often in association with rocky outcrops and within savanna to true desert. In parts of North Africa it is also found on coastal plains.

BEHAVIOUR Most sightings are of solitary animals, or pairs, and most activity takes place at night. Although poorly known, they probably live in loosely associated groupings within a common home range, only foraging being a largely solitary activity. The arid nature of their habitat indicates that they occupy large home ranges but the extent of territoriality is unknown. They show many behavioural similarities to the brown hyaena, and are much less vocal than the spotted hyaena.

FOOD Opportunistic, taking a wide range of animal and plant food; also scavenges.

REPRODUCTION A litter usually consists of 2 to 4 cubs, dropped in a rocky den, or a burrow excavated by another species. In some regions births show seasonal peaks but generally birthings take place at any time of the year. The gestation period is about 90 days.

BROWN HYAENA *Parahyaena brunnea*

Total length 1,3-1,6 m; tail length 17-30 cm;
shoulder height 80 cm; weight 45 kg.
Identification pointers Large; typical hyaena form; long, dark brown
coat; paler neck, shoulders; large head; long, pointed ears; restricted
distribution. **Similar species** Spotted hyaena, aardwolf (separated
on appearance).

DESCRIPTION Typical hyaena, with shoulders standing higher than rump, and large head with dark-coloured muzzle. The body is covered with long, shaggy dark to light brown hair; the mantle is particularly dense on the back and shoulders and lighter in colour than the rest of the coat. The lower legs are striped black and light brown, with the tail being short, bushy and dark. Ears are large, and pointed towards the tip.

DISTRIBUTION Restricted mainly to northern areas of southern Africa, extending into south-western Angola. Stragglers sometimes occur in the south of the region.

STATUS Occurred throughout southern Africa, but now extinct in much of the south.

The striped hyaena is superficially similar to the aardwolf but much larger.

The brown hyaena is distinguished by its long, shaggy coat and pointed ears.

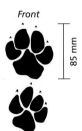

Front

85 mm

Back

Brown Hyaena

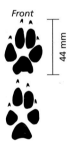

Front

44 mm

Back

Aardwolf

HABITAT Occupies mainly arid and semi-arid areas, as well as some savanna associations. Previous range indicates greater habitat tolerance.

BEHAVIOUR Mainly nocturnal and solitary foragers, but several animals usually share a territory. Territory size varies considerably, from 19 to 480 km^2, depending largely on abundance of habitat and food. Animals sharing a territory are apparently of an extended family unit consisting of four to six individuals and all assist in raising the cubs. Nomadic males, overlapping the territories of several groups, mate with receptive females, while males resident with groups do not. Territories are marked with droppings and anal gland secretions. Their vocalizations are limited and do not carry very far.

FOOD Mainly scavengers but they take a great variety of invertebrates, smaller vertebrates and fruits. Surplus food may be cached for later use.

REPRODUCTION Young may be born at any time of year, and litters usually contain 2 to 3 cubs, dropped after a gestation period of some 90 days.

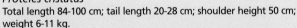

AARDWOLF
Proteles cristatus
Total length 84-100 cm; tail length 20-28 cm; shoulder height 50 cm; weight 6-11 kg.
Identification pointers Hyaena-like, rump lower than shoulders; prominent erectile mane down neck, back; dark, vertical body stripes; feet, muzzle, much of tail black; long, pointed ears.
Similar species Canids (separated on appearance), striped hyaena (separated on size).

DESCRIPTION Medium-sized, and higher at the shoulders than at rump, with longish, coarse hair and a mane of erectile hair on neck and back, which is raised when under stress. General body colour ranges from pale tawny to yellow-white and there are several vertical black stripes on the body, and black bands on the upper parts of the legs. The muzzle, feet and much of the tail are black. The ears are large and pointed.

DISTRIBUTION There are two separate populations, one widely occurring in southern Africa, the other in East Africa, extending through the Horn and along the Red Sea coast to Egypt. The distribution of this animal is largely dictated by the availability of its principal food, the harvester termite.

STATUS Uncommon but secure.

HABITAT Very wide tolerance, from low to high rainfall regions. Avoids forest and dense woodland.

BEHAVIOUR Primarily nocturnal and crepuscular but active on overcast days in areas of low disturbance. Usually solitary animals, pairs, or family parties seen, with two or more animals occupying a home range. Several females may drop their pups in the same den. Although often excavating their own burrows, they will also use and modify those dug by other species. Droppings are deposited in shallow scrapes at latrine sites, and anal gland secretions on grass stalks within the home range.

FOOD Primarily termites, notably the harvester termite, but also other insects. They are falsely accused of killing livestock such as sheep and goats, when in fact dentition is totally inadequate.

REPRODUCTION Between 1 and 4 pups, weighing less than 500 g at birth, are dropped after a gestation period of about 60 days. Births are recorded at most times of the year but summer rainy period peaks are discernible in some areas.

The smallest of the hyaenas, the aardwolf.

The aardwolf is distinguished by its dark, vertical body stripes and long, pointed ears.

THE CATS
Family Felidae
Ten species occur on the African continent, of which only three are endemic. They range in size from the diminutive sand and small spotted cats to the lion.

CHEETAH

Acinonyx jubatus
Total length 1,8-2,2 m; tail length 60-80 cm; shoulder height 80 cm; weight 30-72 (average 40-60) kg (♂ average larger than ♀).
Identification pointers Large; slender, greyhound-like build; long, spotted white-tipped tail, black-ringed towards tip; coat single, rounded black spots; small head, rounded face; black line from inner corner of eye to corner of mouth ('tear-line').
Similar species Leopard (separated on appearance), serval (separated on size).

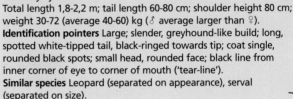

Front

85 mm

Back

Cheetah

DESCRIPTION Sometimes referred to as the 'greyhound of cats', being the fastest of these, with its slender body and long legs. The head is small, with a short muzzle and a clear black line (the 'tear-line') running from the inner corner of each eye to the corner of the mouth. General body colour is off-white to pale fawn and liberally dotted with more or less uniformly-sized black, rounded spots. Numerous small black spots are located on the forehead and crown. Ear tips are white and the long tail is spotted and black, ringed with a white tip. A short, erectile crest is situated on the back and sides. Young cubs have an extensive mantle of longish grey hair. The well-publicized 'king cheetah' is merely an aberrant colour form. The cheetah is the only cat that does not have fully retractile claws.

DISTRIBUTION Wide but highly fragmented distribution in savanna, desert and semi-desert areas, but previously extensive and continuous. The main population centres are located in the northern parts of southern Africa and in East Africa. There is probably some movement between apparently isolated populations, particularly those in the Sahara. Remnant populations survive in parts of the Middle East, particularly Iran.

STATUS Between 9 000 and 12 000 animals (but probably closer to the lower) are estimated to survive. They

are now extinct as viable species in at least 10 countries within their former range, and will slide into extinction in the near future in a further 11 countries, with viable populations probably limited to four countries. The largest national population is found in Namibia.

HABITAT Preference is shown for more open country, such as semi-desert and desert plains, grassland and wooded grassland but they also make use of more closed woodland. Access to drinking water is not essential.

BEHAVIOUR Normally seen singly, in pairs or small family parties consisting of a female and her dependent cubs. Adult males move singly or in small bachelor groups of related animals, while females establish territories from which they will drive other females. Males are apparently not as territorial and may move over the areas held by several females. Group size is variable but appears smaller on average in East Africa. Females in the Serengeti and on Namibian ranches have much larger ranges than males. Ranges of the former average 800 km² and the latter as much as 1 500 km² while groups of males in the Serengeti were found to utilize only 40 km² on average; in the Kruger National Park (South Africa) males and females have similar home ranges of an average 175 km². Mainly diurnal, but most hunting takes place during the cooler hours.

The sleek, long-legged cheetah is built for speed. The black tear-mark running from the eye to the mouth is distinctive.

The so-called 'king cheetah' is merely an aberrant colour form, albeit an attractive one.

They have a complex and drawn-out courtship, leading after seven to 14 days to the female coming into oestrus. Competition for mating rights amongst males is intense and mortality can be high, with up to 50% being recorded in the Serengeti. Cub mortality is also high, particularly in areas where other large predators, such as lion and spotted hyaena, are abundant. Favoured lying-up spots are usually raised above the surrounding area and are marked with urine by both males and females. When hunting, they stalk to within a short distance of their intended prey and then sprint in for the kill at up to 70 km/h but this can only be sustained for a few hundred metres. Speeds of up to 112 km/h as mentioned in the literature are difficult to verify.

FOOD Medium-sized mammals, mainly antelope, up to a weight of about 60 kg, including the young of larger species. Thomson's gazelle is an important prey in East Africa, with impala, springbok, reedbuck and puku being of most importance in southern and Central Africa. They also take other mammals, such as hares, and birds up to the size of the ostrich.

REPRODUCTION Litters of 1 to 5 cubs (usually 3 or 4) may be dropped at any time of the year, but peaks during the rainy season are noticeable in some areas. The gestation period is about 92 days, with the cubs weighing 250 to 300 g at birth. For the first six weeks they are usually hidden in dense vegetation cover.

LEOPARD
Panthera pardus

Total length 1,6-2,1 m; tail length 68-110 cm; shoulder height 70-80 cm; weight ♂ 20-90 kg ♀ 17-60 kg (♂ considerably larger than ♀).
Identification pointers Large, cat-like appearance; rosette spots on body, solid black spots on legs, head, sides, hindquarters; no black facial stripes.
Similar species Cheetah, serval (separated on appearance and size).

Front

92 mm

Back

Leopard

DESCRIPTION Elegant and powerfully built, with a beautifully marked coat. Overall body colour varies from off-white to orange-russet, with black spots on the legs, flanks, hindquarters and the head. The spots over the rest of the body consist of rosettes or broken circles of irregular black spots. The tail is about half of the total length, with rosette spots above and a white tip. Ears are rounded and white-tipped. Underparts are usually white to off-white. Cubs have dark, woolly coats and less distinct spotting. There are some regional differences in size, coloration and patterning but all are easily recognizable.

DISTRIBUTION Has a wide distribution in sub-Saharan Africa, and remnant populations are located in the Atlas Mountains of Morocco and the coastal ranges of South Africa. Elsewhere, it occurs widely in the Middle East and Asia, extending into China.

STATUS Although it has disappeared from some areas and is greatly reduced in others, the leopard is not threatened within its African range.

HABITAT An extremely wide habitat tolerance: from coastal plains to high altitude mountains, from semi-desert areas to tropical rainforests.

BEHAVIOUR Solitary, with the exception of pairs coming together for mating, or when a female is accompanied by cubs. They are mainly active at night but in areas where they are not disturbed they can be observed moving during the cooler daylight hours. Most activity takes place on the ground but they are also capable climbers and swimmers. Adult males mark and defend a territory against other males, and a male's range may overlap those of several females. Territories are marked with urine scrapes, droppings, tree-scratching points and the deep 'sawing', or grunting, call. Females

Leopards have no facial 'tear-mark' and are more powerfully built than the cheetah.

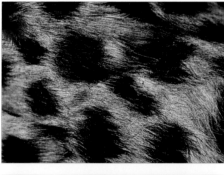

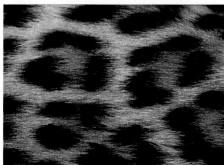

Cheetah spots (above) are 'solid', compared with leopard spots that are mostly in the form of 'rosettes' (below).

Whether in trees or on the ground, leopards are masters of camouflage.

also call but this presumably serves no territorial function. Home ranges may be as small as 10 km² in optimal habitat, to several hundred square kilometres where prey densities are low. They stalk and then pounce on their prey and do not rely on running at high speed like the cheetah.

FOOD Part of their survival success is their ability to utilize a very wide range of animal food, including insects, reptiles, fish and birds, but the bulk of prey is made up of medium-sized antelope and other ungulates. In some areas hyrax form a very important component of their diet. On occasion they kill more than their immediate needs, the surplus being stored for later use. Kills may be dragged considerable distances and hidden amongst dense vegetation or rocks, or in some areas in trees out of reach of other predators. They readily scavenge, even eating rotten carcasses.

REPRODUCTION Litters of 2 to 3 cubs are usual, each weighing about 500 g at birth. There is no fixed breeding season and the gestation period is approximately 100 days.

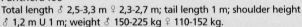

LION
Panthera leo

Total length ♂ 2,5-3,3 m ♀ 2,3-2,7 m; tail length 1 m; shoulder height ♂ 1,2 m U 1 m; weight ♂ 150-225 kg ♀ 110-152 kg.
Identification pointers Large; uniform tawny coloration; most adult males have long mane; dark-tipped tail. **Similar species** None.

■ *High concentration area*
☐ *Total distribution area*

Front

128 mm

Back

Lion

DESCRIPTION The largest of Africa's three 'big cats' and unmistakable. Body colour ranges from pale tawny to reddish-grey, with paler underparts. Faint spotting is present on cubs, particularly on the sides but is usually lost by adulthood. The tail is short-haired with the same colour as the body but the tip is dark brown to black. Only adult males carry manes of long hair, extending from the sides of the face on to the neck, shoulders and chest. Mane ranges from pale tawny to black in colour. Males are noticeably larger than females.

DISTRIBUTION Occurred very widely in Africa but now has a patchy distribution south of the Sahara. Most viable populations are now restricted to the larger savanna conservation areas. An isolated population is located in the Gir Forest, north-western India.

STATUS Some large populations still exist, such as in the Kruger National Park, South Africa, with about 2 000 animals, and in the Serengeti/Mara system of East Africa there are approximately 3 000. However, they are generally in decline, particularly outside established conservation areas, and the total is less than 50 000.

HABITAT Very wide tolerance, from desert fringes to woodland and fairly open grasslands. Absent from true forest.

BEHAVIOUR The most sociable large cat, living in prides of between three and 30 individuals. Pride size is largely dictated by prey availability and varies from region to region. The social groupings are complex, with each composed of a relatively stable core of related females, their dependent offspring, and usually a 'coalition' of two, or more, adult males. In some circumstances a single male may hold tenure over a pride. On reaching maturity, females may stay with their birth pride or leave as a group to form a new pride. Young males always disperse from the birth pride and form coalitions until they are old enough to take over an existing pride, rarely before four years of age. Most males hold tenure for only two to three years, with the larger coalitions usually being able to hold the pride for longer. When new males drive away pride-holding males, the new animals usually kill any younger cubs present. Most hunting is undertaken by the lionesses but males usually take priority when feeding at a kill. Most hunting takes

The lioness does not grow a mane, and is smaller than the lion.

The extent and coloration of the male lion's mane is variable. **Inset:** *Lion cubs have brown spotting, which becomes less distinct, or disappears, with age.*

place at night and during the cooler daylight hours. A pride territory is defended against strange lions by both males and females, but some prides and solitary males may be nomadic. Territories are marked with urine, droppings, earth-scratching and their distinctive roaring. These calls are audible over distances of several kilometres. Pride home ranges vary from 26 to 220 km^2 but in some cases may exceed 2 000 km^2.

FOOD Mainly medium to large mammals, particularly ungulates, including buffalo, giraffe, plains zebra and warthog, but mainly antelope species. Some prides specialize in hunting a particular species, such as hippopotamus and porcupines, and prey preferences vary from region to region. They will drive other predators from their kills and will readily scavenge.

REPRODUCTION There is no fixed breeding season, and 1 to 4 cubs (rarely up to 6), weighing about 1,5 kg, are dropped after a gestation period of some 110 days. Adult pride females often conceive at about the same time, with the advantage that cubs can suckle from any lioness that is lactating. Cubs may remain with the mother for about two years.

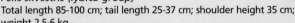

AFRICAN WILD CAT
Felis silvestris (lybica group)
Total length 85-100 cm; tail length 25-37 cm; shoulder height 35 cm; weight 2,5-6 kg.
Identification pointers Similar build, form to domestic cat; very variable in colour, but backs of ears rich reddish-brown; vertical body stripes distinct to very faint. **Similar species** Sand and swamp cats.

Front

36 mm

Back

African Wild Cat

DESCRIPTION At least 13 subspecies have been recognized, based largely on colour variations. Appearance and form similar to domestic cat but it is generally longer in the leg and larger. The diagnostic feature is the reddish hair on the backs of the ears, this being lacking in domestic and feral cats. It hybridizes readily with the domestic cat. Reddish-brown to yellowish fur is usually present on the belly and inner surfaces of hind legs. Overall body colour ranges from pale sandy-brown in drier areas to light or dark grey in moister regions. The body is marked to greater or lesser extent with darker vertical stripes, sometimes dark ringing on limbs. The longish, dark-ringed tail has black tip. The chin and throat are white, and underparts are paler than upperparts.

DISTRIBUTION Widespread but absent from some habitats. Elsewhere extends into Europe, Middle East and western Asia.

STATUS Generally common but threatened in some areas by hybridizing with domestic and feral cats.

HABITAT Absent from much of the lowland tropical rainforest belt and true desert.

BEHAVIOUR Solitary, except during the brief mating period and when the females are accompanied by kittens. They are primarily nocturnal and crepuscular but are occasionally seen on cool, overcast days. They lie up in rock crevices, amongst dense vegetation, in burrows excavated by other species and in trees. Both sexes establish, mark and defend territories, and cat densities may be high in areas of optimal habitat and abundant prey.

FOOD Primarily small rodents (rats and mice) but also mammals up to the size of hares and hyrax (and young of small antelope are recorded). They readily take birds, including ostrich chicks and bustards, and occasionally reptiles and invertebrates.

REPRODUCTION After a gestation period of 56 to 65 days, 1 to 5 kittens are dropped, weighing 40 to 50 g. Most births are recorded during warm, wet summer months.

In higher rainfall areas African wild cats are generally darker in colour than those found in arid regions.

The backs of the ears of the African wild cat are rich red-brown in colour.

SWAMP CAT
Felis chaus

Total length 80-120 cm; tail length 20-30 cm; shoulder height 45 cm; weight 2,5-12 kg.
Identification pointers Medium-sized; overall sandy-brown colour, no distinctive markings; back surface of ears red-brown, short, black tufts; tail shortish and black-tipped.
Similar species African wild cat (separated on size).

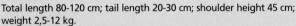

DESCRIPTION Similar in overall appearance to African wild cat but larger and not as distinctly marked. Backs of ears reddish-brown, with short terminal tuft of black hairs. The tail is proportionately shorter than in wild cat. Overall body colour is pale sandy-brown, with indistinct markings on sides and legs, but underparts paler.

DISTRIBUTION Vicinity of lower Nile River and its delta, as well as Mediterranean coast of Egypt. Extends into Middle East and east to Vietnam.

STATUS It is probably severely endangered in its limited African range.

HABITAT Wetland associations with good cover, including agricultural land.

BEHAVIOUR Solitary and nocturnal but not studied within its African range. Probably similar to the wild cat.

FOOD Apparently rodents dominate, but hares, birds, reptiles and fish are also taken. No inventory for Africa.

REPRODUCTION Three to 5 kittens are dropped after a gestation period of about 66 days, with birth weight ranging from 45 to 55 g.

SMALL SPOTTED CAT *Felis nigripes*

Total length 50-63 cm; tail length 16 cm; shoulder height 25 cm; weight 1-2 kg.
Identification pointers Small; pelage colour pale, smallish dark-brown to black spots; backs of ears same as pelage colour; restricted to southern Africa. **Similar species** African wild cat, genets.

DESCRIPTION The small spotted cat is also known as the **black-footed cat** and the **anthill tiger**, and is one of the world's smallest wild cats. Its overall coloration ranges from reddish-fawn within its southern range to a much paler colour northward. Numerous black (red-brown in north) spots and bars occur over the entire body and on the short, black-ringed and -tipped tail. The chin is white, as is the throat, which also has two or three distinct dark bands.

DISTRIBUTION Arid parts of southern and central southern Africa.

STATUS Occurs at low densities and for the most part is uncommon.

HABITAT Arid to semi-arid scrub and grassland, in generally open terrain.

BEHAVIOUR Principally nocturnal but occasionally crepuscular. They are solitary and the males, at least, are probably territorial. During the day they lie up in burrows dug by other species, in hollow termite mounds and amongst rock tumbles.

FOOD Opportunistic hunters that take anything they can overpower but mainly small rodents, hares and birds. Known to scavenge; invertebrates important.

REPRODUCTION Litter of 1 to 3 kittens is born during the summer months after a gestation period of 63 to 68 days.

The swamp cat occurs only marginally in Africa, in northeastern Egypt.

Two subspecies of the small spotted cat are recognized: nigripes *from the south* (left) *and* thomasi *from the north.*

The southern subspecies of the small spotted cat (Felis nigripes nigripes).

SAND CAT *Felis margarita*

Total length 65-85 cm; tail length 23-31 cm; shoulder height
up to 30 cm; weight 1,5-3,5 kg.
Identification pointers Small; proportionately broad face and ears;
mostly uniform pale sandy-buff, indistinct markings; northern
desert distribution. **Similar species** African wild cat (separated on size).

DESCRIPTION The smallest cat in the Saharan belt, with a somewhat broadened face and large, rounded ears. The fur is thick, soft and more or less uniformly pale sandy-buff, with indistinct darker markings. Face paler than rest of body, and dark spots on the backs of the ears. Underparts are off-white.

DISTRIBUTION Restricted to the Sahara, with other populations in Arabia and extending to at least Afghanistan.

STATUS Unknown but probably secure given its desert habitat.

HABITAT Principally sandy desert.

BEHAVIOUR Nocturnal and solitary, and lives in burrows excavated under shrubs and tussocks. Hardly known in the wild.

FOOD Mainly small rodents up to the size of ground squirrels, and also hares, birds, reptiles and invertebrates.

REPRODUCTION Two to 4 kittens, each weighing about 55 g, dropped after a gestation period of some 63 days.

SERVAL *Leptailurus serval*

Total length 96-120 cm; tail length 25-38 cm;
shoulder height 60 cm; weight 8-13 kg.
Identification pointers Slender; pale, usually yellowish-fawn coat,
black-spotted, barred; large, rounded, distinctly marked ears; short,
black-banded and -tipped
tail. **Similar species** leopard, cheetah (separated on size), golden cat.

Front

47 mm

Back

Serval

DESCRIPTION Slender, long-legged and spotted, with a short tail and large, rounded ears. Overall colour ranges from off-white to yellowish-fawn, with pale to white underparts. Numerous black spots and bars scattered over body, with those down centre of back forming more or less straight lines. Tail is banded with black and has a black tip. Back surfaces of ears have black band and tip, separated by distinctive white patch. In West Africa the *servaline* form has an overall greyish coloration, with a speckling of very small, dark spots.

DISTRIBUTION Throughout savanna zone, from Senegal eastward to the Red Sea, through East and Central Africa and south to KwaZulu-Natal, South Africa.

STATUS Common over much of its range.

HABITAT Usually areas with water, with tall grassland, reed beds or forest fringes.

BEHAVIOUR Mainly nocturnal and crepuscular but not infrequently seen on cool days. Although mostly solitary, sightings of pairs and family groups not unusual. Predominantly terrestrial but are agile climbers. Males are territorial, as may be females.

FOOD Variety of small mammals, particularly rodents such as the *Otomys* group, canerats and hares, and possibly the young of small antelope. Birds, reptiles and invertebrates are also taken.

REPRODUCTION Litters are usually dropped during the summer rains, consisting of 1 to 3, rarely 5, kittens averaging 200 g in weight. Gestation is 68 to 79 days.

The sand cat is the smallest cat in the Saharan belt; it has a proportionately broad face and large ears.

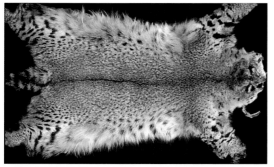

Skin of the servaline, a form of the serval restricted to West Africa.

Serval sub-adult

The serval has distinct black and white markings on the backs of the ears.

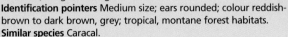

GOLDEN CAT *Profelis aurata*

Total length 1,07-1,35 m; tail length 35-45 cm; shoulder height 38-50 cm; weight 8-16 kg.
Identification pointers Medium size; ears rounded; colour reddish-brown to dark brown, grey; tropical, montane forest habitats.
Similar species Caracal.

DESCRIPTION Robust and medium-sized, with dark-backed, rounded ears. Colour is commonly overall red-brown but in some areas may be dark brown or grey. Dark spots are present to a greater or lesser extent on the underparts, and occasionally also over the entire body. Underparts usually white to off-white.

DISTRIBUTION Restricted to tropical forest belt.

STATUS Probably secure, except in West Africa where loss of habitat is a problem.

HABITAT Tropical and montane forests.

BEHAVIOUR Very little known but probably solitary and the males are territorial. They have been sighted at night as well as during daylight hours, and are both terrestrial and arboreal.

FOOD Rodents, hyrax and duikers important part of diet; recorded as taking birds.

REPRODUCTION Litters said to be denned in trees, amongst dense foliage and rocks.

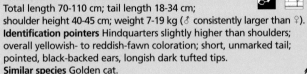

CARACAL *Caracal caracal*

Total length 70-110 cm; tail length 18-34 cm; shoulder height 40-45 cm; weight 7-19 kg (♂ consistently larger than ♀).
Identification pointers Hindquarters slightly higher than shoulders; overall yellowish- to reddish-fawn coloration; short, unmarked tail; pointed, black-backed ears, longish dark tufted tips.
Similar species Golden cat.

Front

47 mm

Back

Caracal

DESCRIPTION Robustly built and medium-sized, with hindquarters somewhat higher than shoulders. Coat is short, dense and soft, and colour ranges from pale yellowish-fawn to rich brick-red, with animals from drier regions tending to be paler than those from high rainfall regions. Underparts may be almost white to slightly paler than general body colour. Ears are long and pointed, with a tuft of longish black hair at tips; the back surfaces are black with a liberal sprinkling of white hairs. The face is prominently marked with black and white patches, especially around the eyes and mouth. Tail is short and uniformly coloured.

DISTRIBUTION Widespread but absent from much of tropical forest belt and the Sahara.

STATUS In decline in some areas but common in others, such as southern Africa.

HABITAT Semi-desert to range of savanna types, and high and low rainfall regions. Present in some forest associations.

BEHAVIOUR Mainly nocturnal but also crepuscular where undisturbed, and solitary. The males appear to be territorial and their home ranges overlap those of at least one and usually two, or more, females. Recorded ranges from 4 to >100 km².

FOOD Mainly small- to medium-sized mammals, from mice to antelope (up to about 40 kg), also birds and reptiles. Considered a major predator of sheep and goats in parts of southern Africa.

REPRODUCTION Litters may be dropped at any time of year but there is a summer peak in southern Africa. After gestation period of about 79 days, 1 to 3 kittens, weighing an average of 250 g, are born.

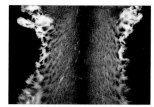
Golden cat skin from Ghana

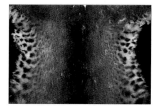
Golden cat skin from Nigeria

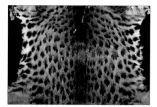
Golden cat skin from the DRC

The golden cat resembles the better-known caracal but lacks the pointed, tufted ears of that species.

Caracal. Inset: The caracal has long tufts of black hair at the tips of its pointed ears.

HYRAXES (DASSIES) Order Hyracoidea

Family Procaviidae
Four species of rock-dwelling hyrax now recognized in genera Procavia and Heterohyrax, and three tree-dwellers. Taxonomy is in a state of flux.

ROCK-DWELLING HYRAXES

TREE-DWELLING HYRAXES
Total length 40-60 cm; shoulder height 15-30 cm; weight 2-5 kg.
Identification pointers Small, stocky build; no tail; small, rounded ears; patch of erectile hairs in centre of back, from black to straw-yellow or white in different species and subspecies. **Similar species** None.

■ *Procavia capensis complex*
■ *Heterohyrax brucei*
■ Area of overlap

■ *Dendrohyrax arboreus*
■ *Dendrohyrax dorsalis*
■ Area of overlap
■ *Dendrohyrax validus*

Heterohyrax antineae is sometimes recognized as a separate species. It only occurs in the Hoggar massif of south-eastern Algeria.

Front   Back

32 mm

Rock Hyrax

DESCRIPTION Small, stoutly built and tailless, with short legs. Overall colour variable both between species as well as within the same population, but mainly light to dark brown. Some populations of the **yellow-spotted rock hyrax** (*Heterohyrax brucei*) are greyish-fawn. Hair length is variable but animals living at higher altitudes and some of the tree hyraxes have fairly long, shaggy coats. All have a gland in the centre of the back that is ringed by longer erectile hair, which may be black, white or yellowish depending on the species.

DISTRIBUTION The most widespread is the **rock hyrax** (*Procavia capensis*), ranging from 'Cape to Cairo', through the Horn and the Sahel, with isolated populations in the mountain ranges of the Sahara. The yellow-spotted occurs throughout the Horn, East Africa and marginally into southern Africa, with an isolated population in Angola. The three **tree hyrax** (*Dendrohyrax* spp.) are largely restricted to the forests and dense woodlands of the tropics, although a few isolated pockets are located in South Africa.

STATUS Common.

HABITAT Rock hyraxes occupy mainly mountain and hill ranges and isolated outcrops. Tree hyraxes have colonized a range of forest, woodland and thicket types.

BEHAVIOUR Rock hyraxes are diurnal, whereas tree hyraxes are principally nocturnal but daylight activity is not unusual. Rock dwellers live in colonies of four to eight individuals but in favourable habitats densities may be very high, whereas tree hyraxes are solitary although large numbers may be concentrated in a small area. Rock hyraxes sunbask in the early morning for an extended period before moving off to feed. During basking an adult will keep watch for predators, uttering a sharp cry when danger threatens. Each colony has a strict pecking order, with a dominant male and female. Most feeding is undertaken in an intensive session in the morning and late afternoon. They rarely move more than a few hundred metres from the rock shelter. Tree hyraxes spend much of their feeding time in trees but will also feed on the ground. During the day they may sunbask or retreat into tree holes. They are far more difficult to observe than their rock cousins but their hair-raising screaming or rattling calls at night are diagnostic.

FOOD Plants, including leaves, flowers, fruits and also bark.

REPRODUCTION Young are well developed at birth and soon able to move around. Gestation averages some 210 days, with 1 to 3 (rarely 5) young being usual. Birth weight varies according to litter size but ranges from 150 to 300 g. Rock hyraxes have distinct birth seasons but this varies from region to region; both yellow-spotted and tree hyraxes may be aseasonal breeders.

Yellow-spotted rock hyrax

Young rock hyraxes suckling

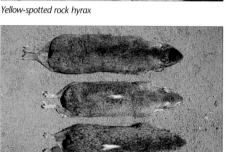
Top to bottom: *Skins of rock hyrax with dark spot, rock hyrax* (northern Namibia) *with white spot, and tree hyrax.*

*Tree hyrax (*Dendrohyrax arboreus*); of the three tree hyrax species this one is the most widespread in East Africa.*

Rock hyraxes favour mountain and hill terrain where they are often seen sunbasking.

AARDVARK Order Tubulidentata

Family Orycteropodidae

Front

90 mm

Back

Aardvark

AARDVARK

Orycteropus afer
Total length 1,4-1,8 m; tail length 45-60 cm; shoulder height 60 cm; weight 40-70 kg.
Identification pointers Unmistakable; large size; elongated pig-like snout; long, tubular ears; heavy build; walks with back arched.
Similar species None.

DESCRIPTION Resembles no other African mammal, with its long, pig-like snout, elongated tubular ears, heavily-muscled 'kangaroo-like' tail and powerful, stout legs which terminate in spade-like nails. Body is sparsely covered with coarse, bristle-like hairs, with those at base of tail and on the legs being darker than rest of body, which is usually grey-fawn but often tinged the colour of local soil. The back is distinctly arched.

DISTRIBUTION Widespread south of the Sahara but absent from much of the equatorial lowland forest belt. Largely dictated by distribution of its food.

STATUS Usually occurs at low densities.

HABITAT Shows preference for open woodland, sparse scrub and grassland but can be expected in most habitats, including forest areas.

BEHAVIOUR Predominantly nocturnal but occasionally crepuscular. Most sightings are of solitary animals but females may be accompanied by a single young. They excavate extensive burrow systems, with those of males tending to be shallower. Occupied burrows are characterized by numerous small flies in the entrance. Whilst foraging they may walk several kilometres each night, depending on termite abundance. If observed they appear to wander aimlessly, nose close to the ground. When they locate an ant or termite colony they tear into it with the massive claws on the front feet.

FOOD Mainly ants and termites, with the former tending to be more important in the dry season in some areas. Once the colony has been opened, the long, sticky tongue probes for the small insects, as well as their eggs and larvae. On occasion other insects are taken, and fruits of the wild cucumber have been recorded as food.

REPRODUCTION Very little information is available but births, at least in some areas, may be seasonal and co-ordinate with the rains. A single young weighing about 2 kg is dropped after a gestation period of some 210 days.

The aardvark with its long, pig-like snout, elongated tubular ears and heavily muscled 'kangaroo-like' tail cannot be confused with any other African mammal.

PANGOLINS Order Pholidota

Family Manidae

- ■ *Manis temmincki*
- ■ *Manis gigantea*

- ■ *Manis tricuspis*
- ■ *Manis tetradactyla*
- ■ Area of overlap

Ground Pangolin

GIANT GROUND PANGOLIN
Manis gigantea
Total length 1,2-1,7 m; tail length 50-70 cm; weight 30-35 kg.

GROUND PANGOLIN
Manis temminicki
Total length 70-110 cm; tail length 30-50 cm; weight 5-18 kg.

LONG-TAILED TREE PANGOLIN
Manis tetradactyla
Total length 90-120 cm; tail length 60-80 cm; weight 2,5-3,2 kg.

WHITE-BELLIED TREE PANGOLIN
Manis tricuspis
Total length 80-100 cm; tail length 50-62 cm; weight 2-3 kg.
Identification pointers Large, brown overlapping scales; tiny head; heavy hindquarters, tail; small forelegs.
Similar species None.

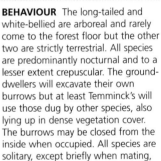

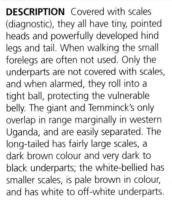

DESCRIPTION Covered with scales (diagnostic), they all have tiny, pointed heads and powerfully developed hind legs and tail. When walking the small forelegs are often not used. Only the underparts are not covered with scales, and when alarmed, they roll into a tight ball, protecting the vulnerable belly. The giant and Temminck's only overlap in range marginally in western Uganda, and are easily separated. The long-tailed has fairly large scales, a dark brown colour and very dark to black underparts; the white-bellied has smaller scales, is pale brown in colour, and has white to off-white underparts.

DISTRIBUTION Giant through West and northern Central Africa, Temminck's through East, much of southern Africa and the southern parts of Central Africa, and the long-tailed and white-bellied in the tropical lowland forest belt, extending marginally into East Africa.

STATUS All uncommon to rare.

HABITAT Both the long-tailed and white-bellied are rainforest inhabitants. The giant occupies forest and moist savanna, while Temminck's occupies dry woodland savanna.

BEHAVIOUR The long-tailed and white-bellied are arboreal and rarely come to the forest floor but the other two are strictly terrestrial. All species are predominantly nocturnal and to a lesser extent crepuscular. The ground-dwellers will excavate their own burrows but at least Temminck's will use those dug by other species, also lying up in dense vegetation cover. The burrows may be closed from the inside when occupied. All species are solitary, except briefly when mating, or a female accompanied by a single young, the latter travelling clinging to the base of the mother's tail.

FOOD Certain species of ants and termites.

REPRODUCTION The three species restricted to the tropics probably breed throughout the year but Temminck's, at least in the south, drops its young mainly during the winter months. A single young, weighing 100 to 150 g in the long-tailed and white-bellied, 330 to 450 g in Temminck's and up to 500 g in the giant, is dropped after a gestation period of approximately 135 to 150 days.

All pangolins curl into a ball to protect the vulnerable underparts when they are threatened.

The long-tailed tree pangolin inhabits rainforests where it rarely comes to the forest floor.

Ground pangolin is the only pangolin species encountered in southern and most of East Africa.

INSECTIVORES Order Eulipotyphla

HEDGEHOGS
Family Erinaceidae
Five species of hedgehog occur in Africa, all easily recognized from their dorsal covering of short spines.

- ■ *Atelerix albiventris*
- ■ *Hemiechinus auritus*
- ■ *Erinaceus algirus*
- ■ Area of overlap

- ■ *Paraechinus aethiopicus*
- ■ *Atelerix frontalis*

Front

26 mm

Back

Hedghog

HEDGEHOGS

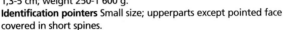 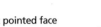

Total length 15-32 cm; tail length 1,3-5 cm; weight 250-1 600 g.
Identification pointers Small size; upperparts except pointed face covered in short spines.
Similar species Porcupines (separated on size).

DESCRIPTION All have a distinctive covering of short spines on the upperparts, with hair-covered underparts, usually paler in colour. Spines are alternately banded brown/black and white. The three North African species – the **Ethiopian hedgehog** (*Paraechinus aethiopicus*), **Algerian hedgehog** (*Erinaceus algirus*), and the **long-eared hedgehog** (*Hemiechinus auritus*) – have long ears, this being particularly pronounced in the last-mentioned. The two species most likely to be encountered in the main tourist areas are the **white-bellied hedgehog** (*Atelerix albiventris*) in East Africa and the **southern African hedgehog** (*Atelerix frontalis*) in that region, both of which have shorter, rounded ears; the former has entirely white underparts, whereas the latter is darker, with a black muzzle and a contrasting white band across its forehead and beyond each ear. They roll into a tight ball if threatened.

DISTRIBUTION Virtually throughout Africa, although absent from high rainfall areas.

STATUS Although common in some regions, hedgehogs tend to have very localized distributional ranges and in areas with seemingly optimal habitats may be entirely absent. In some areas, most notably southern and eastern Africa, there seems to have been a decline in hedgehog numbers in recent years. This appears to be due to a number of reasons, including road mortality, predation by humans, detrimental agricultural practices and possibly climatic factors such as extended droughts. Predation by man for food or for the alleged medicinal and magical properties of the skin and spines is common in some parts of Africa.

HABITAT Occupy desert, arid and wooded savanna, but absent from forest.

BEHAVIOUR Nocturnal and solitary except when a female is accompanied by her young. Hibernation is recorded for some species, in the south mainly from May to July. Although hedgehogs generally move about slowly, they can put on an amazing turn of speed given the required situation; whenever severely alarmed they usually curl into a tight, prickly ball. This defensive posture is usually adequate to frustrate the attentions of even the most determined predator, including the lion. However, the giant eagle-owl (*Bubo lacteus*) with its long talons is an important hunter of these insectivores.
Hedgehogs have a well-developed sense of smell and acute hearing, but their sight is very poor.

FOOD By and large opportunistic feeders, and with their high metabolic rate consume about one third of their body weight in animal food every night. Mainly invertebrates, and occasionally mice and lizards, also fungi and fruits.

REPRODUCTION Two to 10 (average 5) young, weighing between 8 and 18 g, are dropped after a gestation period of 35 to 48 days.

Southern African hedgehog

White-bellied hedgehog

Long-eared hedgehog female with young

Ethiopian or desert hedgehog

Algerian hedgehogs

HARES AND RABBITS Order Lagomorpha

Family Leporidae

Some taxonomists recognize more species (eg. *L. habessinicus; L. whytei*) but this situation remains in flux. Only the two species discussed below are common and widespread. Both show considerable variation in size and coloration through their range. In Southern Africa the Cape hare averages smaller than the scrub hare but in some areas the latter is smaller. Both species easily recognized as hares.

■ *Lepus saxatilis*
■ *Lepus capensis*
▨ *Areas of overlap*

CAPE HARE

Lepus capensis (europaeus)
Total length 45-60 cm; tail length 7-14 cm; weight 1,5-2,5 kg.

SCRUB HARE

Lepus saxatilis
Total length 45-70 cm; tail length 7-17 cm; weight 1,5-4,5 kg.
Identification pointers Very long ears; long, well-developed hind limbs; tail black above, white below; progress by hopping.
Similar species Rabbits.

Some authorities recognize additional species *Lepus habessinicus* from Ethiopia, as well as *Lepus whytei* but this is an issue that is far from resolved. *Lepus victoriae* now replaces *Lepus saxatilis* over much of its African range, with the latter now only in South Africa. The Ethiopian Highland Hare *Lepus starcki* is recognized by some authorities.

DESCRIPTION Both range from brown-grey to almost grey (particularly Cape hare), with black flecking or pencilling. The scrub hare has white underparts, whereas the Cape hare usually only has a white abdomen in the south, while elsewhere it is white throughout. The face may be lighter than the upperparts. The colour of hair on the nape of the neck behind the ears is brownish-pink to grey in the Cape hare and reddish-brown in the scrub hare. A white spot on the forehead is often present on the scrub hare, and occasionally on the Cape hare.

DISTRIBUTION See maps.

STATUS Both are common to very common over much of their ranges.

HABITAT Although there is some overlap, the Cape hare prefers drier, open areas, whereas the scrub hare favours woodland and bush cover with grass, and in the south it is commonly associated with cultivation.

BEHAVIOUR Nocturnal, crepuscular and solitary, but both can reach high densities.

FOOD Graze and to a lesser extent browse.

REPRODUCTION Births occur throughout the year, up to four litters per annum in Cape hare. The gestation period is about 42 days, when 1 to 3 leverets are born. Young are well developed at birth.

Ear structure of true hares

Ear structure of most true rabbits

The Cape hare is considered by many to be part of the European hare complex.

Scrub hare. Right: *Typical skins of Cape hare* (left) *and scrub hare* (right); *however, considerable variation in size occurs throughout the extensive ranges of both species.*

Pronolagus rupestris
Pronolagus randensis
Pronolagus crassicaudatus
Area of overlap between
Pronolagus rupestris and
Pronolagus crassicaudatus

Oryctolagus cuniculus
Poelagus marjorita
Bunolagus monticularis

A fourth species is now recognized from western and eastern Cape regions of South Africa, Hewitt's Red Rock Rabbit *Pronolagus saundersiae*, but it cannot be recognized in the field.

RED ROCK RABBITS

JAMESON'S RED ROCK RABBIT
Pronolagus randensis

NATAL RED ROCK RABBIT
Pronolagus crassicaudatus

SMITH'S RED ROCK RABBIT
Pronolagus rupestris
Total length 43-67 cm; tail length 3-13 cm; weight 1,3-3 kg.
Identification pointers 'Rabbit-like'; shorter ears and hind limbs than hares; largely separated by distribution; rocky habitats.
Similar species Hares.

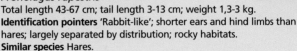

DESCRIPTION All similar in appearance. Coloration is variable but the soft coat is usually reddish-brown, grizzled black and grey. Underparts pinkish- to reddish-brown. In Jameson's, the rump and hind legs are paler than the back and sides but in the others are bright red-brown. Tail of Jameson's and Smith's is dark- to red-brown with black tip; that of the Natal has no black tip. Faces are greyish.

DISTRIBUTION See maps.

STATUS Common.

HABITAT Rocky habitats, from isolated outcrops to mountain ranges.

BEHAVIOUR Nocturnal, lying up during day in rock crevices or boulder tumbles, or in dense cover. Solitary but can reach high densities. Unlike hares, they deposit droppings at latrine sites in home range.

FOOD Graze and browse.

REPRODUCTION One or 2 helpless young are born in a cup-shaped nest which is lined with the belly fur of the female.

Three other rabbit species deserve mention: The **riverine rabbit** (*Bunolagus monticularis*) is restricted to a small area of the semi-arid interior plain of the Northern Cape (South Africa) and is considered to be one of Africa's most threatened mammals; although it is more hare-like in appearance, its naked and helpless young are dropped in a shallow burrow, which is typical of rabbits. The small **Uganda grass rabbit** (*Poelagus marjorita*) has short ears and coarse, dull grey-fawn upperparts and white underparts; it occupies woodland and forest clearings through a great part of Uganda, and there are apparently isolated populations in the Central African Republic and Angola but it is probably much more widespread. The **European rabbit** (*Oryctolagus cuniculus*) occurs naturally in a limited area of north-western Africa and has been introduced to a number of islands off the South African coast. The only hare present in its North African range and for which it could be mistaken is the Cape hare. However, the European rabbit has much shorter ears and hind legs and lives in burrows.

Ear structure of true hares

Ear structure of most true rabbits

The European rabbit occurs naturally in a limited area of north-western Africa but has been introduced to islands off the South African coast.

The riverine rabbit is one of Africa's most endangered mammals.

Jameson's red rock rabbit

Skins (left to right): Riverine rabbit, Jameson's, Natal and Smith's red rock rabbits

A young Smith's red rock rabbit

RODENTS Order Rodentia

SPRINGHARE
Family Pedetidae

SPRINGHARE *Pedetes capensis* and *Pedetes surdaster*
Total length 75-85 cm; tail length 35-45 cm; weight 2,5-3,8 kg.
Identification pointers Kangaroo-like appearance; long, powerful
hind legs; long, well-haired tail with black tip; ears, eyes fairly large;
nocturnal. **Similar species** None.

Left   Right

Springhare

DESCRIPTION A true rodent despite its name, and resembling a small kangaroo or wallaby although not related. The hind legs and feet are long and well developed; progresses with hopping gait, but the front legs are small and not used in locomotion. The tail is long, bushy and black towards the tip. Upperparts are yellowish or reddish-fawn but underparts are paler to white.

DISTRIBUTION Occurs extensively in southern Africa but absent from the south-west region, with a separate population in East Africa. Its absence from the Central African Rift is difficult to explain.

STATUS Very common.

HABITAT Compacted sandy soils with short vegetation cover.

BEHAVIOUR Nocturnal, terrestrial, not territorial. Although several burrows, housing several individuals, may be situated in close proximity, each burrow is occupied by a single individual or a female with young.

FOOD Grass, grass roots and other plants.

REPRODUCTION A single young, weighing about 300 g, may be born at any time of year.

> The East African population is now recognized as a separate species, *Pedetes surdaster*, based on some anatomical and behavioural differences.

GROUND SQUIRRELS
Family Sciuridae
These are the most frequently observed squirrels of Africa's drier savannas and semi-desert. Five species are recognized, all being similar in size and appearance.

GROUND SQUIRRELS
Total length 40-70 cm; tail length 18-30 cm;
weight 500-1 000 g.
Identification pointers Typically 'squirrel-like'; bushy black and white
tail; short, coarse hair covers body, grey, grey-fawn to rich reddish-
brown; four species have white stripe down each side, one lacks
stripes; underparts sparsely haired, paler than rest of body.
Similar species Mongooses, e.g. suricate, yellow mongoose in south.

■ *Xerus erythropus*
■ *Atlantoxerus getulus*
■ *X. erythropus* and *A. getulus*
■ *Xerus rutilus*
■ Area of overlap
■ *Xerus inauris*
■ *Xerus princeps*
□ Area of overlap

DESCRIPTION Ground-dwellers, all similar in appearance, with long, bushy black and white tails. Hair on the body is short and coarse, but sparse on underparts. Ears are very small.

DISTRIBUTION The common species through the drier parts of southern Africa is the **ground squirrel** (*Xerus inauris*), with the **Damara ground**

squirrel (*X. princeps*) being restricted to the western escarpment; these cannot be distinguished in the field. In west-central parts of East Africa and in West Africa the only species with side stripes is the **western ground squirrel** (*X. erythropus*). The unstriped ground squirrel (*X. rutilus*) is restricted to East Africa and the Horn, the **Barbary**

Springhares resemble miniature kangaroos but are in no way related.

The unstriped, or plain, ground squirrel occurs only in East Africa.

Although the western ground squirrel is the most widely distributed ground squirrel, virtually nothing is known about it.

Front

22 mm

Back

Ground Squirrel

■ Hystrix africaeaustralis
■ Hystrix cristata
▨ Area of overlap

■ Atherurus africanus

Southern porcupine

Front   Back

70 mm

Porcupine

ground squirrel (*Atlantoxerus getulus*) to Morocco and north-west Algeria.

STATUS Common.

HABITAT Arid to semi-arid regions, showing preference for areas with sparse and open vegetation. In some areas they are associated with rock outcrops.

BEHAVIOUR Strictly diurnal, terrestrial and colonial. Excavate their own burrow systems, even in hard soils such as calcrete. Group size averages from five to 30 individuals in the case of the southern species. Females and young of *inauris* remain in close proximity to the burrows but males wander from colony to colony. They frequently sit on their haunches, increasing visibility and making it easier to hold food in the front paws. The bushy tails are used as 'sunshades' when feeding.

FOOD Wide range of plant food. They excavate extensively for roots and bulbs. Termites and other insects also eaten.

REPRODUCTION The gestation period is about 45 days, after which 1 to 3 helpless young, each weighing some 20 g, are dropped in a nest within the burrow system.

PORCUPINES Family Hystricidae

Three species are recognized: both **southern porcupine** (*Hystrix africaeaustralis*) and **North African porcupine** (*H. cristata*) are very similar and easily recognized in field, while **African brush-tailed porcupine** (*Atherurus africanus*) looks very different.

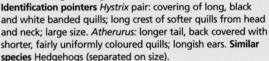

SOUTHERN/NORTH AFRICAN PORCUPINES
Total length 75-100 cm; tail length 10-15cm; shoulder height 25 cm (>45 cm when quills are raised); weight 10-24 kg.

AFRICAN BRUSH-TAILED PORCUPINE
Total length 55-85 cm; tail length 15-23 cm; shoulder height 20-25 cm; weight 2-4 kg.
Identification pointers *Hystrix* pair: covering of long, black and white banded quills; long crest of softer quills from head and neck; large size. *Atherurus:* longer tail, back covered with shorter, fairly uniformly coloured quills; longish ears. **Similar species** Hedgehogs (separated on size).

DESCRIPTION Large size and presence of quills diagnostic. When relaxed quills lie flat but if threatened or disturbed are raised and greatly increase animal's outline.

DISTRIBUTION *Hystrix* species occur very widely, being absent only from true desert and central Congolean lowland forests. Brush-tailed restricted to tropical forest belt.

STATUS Common.

HABITAT Very wide, but the brush-tailed is restricted to lowland rainforest.

BEHAVIOUR Strictly nocturnal; although foraging is primarily a solitary activity, several animals may use same burrow system; up to eight individuals recorded for the brush-tailed. During the day they lie up in self-excavated burrows, those dug by other species, in caves, amongst rocks or in dense vegetation tangles. Within its range, regular pathways are used when foraging, along which are numerous shallow excavations from which bulbs and roots are extracted. Both *Hystrix* species strictly terrestrial but brush-tailed is adept at climbing.

FOOD Roots, bulbs, corms, tubers and tree bark favoured. Scavenge occasionally.

REPRODUCTION Litters of 1 to 4 (usually 1 to 2) young, weighing 100 to 300 g; well developed at birth; quills harden in second week. Seasonal breeders in some areas.

Southern ground squirrel. Inset: *Note the different colour form of this southern ground squirrel.*

Top and above: *The porcupine that occupies Africa south of the equator; the North African porcupine is very similar and cannot be separated in the field.* Right: *The African brush-tailed porcupine has a distinctive white, brush-like tail.*

SKULLS

On occasion all there is to view of an animal is its skeletal remains. Of these, probably the most recognizable is the skull, which can be identified to a particular species. In some cases, even a cursory examination will show whether the skull belonged to a male or female. Hence, this section has been included to aid identification and enhance knowledge with regard to the dentition and skull form of the species. Where relevant, the horns have also been included and are often a clue to the animal's gender.

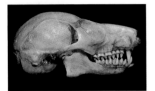

ANGWANTIBO
Arctocebus calabarensis
pg 16

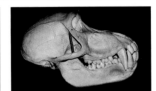

HAMADRYAS (MALE)
Papio hamadryas
pg 22

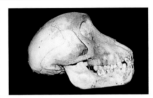

SAVANNA (COMMON) BABOON (FEMALE)
Papio cynocephalus pg 24

SAVANNA (COMMON) BABOON (MALE)
Papio cynocephalus pg 24

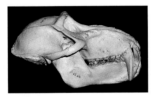

MANDRILL (MALE)
Papio (Mandrillus) sphinx
Pg 26

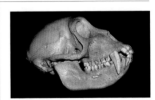

MANGABEY (TYPICAL)
Cercocebus fuliginosus
pg 32

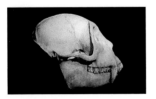

BLUE/SYKES' MONKEY
Cercopithecus albogularis
pg 38

DIANA MONKEY
Cercopithecus diana
pg 42

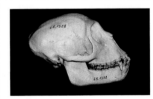

L'HOEST'S GUENON
Cercopithecus l'hoesti
pg 44

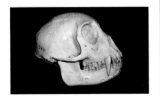

CROWNED GUENON
Cercopithecus pogonias
pg 46

MONA MONKEY
Cercopithecus mona
pg 46

PATAS MONKEY
Erythrocebus patas
pg 48

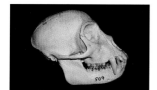

RED-EARED GUENON
Cercopithecus erythrotis
pg 50

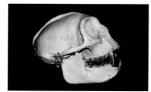

OLIVE (VAN BENEDEN'S) COLOBUS
Procolobus verus
pg 54

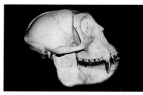

WESTERN RED COLOBUS
Procolobus badius
pg 58

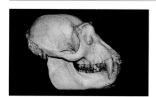

WESTERN BLACK AND WHITE COLOBUS
Colobus polykomos *pg 60*

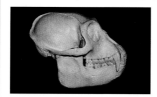

GUEREZA (ABYSSINIAN) BLACK AND WHITE COLOBUS
Colobus guereza (abyssinicus) *pg 60*

CHIMPANZEE
Pan troglodytes
pg 62

GORILLA
Gorilla gorilla
pg 66

HARTMANN'S MOUNTAIN ZEBRA
Equus zebra hartmannae
pg 70

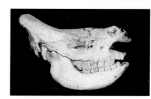

SQUARE-LIPPED (WHITE) RHINOCEROS
Ceratotherium simum *pg 78*

BUSHPIG
Potamochoerus larvatus
pg 88

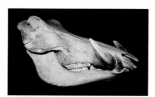

COMMON WARTHOG
Phacochoerus africanus
pg 88

GIANT FOREST HOG
Hylochoerus meinertzhageni
pg 94

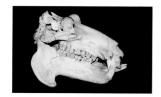

COMMON HIPPOPOTAMUS
Hippopotamus amphibius
pg 90

GIRAFFE
Giraffa camelopardalis
pg 96

GERENUK RAM
Litocranius walleri
pg 164

DIBATAG RAM
Ammodorcas clarkei
pg 166

DAMA GAZELLE RAM
Gazella dama
pg 166

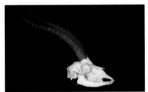

SOEMMERING'S GAZELLE RAM
Gazella soemmeringi
pg 168

SPEKE'S GAZELLE RAM
Gazella spekei
pg 170

DORCAS GAZELLE RAM
Gazella dorcas
pg 176

THOMSON'S GAZELLE RAM
Gazella thomsoni
pg 178

ROYAL ANTELOPE
Neotragus pygmaeus
pg 182

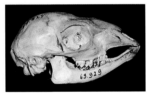

BATES'S PYGMY ANTELOPE
Neotragus batesi
pg 184

SUNI RAM
Neotragus moschatus
pg 182

ORIBI RAM
Ourebia ourebi
pg 186

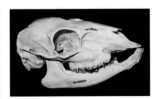

CAPE GRYSBOK EWE
Raphicerus melanotis
pg 190

BEIRA EWE
Dorcatragus megalotis
pg 192

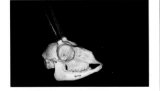

KLIPSPRINGER RAM
Oreotragus oreotragus
pg 192

KIRK'S DIK-DIK
Madoqua kirki
pg 194

COMMON (GREY) DUIKER RAM
Sylvicapra grimmia
pg 198

BLUE DUIKER
Cephalophus monticola pg 214
AND YELLOW-BACKED DUIKER
Cephalophus silvicultor pg 206

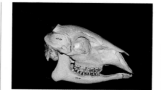

BLACK DUIKER
Cephalophus niger
pg 210

MAXWELL'S DUIKER
Cephalophus maxwellii
pg 208

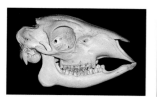

ZEBRA (BANDED) DUIKER
Cephalophus zebra
pg 206

OGILBY'S DUIKER
Cephalophus ogilbyi
pg 204

BARBARY SHEEP RAM
Ammotragus lervia
pg 218

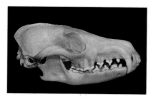

RED FOX
Vulpes vulpes
pg 224

BAT-EARED FOX
Otocyon megalotis
pg 226

RÜPPELL'S FOX
Vulpes rüppelli
pg 228

PALE FOX
Vulpes pallida
pg 228

FENNEC
Fennecus zerda
pg 230

ETHIOPIAN WOLF
Canis simensis
pg 230

BLACK-BACKED JACKAL
Canis mesomelas
pg 232

GOLDEN (COMMON) JACKAL
Canis aureus
pg 234

CONGO CLAWLESS OTTER
Aonyx congica
pg 238

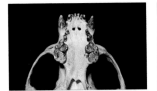

CONGO CLAWLESS OTTER MOLARS
Aonyx congica
pg 238

EURASIAN OTTER
Lutra lutra
pg 240

LIBYAN STRIPED WEASEL
Poecilictis Ictonyx libyca
pg 242

WEASEL
Mustela nivalis
pg 244

AFRICAN CIVET
Civettictis civetta
pg 246

AFRICAN PALM CIVET
Nandinia binotata
pg 250

YELLOW MONGOOSE
Cynictis penicillata
pg 252

AFRICAN LINSANG
Poiana richardsoni
pg 246

AQUATIC GENET
Genetta piscivora
pg 246

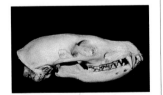

LIBERIAN MONGOOSE
Liberiictis kuhni
pg 250

LONG-NOSED MONGOOSE
Herpestes naso
pg 250

SELOUS' MONGOOSE
Paracynictis selousi
pg 252

GIANT GENET
Genetta victoriae
pg 246

LARGE GREY MONGOOSE
Herpestes ichneumon
pg 256

WATER (MARSH) MONGOOSE
Atilax paludinosus
pg 258

MELLER'S MONGOOSE
Rhynchogale melleri
pg 258

WHITE-TAILED MONGOOSE
Ichneumia albicauda
pg 260

BANDED MONGOOSE
Mungos mungo
pg 260

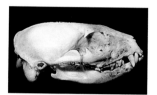

GAMBIAN MONGOOSE
Mungos gambianus
pg 260

FLAT-HEADED CUSIMANSE
Crossarchus platycephalus
pg 262

ANSORGE'S CUSIMANSE
Crossarchus ansorgei
pg 262

ALEXANDER'S CUSIMANSE
Crossarchus alexandri
pg 262

CUSIMANSE
Crossarchus obscurus
pg 262

STRIPED HYAENA
Hyaena hyaena
pg 268

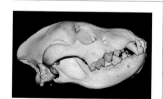

BROWN HYAENA
Parahyaena brunnea
pg 268

AARDWOLF
Proteles cristatus
pg 270

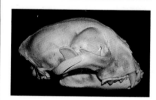

CHEETAH
Acinonyx jubatus
pg 272

LEOPARD
Panthera pardus
pg 274

LION
Panthera leo
pg 276

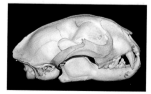

CARACAL
Caracal caracal
pg 284

SWAMP CAT
Felis chaus
pg 280

SMALL SPOTTED CAT
Felis nigripes
pg 280

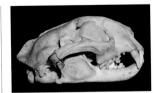

GOLDEN CAT
Profelis aurata
pg 284

AFRICAN WILD CAT
Felis silvestris
pg 278

ROCK HYRAX MALE
Procavia capensis
pg 286

ROCK HYRAX FEMALE
Procavia capensis
pg 286

ROCK HYRAX
Procavia capensis
pg 286

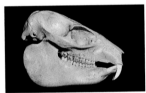

SOUTHERN TREE HYRAX
Dendrohyrax arboreus
pg 286

TROPICAL TREE HYRAX
Dendrohyrax dorsalis
pg 286

AARDVARK
Orycteropus afer
pg 288

GROUND PANGOLIN
Manis temmincki
pg 290

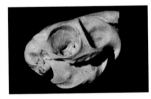

SPRINGHARE
Pedetes capensis
pg 298

GROUND SQUIRREL
Xerus inauris
pg 298

SCRUB HARE
Lepus saxatilis
pg 294

CAPE HARE
Lepus capensis
pg 294

SUGGESTED FURTHER READING

There is a vast amount of literature covering Africa's mammalian fauna but much is outdated, highly specialized or largely hidden away in scientific journals. The following list covers only those books that we know to be available in libraries and consider to be of general use to the average reader.

Corbet, G.B. & Hill, J.E. 1980. *A World List of Mammalian Species*. British Museum & Cornell University Press, London & New York.

Dorst, J. & Dandelot, P. 1983. *A Field Guide to the Larger Mammals of Africa*. Collins, London.

Haltenorth, T. & Diller, H. 1984. *A Field Guide to the Mammals of Africa including Madagascar*. Collins, London.

Kingdon, J. 1971-1982. *East African Mammals, an Atlas of Evolution in Africa*. Academic Press, London.

Leuthold, W. 1977. *African Ungulates: A Comparative Review of their Ethology and Behavioural Ecology*. Springer-Verlag, Berlin.

Nowak, R.M. & Paradiso, J.L. (Eds). 1983. *Walkers' Mammals of the World* 2 vols. John Hopkins University Press, Baltimore.

Skinner, J.D. & Chimimba, C.T., 2005. *The Mammals of the Southern African Subregion*. Cambridge University Press, Cape Town.

Stuart, C. & Stuart, T. 2001. *A Field Guide to the Tracks and Signs of Southern and East African Wildlife*. Struiik Publishers, Cape Town.

Stuart, C. & Stuart, T. 1995. *Africa: A Natural History*. Southern Publishers, Halfway House, South Africa.

Stuart, C. & Stuart, T. 1996. *Africa's Vanishing Wildlife*. Southern Publishers, Halfway House, South Africa.

Stuart, C. & Stuart, T. 1995. *Field Guide to the Mammals of Southern Africa*. Struik Publishers, Cape Town.

Stuart, C. & Stuart, T. 1995. *Southern, Central and East African mammals*. Struik Publishers, Cape Town.

GLOSSARY

ADULT Fully developed, mature animal, capable of breeding but not necessarily doing so until social and/or ecological conditions allow.

AMPHIBIOUS Able to live both in water and on land.

AQUATIC Living mainly, or entirely, in water.

ARBOREAL Living in trees.

ARTIODACTYL Member of the Order Artiodactyla (even-toed ungulates).

ASSOCIATION Mixed-species group involving two, or more, species; most common in forest-dwelling guenons.

BOVID Member of the cow-like artiodactyl family, Bovidae.

BRINDLED Having inconspicuous dark streaks or flecks on a grey or tawny background.

BROWSER Herbivore which feeds on shoots and leaves of trees, bushes and shrubs.

CACHE Hidden store of food; to hide for future use.

CALLOSITY Hardened, thickened area of skin.

CARNIVORE Meat-eating animal.

CHEEK POUCH Pouch (in the cheek) used for temporary storage of food.

CHEEK-TEETH Teeth lying behind the canines in mammals, including the molars and premolars.

CREPUSCULAR Active in twilight.

DEWLAP Loose fold of skin hanging from the throat.

DISPERSAL Movements of animals, often on reaching maturity, away from the previous home range.

DIURNAL Active during daylight hours.

DORSAL On upper surface, or top side.

ECOSYSTEM Unit of the environment within which living and non-living elements interact.

ENDEMIC Native to a particular region or restricted area.

ERECTILE Capable of being raised to an erect position.

FERAL Domesticated animals living in a wild state.

FETLOCK A projection behind and above an animal's hoof. Also: The tuft of hair growing from this part.

FOLIVORE Animal which eats mainly leaves.

FORAGING Searching for food.

FOSSORIAL Burrowing animals that spend most, or part, of their time underground.

FRUGIVORE Animal which eats mostly fruits.

GESTATION Period of development of young within the uterus.

GRAZER Herbivore which feeds on grasses.

GREGARIOUS Living together in groups, herds or colonies.

GRIZZLED Sprinkled, or streaked, with grey.

HAREM GROUP Social grouping consisting of a single adult male and two, or more, females and their accompanying young.

HERBIVORE Animal which eats plants, or parts of plants.

HOME RANGE Area in which an animal normally lives and carries out its day-to-day activities, irrespective of whether or not the area is defended against other animals.

INCISORS Sharp-edged front teeth.

INSECTIVORE Animal which eats mainly arthropods (type of invertebrate).

INTRODUCED (also alien, exotic) Species brought by man from areas where it occurs naturally, to areas where it has not previously occurred. Some introductions are deliberate, others by accident.

LATRINE (midden) Place where droppings/scats are regularly deposited.

MELANISM Unusual dark colouring due to the presence of the pigment melanin.

MIGRATION Movement, usually seasonal, from one region, or climate, to another for purposes of feeding or breeding.

NOCTURNAL Active during the hours of darkness.

OESTRUS (heat) Period during which female mammals are sexually receptive to males.

OMNIVORE Animal with a varied diet which includes both animals and plants.

OPPORTUNIST Flexible behaviour of exploiting circumstances to take a wide range of food items.

PALAEARCTIC Geographical region encompassing Europe, Asia north of the Himalayas and Africa north of the Sahara Desert.

PARTURITION Process of giving birth.

PELAGE Hair covering or coat.

PERISSODACTYL Member of the Order Perissodactyla (odd-toed ungulates).

PREDATOR Animal which forages for live prey.

PRECOCIAL Young born at a relatively advanced stage of development.

PREORBITAL GLANDS Glands located just in front of the eyes.

RIPARIAN In close association with rivers and river-bank habitats.

RUMINANT Mammal with a specialized digestive system typified by behaviour of chewing the cud; an adaptation to digesting the cellulose walls of plant cells.

RUT Period of sexual excitement (in male animals) associated with the mating season.

SEXUAL DIMORPHISM Where males and females of a species differ consistently in form.

SOLITARY Living on its own.

SOUNDER Collective name given to pigs.

SPECIES Group of interbreeding individuals of common ancestry, reproductively isolated from other groups.

SUPERSPECIES A group of species (two, or more) considered by taxonomists to be very closely related but basically distinct enough to be given their own species standing.

TERRESTRIAL Living on land.

TERRITORY Area defended from intruders by an individual or group.

UNGULATE Mammal which has its feet modified as hoofs (of various types).

VENTRAL On the lower, or under, side.

VIBRISSAE Stiff, coarse hairs (usually on the face) that are richly supplied with nerves.

WITHERS Area behind the neck and between the shoulders of an animal.

PHOTOGRAPHIC CREDITS

All photographs in this book have been taken by the authors with the exception of those listed below.

ABPL = Anthony Bannister Photo Library; FLPA = Frank Lane Picture Agency; NHPA = Natural History Photographic Agency; SIL = Struik Image Library.

ABPL/Anthony Bannister: 183 (bottom); **ABPL/Nigel Dennis:** 161 (top); **ABPL/Richard du Toit:** 261 (top); **ABPL/Clem Haagner:** 183 (top); **ABPL/Joan Ryder:** 269 (bottom); **ABPL/Lorna Stanton:** 19 (top); **ABPL/Gavin Thomson:** 119; **Antwerp Zoo:** 17 (bottom), 19 (bottom left), 109 (bottom), 113, 231 (top); **Ardea London Ltd/Nick Gordon:** 35 (top left) **Ardea London Ltd/Kenneth W. Fink:** 153 (top left); **Ardea London Ltd/Caroline Weaver:** 197 (bottom); **Ardea London Ltd/Alan Weaving:** 53 (top right); **Keith Begg:** 245 (bottom); **Phil Berry:** 139 (insets - bottom); **Bios/Ancrenaz Marc:** 53 (bottom left); **Bios/Dominique Halleux:** 211 (top, bottom right); **Bios/Mathieu Laboureur:** 209 (bottom left); **Duncan Butchart:** 107 (bottom left); **John Carlyon:** 235 (inset - top), 299 (top); **Bruce Coleman Ltd/Rod Williams:** 35 (bottom right), 43 (bottom right), 45 (inset); **Bruce Coleman Ltd/Dr M.P. Kahl:** 95 (bottom); **Bruce Coleman Ltd/Peter Davey:** 207 (bottom); **Bruce Coleman Ltd/Leonard Lee Rue:** 235 (bottom); **Nigel Dennis:** 63 (top right), 147 (bottom), 203 (bottom right), 243 (bottom), 265 (bottom); **Dr James M. Dolan Jr:** 103 (top, bottom); **Andrew Duthie:** 297 (top right); **Tony Farrell (Kimbla Safaris):** 67 (top right); **FLPA/Terry Whittaker:** 55; **FLPA/Mark Newman:** 63 (top left); **FLPA/Michael Gore:** 205, 209 (bottom right); **Pat J. Frere:** 61 (bottom left), 287 (middle right); **Christian Gross:** 293 (bottom left); **Peter Jackson:** 49; **Thomas Kaufmann:** 29 (bottom); **Ian Manning:** 123 (right middle, right bottom); **Penny Meakin:** 139 (bottom), 291 (top left, bottom); **NHPA/Daniel Heuclin:** 33, 291 (top right); **NHPA/Laurie Campbell:** 297 (top left); **Prof. Dr B. Nievergelt:** 217 (bottom left); **Photo Access/David Steele:** 151 (bottom); **Walter Poduschka:** 293 (middle left, middle right, bottom right); **Klaus Rudloff:** 27 (right), 101 (top), 141 (bottom), 209 (top), 299 (bottom left); **Roland Seitre:** 49 (inset), 203 (bottom left); **SIL/Peter Blackwell:** 57 (top), 59 (top left, top right); **SIL/Nigel Dennis:** 159 (bottom right); **Claudio Sillero-Zubiri and Dada Gottelli:** 231 (bottom left and right); **Alexander Sliwa:** 53 (top left); **Hazel Smithers:** 253 (top right); **Station Biologique de Poiunpont, France:** 51; Mark Taylor: 251 (top right); **Roland van Bockstaele:** 95 (top); **Linda van Elsakher:** 65 (bottom); **Harry van Rompaey:** 19 (bottom right), 35 (bottom left), 41 (bottom left), 247 (inset), 261 (bottom left), 263 (top left); **Paul Vercammen:** 59 (bottom), 285 (middle); **John Visser:** 87 (bottom), 263 (bottom); **Alan Weaving:** 189 (bottom left); **Roland Wirth:** 29 (top), 35 (bottom left), 37 (top right), 41 (bottom right), 43 (top, bottom left), 53 (bottom right), 61 (top), 131, 151 (top left), 167 (bottom right), 175, 185, 197 (top), 199 (top), 211 (bottom left), 215 (bottom left), 281 (top left).

INDEX TO SCIENTIFIC NAMES

INDEX TO GERMAN COMMON NAMES

INDEX TO FRENCH COMMON NAMES

INDEX TO ENGLISH COMMON NAMES